Europe in Transition
Politics and Nuclear Security

TAPRI Studies in International Relations

This series, edited jointly by Dr Vilho Harle and Dr Jyrki Käkönen of the Tampere Peace Research Institute (TAPRI) at Tampere in Finland, is based on the work of TAPRI on peace studies. The series is launched with publications from TAPRI Workshops on European Futures: Bases & Choices. The workshops have concentrated on European issues concerning international relations, security, disarmament, human rights, technology and co-operation.

List of publications:

Vilho Harle and Pekka Sivonen (eds), *Europe in Transition: Politics and Nuclear Security*

Vilho Harle (ed.), *European Values in International Relations*

Vilho Harle and Jyrki Iivonen (eds), *Gorbachev and Europe*

Europe in Transition

Politics and Nuclear Security

Edited by

Vilho Harle and Pekka Sivonen

Pinter Publishers
London and New York

© Vilho Harle and Pekka Sivonen 1989

First published in Great Britain in 1989 by
Pinter Publishers Limited
25 Floral Street, London WC2E 9DS

British Library Cataloguing in Publication Data

A CIP catalogue record for this book is available from the
British Library
ISBN 0-86187-812-4

Library of Congress Cataloging-in-Publication Data

Europe in transition : politics and nuclear security / edited by Vilho
 Harle and Pekka Sivonen.
   p.   cm.
   Papers based on the 1st meeting of a TAPRI workshop held in
Tampere, June, 8–10, 1987, launched by the Tampere Research
Institute.
   ISBN 0-86187-812-4
   1. Nuclear disarmament—Europe—Congresses. I. Harle, Vilho.
II. Sivonen, Pekka. III. Rauhan- ja konfliktintutkimuslaitos
(Tampere, Finland)
JX1974.7.E87 1989
327.1′74′094—dc20   89-39050
                                                            CIP

Typeset by Florencetype, Kewstoke, Avon
Printed and bound in Great Britain by
Biddles Limited, Guildford and King's Lynn

Contents

Contributors

BRAUCH, HANS GÜNTER. D.Phil. (Heidelberg University, 1976); Chairman of AFES-PRESS; Lecturer in International Relations, Heidelberg University (1988–). Editor of *Military Technology, Armament Dynamics and Disarmament* (Macmillan, 1989).

BRYANT, JANET. M.A. (University of Reading, 1988); Lecturer, Portsmouth Polytechnic, School of Languages and Area Studies (1989–).

DUKE, SIMON. D.Phil. (Oxford University, 1985); Research Fellow, SIPRI, Stockholm (1987–9); Post-doctoral Fellow, The Mershon Center (1989–). Author of *US Military Installations and Forces in Europe* (Oxford University Press, 1989).

HARLE, VILHO, D.Phil. (University of Tampere, 1975); Senior Research Fellow, Tampere Peace Research Institute (1988–). Editor of *Tapri Yearbook 1986* (Avebury, 1987), and of *Essays in Peace Studies* (Avebury, 1987).

JONES, PETER, Ph.D. (University of London, 1977); Lecturer in Politics, University of Reading (1970–). Author of *British Public Attitudes to Nuclear Defence* (forthcoming from Macmillan).

RICHARDSON, DICK, Ph.D. (University of London, 1983); Senior Lecturer in International Relations, Teeside Polytechnic (1979–). Author of *The Evolution of British Disarmament Policy in the 1920s* (Pinter Publishers, 1989).

SIVONEN, PEKKA, Pol.Lic. (University of Helsinki, 1985); Research Fellow, Tampere Peace Research Institute (1986–).

VISURI, PEKKA, D.Phil. (University of Helsinki, 1989), Lt.Col.(G.S.), Lecturer in Strategy, Defence College, Helsinki (1981–). Author of *From Total War to Crisis Management* (in Finnish; Otava, 1989).

VÄYRYNEN, RAIMO, D.Phil. (University of Tampere, 1973); Professor in International Politics, Department of Political Science, University of Helsinki (1979–). Editor of *The Quest for Peace* (Sage, 1987).

WÆVER, OLE, Cand.phil. (University of Copenhagen, 1985); Research Fellow, The Center of Peace and Conflict Research, Copenhagen (1986–). Co-editor of *European Polyphony* (Macmillan, 1989).

Preface

In 1987 The Tampere Peace Research Institute (TAPRI) launched international TAPRI Workshops on 'European Futures: Bases & Choices'. The workshops deal with European values in international relations; human rights in an East–West perspective; technology, co-operation and political order in Europe; the Soviet Union and Europe; superpower stereotypes; alternative security in the Arctic region; and the political consequences of nuclear disarmament in Europe. The workshops have had two or three meetings, and about sixty scholars have taken part.

The present work comes from the workshop on the political consequences of nuclear disarmament in Europe, and is mainly based on its first meeting in Tampere, 8–10 June 1988. In addition to the project members, the editors invited Professor Raimo Väyrynen, Dr Pekka Visuri and Dr Dick Richardson to contribute to the book. For technical reasons, some topics—especially those concentrating on the Soviet Union, the Arctic and the superpower images—relevant to the present work will be included in the forthcoming publications in this series from other workshops.

The TAPRI Workshops have been financed mainly by a grant from the John D. and Catherine T. MacArthur Foundation, to which we wish to extend our thanks. Needless to say, the Foundation bears no responsibility for Workshop publications or other activities.

Tampere, Finland
April 1989

1 Introduction: Stability versus Dynamic Security Order

Pekka Sivonen

Efforts to reduce the risk of war and to contain its possible destructiveness by means of arms limitations, agreements on confidence-building measures and on ways to reduce the danger of inadvertent war, are called *arms control*. On the other hand, *disarmament* has stood for real cuts in the quantity of armaments, not to be replaced by new deployments.

In peace research the arms control approach has been criticized for what is perceived as its tendency to 'legitimize' the arms race: according to arms control theory drastic cuts in armaments stockpiles of the leading powers would destabilize both 'the balance of terror' and the existing overall power configuration in the world.

The mainstream of arms control theory has traditionally dominated great power politics in these issues. This is why the negotiations between Ronald Reagan and Mikhail Gorbachev on 11 and 12 October 1986 in Reykjavik were such a surprise to establishment-oriented arms control specialists. Serious negotiations on the possibility of sharp reductions in nuclear arsenals were not compatible with the traditional arms control way of doing things.

The Reykjavik summit never reached a mutual understanding, and was therefore soon deemed a failure. However, since Reykjavik many far-reaching disarmament measures have been taken or are currently under negotiation. The superpowers have signed the INF treaty and are working on an agreement that would mean a 50 per cent cut in their strategic nuclear arsenals. Within the Conference on Security and Co-operation in Europe (CSCE) process, twenty-three allied nations began negotiations in March 1989 on conventional disarmament. These talks, held in Vienna, cover the area from the Atlantic to the Urals, and the objective is to attain real reductions in troop levels and equipment. In Geneva, a total ban on chemical armaments is under negotiation within the Conference on Disarmament (CD) process.

In addition to the agreement reached and the negotiations in progress, unilateral moves constitute an important part of the overall picture. These are unilateral disarmament steps and unilateral restraints.

1

The most important unilateral disarmament step so far has been the UN speech by Soviet leader Mikhail Gorbachev on 7 December 1988. In this speech, Gorbachev announced that within two years the Soviet Union would cut its military manpower by half a million troops and withdraw from the European part of the Soviet Union 10,000 main battle tanks, 8,500 artillery pieces and 800 fighter aircraft. From the territories of its Eastern European allies, the Soviet Union would withdraw six armoured divisions.

Pressures for significant unilateral moves are also mounting in allied Western Europe. However, because of military asymmetries, these pressures are not so much for unilateral disarmament measures as for unilateral restraints on deployment. At the time of writing (spring 1989), these pressures were most visible and most effective in West Germany. There was a general domestic consensus among the West Germans that they would be unwilling to consider the modernization of German-based American tactical nuclear weapons as an urgent task. The modernization of nuclear artillery seemed politically impossible in any case, while the replacement of Lance missiles seemed to be politically impossible at least for some years to come.

There were also political pressures for unilateral restraints on the other side of the Atlantic. The US Congress had set budgetary limits to the SDI programme, curbing the government's possibilities of using 'bargaining chips' tactics, and generally supporting a relatively conciliatory approach to arms control and disarmament issues. Also, the Bush administration seemed to be showing a lesser commitment to certain armament programmes (notably SDI) than did Reagan's administration. From all this it was clear that, with East–West relations as they were in the spring of 1989, disarmament was enjoying more respectability than ever before. Increasingly, calls for disarmament measures were seen as *realism*, not as idealism.

Accordingly, Reykjavik was no failure as such. It was certainly poor diplomacy, and did not produce even an agreement on disarmament principles. However, the readiness to negotiate on deep cuts in nuclear weaponry in Reykjavik has been preserved. This readiness has transformed the post-war realities in questions of nuclear security. It is most important to notice that disarmament has become a new norm of success for arms control, contrary to the old assumptions. In this respect, we have already passed the point of no return in the change of attitudes to arms control. Disarmament and arms control are seen increasingly as compatible rather than rival approaches.

What does this mean for the present international power structure? It would be too simplistic to assume that the leading nuclear powers are willingly giving up a great deal of their political power. They are not. Rather, it is more and more anachronistic to think that nuclear armaments are one of the most successful ways to gain and maintain that power. The Cold War system is fading away; public opinion is less and less willing to support military overarming. Accordingly, there has emerged new great power willingness to perceive nuclear disarmament measures as a natural adjustment to the changing situation rather than as a threat to their own power position.

Meaningful nuclear disarmament can be started in the context of the present international power structures. In fact, in order to succeed, it must serve the security interests of the superpowers and existing military alliances. It would be hopelessly idealistic to analyse the situational dynamics otherwise. This means that the process can only be a step-by-step one. But who could have imagined just a decade ago that the steps taken and under consideration would be so significant and that the pace would be so fast?

In time nuclear disarmament could bring about considerable changes in the whole armament culture and international power structure in the industrialized world. Disarmament could have especially far-reaching political consequences in Europe, not least in the eastern parts of the continent.

Such a process of change might at some point frighten the decision-makers and make them turn back. Or it could reinforce itself, if the frightening prospects of unpredictability could be alleviated. To choose the latter alternative, the decision-makers would have to be confident enough of their ability to manage this change. Nuclear disarmament could be developed into a *regime*, a security system for the regulation of East–West relations.

This kind of regime would consist of an increasingly comprehensive network of disarmament and arms control agreements, mutually agreed-upon military principles and restraints, increased observability of military forces, improved economic ties between East and West, better possibilities for human contact across borders, and a continuing process of liberalization and opening up of the hitherto relatively closed societies of the East.

Something along these lines is in fact already happening; we have a more comprehensive and promising process than ever before since the beginning of the Cold War. In addition to the actual arms control and disarmament measures and negotiations, we can identify three main contributing elements to such a regime-building process.

First—and this is also a precondition for continuous progress in all other aspects—there is the process of political and economic reform in the Soviet Union and Eastern European countries. The Cold War has consisted primarily in ideological antagonism. By getting rid of the worst kind of ideological dogmatism, the Soviet and Eastern European powerholders can greatly alleviate Western fears about the intentions of the Eastern bloc. Increasing freedom strengthens peace.

Second, there is encouraging development in the CSCE process. The concluding document signed in Vienna in February 1989 represents a remarkable widening of the role of the CSCE, if and when it is implemented. Along with the above-mentioned new talks on Conventional Forces in Europe (CFE), the most important achievement of the Vienna follow-up meeting was the new emphasis given to the 'human dimension'. Now, more than ever, the CSCE process stands for improvement in human rights and human contact. International security cannot be merely a question of inter-state relations; it is increasingly a question of domestic conditions and non-governmental international relations. In Europe it is security for the people and for the peoples, not only for the states.

Third, economic integration in Europe, a process led by the EC, can have a positive effect on European security. Increasingly, European economic integration has an East-West dimension. As regards the Soviet Union, the effects of this are slow in coming, but it is already strongly present in Eastern Europe, particularly in Hungary. According to the traditional liberal view, economic interaction strengthens peace. Crossing the political division line, and containing strong elements of actual economic integration, it could very well do that in the Europe of our times.

In sum, then, there are many parallel mechanisms for managing the evolving European security order. It is becoming increasingly superficial and narrow-minded to analyse European security in military terms, to consider it as a question of comparative strength and mobilization potentials.

Johan Galtung, the Norwegian-born world-famous peace researcher, developed in the late 1950s the concept of 'positive peace'. Briefly, this stands for the idea that peace must be more than the absence of war. Peace must include, among other things, improving international relations and less 'structural violence' in domestic conditions. Multidimensional development towards a European security order, as it is described here, contains characteristics which resemble this notion of 'positive peace'. We do not yet know whether that development is going to continue long enough for these hopes to materialize. However, we can and must work to influence the changes occurring within that security system.

In such a system change there have to be strong elements of reassurance, predictability and clear-cut mutual benefits. Nuclear disarmament has to be closely connected with conventional and chemical disarmament, confidence-building measures, verification procedures, and political *détente*. And, one has to bear in mind, total disarmament is not on the cards. Adequate national defences and the existence of military alliances have to be accepted as necessary requirements for any substantial disarmament—and this will be the case for some time to come.

Elements of predictability have usually been characterized as *stability*. However, international relations under substantial change cannot be stable! Rather, it is more appropriate to talk about *orderly change*. 'Stability' as a term resembles too much the old arms control wisdom of arms race stability.

European security is in a process of transformation. It remains to be seen whether that transformation will develop into such an integral process as the one described above. However, the present direction of change can be analysed in terms of an evolving *dynamic security order*. Maintaining the old configuration would not preserve stability, because pressures towards change would accumulate. Creativity and adaptation are needed.

European nuclear security must be analysed within a conceptual context of overall systemic transformation. New types of international conflict emerge. Evolving domestic political situations set new directions for external security policies. The disarmament process has uneven effects on public opinion in different countries and political systems. Various political and military alternatives are put forth in political discussion as attainable arrangements.

This book is about nuclear security and politics in European transition. Eight different perspectives are presented, without any aim of reaching uniformity.

2 Arms Race: Theory and Action

Raimo Väyrynen

Strategic theory and reality

The major mistake in the analysis of arms races is that the process of armament is separated from the totality of international relations, their structures and actors. This applies to a considerable part of strategic theory, which attempts to construct a coherent picture of the relationship between the technology of weapons systems, their military functions and political decisions. To take an example, the improved accuracy of the adversary's offensive missiles and the increased number of their warheads means, the strategy to target military objects prevailing, that the vulnerability of one's own missiles system will grow. This calls for certain countermeasures: the development of defensive systems, the strengthening of missile silos or adoption of a policy of launching missiles on warning. The development of defensive systems again increases the likelihood that the adversary reinforces its offensive power and, in addition to that, starts developing its own defence. Strategic theory aims at the systematic and logical presentation of military reality. In this presentation the compatibility between different constituents of the theory is more essential than its testable correspondence with reality.

However, strategic theory cannot normally be tested, which is the reason for its epistemologically problematic position; which criterion should be applied in assessing the truth value of its propositions? Strategic theory is, in fact, a part of the political process of society, which means that a criterion based on this process ought to be applied instead of a scientific one. In order to facilitate further discussion, it is necessary to divide strategic theory into two subdisciplines: one aims at the accurate, often mathematical, presentation of the logic of action of the armament system, and the other at its application to political needs. The character and functions of these two approaches differ from each other to a great extent.

The intention to present the armament system as a logical unity is based on the mechanical conception of the world that originated along with the Industrial Revolution. Within this conception, reality can be

6

expressed as different kinds of quantities as well as logical and functional relations between them. As far as armament is concerned, the most important weapons systems, which all have military functions of their own, are typical artefacts of the productional processes of society. Military power based on weapons systems can be utilized rationally in order to promote political aims. This requires, however, that political solutions are in harmony with the action of logic of the armament system. This does not necessarily mean support for the armament policy, for arms control policy can also follow the technological imperative. As a matter of fact, the supporters and opponents of armament can both base their activities on strategic theory, the central feature of which is mechanical political rationality. As far as arms control is concerned, the control and restriction of weapons systems must conform to the limits and requirements set for decision-makers by the nature and functions of these systems.

The strategic theory based on the technological imperative and on model construction is alluring due to the accurate, and sometimes relevant, answers offered by it. On the other hand, these answers are often of little value because their conception of politics is very naive.[1] When it comes to applied strategic analysis, the situation is more complicated and in a way more interesting. It can be judged at two different levels: one of them is connected with the analysis of the scientific characteristics and problems of strategic theory, and the other with its goals, i.e. the normative side. It is important, in my opinion, to see clearly that topics can be discussed at two levels: theory and research as well as politics. These levels are, by no means, completely distinct; on the contrary; they meet in the analysis of deterrence theory and policy, for example.

It is, however, necessary to make a distinction between them, because scientific research cannot set social objectives. Setting objectives is a part of the political process that belongs to the representative institutions of society. This also applies to the decision-making connected with armament and arms control, in which researchers can naturally participate on socio-political terms. This kind of participation is not, however, research, the primary task of which is, as far as social sciences are concerned, critical interpretation of reality. The political elite usually aims at the unidimensional description of reality.

The task of the researcher is to break and diversify this image but not to begin dictating the goals and methods of politics. Johan Galtung and Erik Allardt have stated that the task of the researcher is not only to confirm regularities but also to break them. As far as I can see, this means that they are broken interpretatively. Interpretation means a change in the concept of social reality, which, consequently, has a special effect on the selection of goals and methods of politics.

Applied strategic analysis works in terms of the goals set by political decision-makers. This may mean promoting the goals of either the government or the opposition. Applied strategic analysis may, therefore, cross in its applications some internal divisions of the political elite of society, but it seldom questions the prevailing strategic world or creates alternatives for it.[2] For this reason, the applications of strategic theory are artificially directed at a routine level: within the limits set by resources and political consensus, means are searched which enable one to realize political goals. The more ambitious appliers of strategic theory are not, however, content with this. They do admit that the breakthrough of new strategic thinking requires special circumstances—either a lost war or a thorough change in the attitudes of political elite. Still, the fundamental elements of strategic theory usually change by gradations. According to Colin Gray, the task of strategic theory is to guide decision-makers in their choices between different weapons systems, keeping an eye on the set goals of foreign policy. In this sense the strategic theory created by experts is a basis for a state's security policy, though it is, on the other hand, affected by both the technological imperative and the outlines laid down by political decision-makers (Gray, 1982a, pp. 16–28).

The task of strategic theory is, in other words, either to guide or to serve politics, depending on the degree of ambition of the political goals set by the supporters of this theory. The extent of ambition is not, however, the most crucial thing when we are looking at the scientific nature of strategic theory. The essential fact is that it is in a particular relation to practice: it is instrumental and, in most cases, preserving as far as its basis is concerned. The instrumental nature of strategic theory inevitably links its pursuers with the aims of a part of some official decision-making machinery or a political interest group.

In the era of nuclear weapons the application of strategic theory is connected with special normative problems due to the qualitative changes in military power. These problems concern the consequences of a recommended strategy as well as the relations of a state with its citizens. The devastations of a potential nuclear war are only a part of the problem. While weapons systems are becoming more dominant, their juxtaposition with civil society is more marked. Armament based on weapons of mass destruction creates a national security bureaucracy and an ideology that strengthens the state at the expense of individual rights. This development is an indication of the fact that the relationship between the state and individual security is, even at its best, problematic (Buzan, 1983, pp. 21–34; Lawrence, 1985).

Strategic theory is a part of national policy and it must, therefore, be assessed by socio-political standards. It should, however, be evaluated by scientific standards, too, in so far as its developers and appliers declare themselves to conduct scientific research. In this respect, one has often made a distinction between the developers of abstract, above all game-theoretical, and neo-realistic strategic theory. The former have been criticized for the non-politicization of international relations, and the latter for their one-sided power-political interpretation (Rapoport, 1964, pp. 176–86). Colin Gray has acknowledged a certain inclination towards abstractionism, but he has, on the other hand, claimed the world picture of strategy to be justified in that it always understands the political value of military power. In order to impress this understanding upon strategic theory, he strongly emphasizes the need to base it on the axioms of neo-realism (Gray, 1982a, pp. 188–91; 1982b, pp. 65–74).

There is, however, a limit in this co-operation of strategic theory and neo-realism. Neo-realism aiming at deductiveness (as exemplified by Kenneth Waltz) could hardly accept the instrumental nature of strategic theory—a deductive theory as such is a goal for him. Another problem in strategic theory is, from the point of view of neo-realism, the difficulty in testing it. At least as far as nuclear strategies are concerned, it is not possible to test the equivalence between strategic theory and reality. It is, consequently, not a question of an empirical theory that could be proved right or wrong; rather, the aim is to construct hypothetical models to support different decision-making situations. Testing strategic theory means, in fact, that statements concerning its weapons systems, their military employment doctrines and political functions are compared with the state's existing military capacity and the plans for using it (Gray, 1982a, pp. 12–13). It is not, in other words, a question of testing these statements in the ordeal of a (nuclear) war; rather, we are talking about projecting the present equivalence between words and deeds on the circumstances of a war. Due to these problems, not even the most active supporters of strategic theory necessarily characterize their field as scientific research; they rather talk about producing information in order to stimulate thinking and give material for the planning and implementing of politics (Gray, 1982b, pp. 128–33).

The problem of explaining armament

In reality, the activities of a strategic community are a factor that stimulates armament. This clearly follows from the definition of the study of strategy, according to which such study aims at analysing 'the employment of military means in order to further political goals'. The study of strategy is, therefore, tied up with a conflict between states competing against each other, and it attempts, on both sides, to find means for promoting one's own goals (Freedman, 1985, pp. 29–31). The question of the causes of the arms race is more important in the scientific study of international relations than in strategic analysis in which the military objectives dominate. Instead, a better understanding of the causes for armament provides answers to the problem of preserving peace between nations.

It is useful to distinguish here between two models of explanation— teleologic and genetic.[3] A genuine teleologic explanation interprets the activities of a person or a collective to be the result of a conscious striving for a certain goal. Explaining armament as an attempt to promote national interests or national security is a typical teleologic explanation. A quasi-teleologic explanation is adapted for the self-regulating system, for example, the functioning of which, based on correcting its own mistakes, is directed towards a certain goal. A teleologic explanation emphasizes the ability of political collectives to function in an objective-oriented way in order to reach positive goals. Its application in the study of armament and disarmament stresses the significance of political powers and processes.

A genetic explanation is concentrated on the historical chains of events deriving their origin from certain starting points. In these chains of events a preceding event always creates preconditions for the realization of the next one. A phenomenon at the end of the chain of events can be genetically explained by tracing the sequence of realized events. A model of explanation like this may come closer to determinism in that a realized chain of events is seen, to a certain extent, as inevitable, and there is practically no room for 'history of the possible'. The application of a genetic explanation in the study of armament means, among other things, that a researcher first locates the techno-bureaucratic basis of weapons systems and then traces the stages through which this system is put into use.

A genetic explanation is clearly used in the studies which analyse armament as chains of successive weapon systems (a weapon succession process), in which the important weapons producers get a new system on their production line as soon as the previous system goes out of date (follow-on imperative) (Kurth, 1973; Kaldor, 1986). This way of approaching things naturally requires the analysis of the interest groups participating in the process of acquiring weapons. However, instead of wider, political intentionality, the activities of these groups are seen as reflecting an aspiration to their own material interest.

Hence, a genetic model of explanation draws the following picture of armament: it proceeds from one phase to another without any real alternatives created by political considerations.

The idea of politics expressed by a genetic explanation is inadequate for illuminating reality. The same also applies to the rather functional explanation of armament deriving from the needs of capitalism. According to this explanation, armament is necessary for capitalism as a producer of technological innovations, to increase demand in order to solve the problems caused by underconsumption, or to retard the decline of the rate of profit. This explanation, deriving from Marxist economics, has also been put forward as a counterbalance to the theory of the military-industrial complex as an explanation for armament. The theory in question is not considered to take sufficiently into account the importance of armament for the whole of the capitalistic system.[4] The thesis concerning armament as a consequence of the 'permanent armament economy' of capitalist countries is, however, questionable.

The direction of resources towards developing weapons has slowed down rather than accelerated technological innovations and the structural changes connected with them. The fact that increasing military expenditures tend to spend the capital needed for investments and for increasing the efficiency of production has a negative effect, too. During the period of rapid economic growth from the late 1940s till the end of the 1960s, armament could, together with other forms of public consumption, stimulate economic development. Since then the costs of armament have become, especially in highly militarized countries, an ever-increasing economic burden under the circumstances of retarded and lopsided economic growth. As far as the capitalist world is concerned, the United States and the United Kingdom, in particular, have had to put up with this development. The experiences of the past few years show that not even the economy of the United States is strong enough to carry the burden of the financial costs created by its armament policy and international commitments. The same conclusion applies, even more forcefully, to the Soviet Union and the carrying capacity of its economy.

These facts make us doubt the ability of theories of capitalism and, in a general sense, of the theories deriving from economic needs to explain the increase of armament. One of the problems of these theories is, in fact, nuclear weapons. They can be produced at a considerably lower price than conventional weapons, especially if the costs are calculated per unit of destructive power. In addition, the production of nuclear weapons has fewer positive demonstration effects on the civil economy than that of conventional weapons. Hence, according to the thesis of 'permanent armament economy', weapons production should be concentrated on conventional armaments. The expensiveness of NATO's conventional weapons as well as the fading of the perceived threat posed by the Soviet Union and the resistance of public opinion were, however, the most important reasons why NATO decided, in the late 1950s, to develop nuclear weapons, which were less of a burden to the economy. Similar reasons made the Soviet Union adopt a new military strategy based on nuclear weapons at the beginning of the 1960s.

This general examination refers to the fact that an adequate explanation of armament requires a theory of action, in which armament and its opposition manifest object-oriented activity. This kind of theory cannot, of course, totally deny the effect of economy, technology and organizations on the genetics of armament. Their influence is, however, partial and even mutually contradictory. Economy and organizations set limits to organized political will and to the activities based on them, which, on the other hand, use them as resources. Armament and militarism have, consequently, also to be seen, perhaps primarily, as the products of organized political will. This point of view does not release political leaders from the responsibility for armament and its consequences in the same way as the genetic model of explanation, for instance, does. This approach also renders possible the opposition directed towards armament and promotive political decisions; in other words, it enables us to outline the activities of the peace movement, which the genetic model of explanation is unable to do (Väyrynen, 1984).

When we are trying to develop this kind of theory of action, we have to make the important choice between purely rational and more extensive theories of action. Game theory is a conventional way of presenting both armament and arms control as a rational activity on the part of the participating actors. It has been emphasized recently that, in addition to the analogous description of the reality and the construction of models, game theory is able to provide a basis for the creation of the theory of international politics. As a matter of fact, models cannot be interpreted without any information about the surrounding theory. Duncan Snidal (1985) has pointed out that game theory as a theory of international politics differs from traditional politic realism in that it is based on strategic rationality instead of the non-strategic rationality of realism. Realism stresses the factor that state rationality means an attempt to maximize power and promote other national interests in an anarchic world. However, this kind of pure confrontation of interests will only be realized under certain circumstances. The strategic rationality of game theory describes a reality where the opportunities of a state to reach its goals are dependent on the choices made by other states. When making decisions, states depend on each other both statically, due to the interaction between the alternatives of their strategies of action, and dynamically, when the choices made at a certain moment affect the future choices of a state between different alternatives.

The assumption of the strategic rationality of the actors in international politics renders possible the intentional interpretation of their choices. The goals of activity are, hence, determined apart from the underlying separate solutions. If we want to define the preferences of the actor and their utility values apart from the activity itself, we need a theory which the preferences can be derived from (Snidal, 1985, pp. 42–3). The description of armament and arms control as a game theory attempts to preserve the scientific status of strategic theory, which the strategic analysis providing for political decision-making has questioned. It is true that outlining rational activity with the help of game theory as a part of the totality of interdependent strategic choices means progress in comparison with the model of explanation embedded in standard realism. On the other hand, game theory as an analogy or model of decision-making situations has at least the possibility of becoming a tool in applied strategic analysis. Game theory as a method cannot yet offer a theory of international politics. Snidal (1985, pp. 55–7) points out that this point of view is most appropriate for developing a theory of governmental activity and that it is able, in this purpose, to absorb most different starting points. So far this point of view has not, however, been able to develop a theory which the goals of actors, for instance, could be derived from. Neither can it explain the change in the international system.

Game theory provides, for example, a possible solution to the explanation of the goal-directed activity of states in armament policy. The strategic choice situations determined by game theory require that actors making decisions are unitary; both preferences and their utility values must be able to be accurately defined. The anarchy of international relations or co-operation based on mutuality describe the relations of state-like unitary actors in a system working without any central authority. Hence, international anarchy, which is considered perhaps the most important explainer of armament in realistic tradition, is a characteristic of the system, not of its units. Game theory does not make a distinction between the size of state actors and their character (which is one of its most crucial limitations as a theory). This means that it cannot take into account the internal roots of anarchy and armament. In addition to the nature of the international system, these phenomena can, to take an example, be the result of the dictatorial and aggressive nature of the internal system of the central state actors.

Armament is a product of the internal forces of a state as well as of the prevailing international order. Furthermore, these factors interact in a complex fashion with each other. The anarchic and unequal nature of the international system helps to justify states' decisions on armament acquisition, though it may hinder such decisions in smaller states. Armament decisions made by the superpowers have a crucial effect on international relations, and they even mould—as the influence of nuclear weapons indicates—international order. On the whole, an approach is needed in which the external and internal causes for armament as well as their interaction are outlined as a functional unity. Game theory cannot perform this task; in a way, what is needed instead is a cybernetic approach.

Among others Dieter Senghaas (1969; 1972) has attempted to create an approach like this. He emphasizes the need to interpret armament as a whole. In his opinion, armament cannot be outlined by using unconnected conceptions and indicators, or, in other words, simple causal relations. A successful model of explanation must include a unified view about intergovernmental relations and social activity (the *Gesamtkomplex*) pertaining to armament. According to Senghaas, organized peacelessness (*organisierte Friedlosigkeit*) is typical of this unity. The first part of the concept refers to the system in the background of armament; the last part, in its turn, refers to the difficulties in controlling the violence and other various consequences caused by it. Two factors are combined in Senghaas's configurative concept of causality: the internal tendency of societies to produce armament and violence (*Autismus*) and, on the other hand, the influence of prevailing international order that fuels the arms race.

The influence of the international order on armament policy is mediated through national decision-making. This mediation can be either technocratic or political. In the former case armament originates from experts' decisions to acquire weapons systems, which can be seen as a response to the challenges of the international weapons-technological environment. In the latter case armament policy is seen as a result of the interaction between different organizations and their political activities. The unregulated nature of international politics indicates the existence of various kinds of perceived threat and of factors of uncertainty. They are not, however, perceived in a uniform manner inside a state; rather, different organizations interpret them—selectively and often distortedly—in accordance with their interests and goals. Hence, the reactions of these organizations to the armament measures adopted or planned by other states must be interpreted by means of their own goals. The effect of the international order on national armament policy is, in other words, conveyed through the self-interested interpretations and decisions made by the actors exerting influence on this policy. These internal influences of a state are, however, directed by the foreign policy strategy created by political decision-makers.[5]

Means and goals

Applied strategic theory regards the general goals of politics as given and undertakes to search for optimum military means in order to reach the goals set. The nature and content of these goals are especially important in the teleological model of explanation, which explains the decisions made by actors with their help. When the goals of security policy have been set, it is time to discuss the means. A successful foreign policy strategy requires, in fact, that the goals be set in a way that they are sufficiently likely to be reached by using available resources and means based on them. The relationship between means and goals is an issue connected with both efficiency and morality.

The motives behind armaments decisions are diverse. Their objective is usually to increase the national sense of security by adding to one's own military resources in competitive international relations. The demand for national security is of a normative nature. The degree of security depends on the severity of threat directed against defendable values and is defined by values which members of society primarily want to defend. These values can vary from territorial integrity and the protection of culture and political institutions to foreign spheres of interest and sources of raw material. The components of national security can be either compatible (e.g. the defence of one's own territory and social order) or incompatible (e.g. the destabilization of another government) with the goals set by other state actors. It is obvious that the concentration of states on promoting compatible security goals will create better opportunities for stable international relations. This basic idea underlies, for instance, the policy of non-offensive defence.

The components of national security are not necessarily in harmony with each other. Different combinations of these components can also be promoted by using means that differ from each other in terms of both efficiency and morality. This means that the choices between different combinations of goals and means are inevitably normative. Besides, the consolidation of national security is often felt to be a burden rather than a positive goal. Arnold Wolfers has stated that security is a negative goal in that it in fact only means freedom from a certain evil, i.e. insecurity. The promotion of this negative goal swallows up resources which could alternatively be used to promote positive goals, such as welfare.[6]

The rational relationship between armament and national security assumed by strategic theory is only true when the definition of security is limited to values obtainable by military means. And this statement is only true when security is solely analysed from the point of view of one's own state, it is not true in the sphere of strategic interaction between several states. Not all security values can be obtained by increasing military power, and some of these values actually suffer from armament policy. From the 1970s onwards it has been emphasized in the study of international relations (by among others Seyom Brown, Alastair Buchan, Robert O. Keohane and Joseph S. Nye) that the political feasibility of military power, whether based on nuclear or conventional weapons, is on the decrease. This is due to the fact that international relations have become more complicated and the restraints on the use of force have strengthened. In my view, the opportunities for using force and the advantages derived from it are historically on the decrease. This development is not, however of a linear nature; rather, the feasibility of military power may temporarily increase due to the cyclical factors of international politics (Bull, 1981, pp. 17–33).

The multi-dimensional nature of security as a national value and the increasingly powerful restraints on the use of military power show concretely that the relationship between armament and security is normative rather than empirical. On the other hand, it may be more appropriate to make a distinction between Max Weber's goal rationality (*Zweckrationalität*) and value rationality (*Wertrationalität*). Goal rationality is realized when the costs of the means needed to reach a certain goal as well as the indirect effects of their application are taken, as far as possible, 'rationally' into account. In this kind of examination military power may, under certain circumstances, prove to be goal-rational. Under most circumstances it is not. Security policy has, however, features connected with value rationality (Eskola, 1987, pp. 19–34). Security, sovereignty and peace—in different combinations—are often considered almost absolute values, with the help of which one chooses means without even thinking about their costs. In this respect both the pacifist demand for the creation of security by non-violent means and the militaristic view that armament increases security are of a value-rational nature. Moreover, the teleologic model of explanation seems to be very suitable for the explanation of this kind of value-rational activity.

With the help of these models of explanation and forms of rationality we can analyse E.P. Thompson's theory of the nature of nuclear armament. His idea on armament and its development includes a lot of genetic material. Nuclear weapons grow 'spontaneously, as if they owned an independent will'; indeed 'the innovations of weapons systems themselves produce themselves'. On the other hand, Thompson admits that political decisions affect the increase of weapons and that weapons systems are not politically neutral. However, he does not reject the genetic model of explanation on the grounds that nuclear armament militarizes politics, which, under these circumstances, loses its alternatives. Weapons systems become political factors that determine the content of the decisions made both in the present and in the future (Thompson, 1982, pp. 46–9). Armament leads, in the long run, to the destruction of mankind, exterminism, which is not, however, a result of a fateful coincidence but 'a direct consequence of previous political decisions'. These decisions have created such strong structures of destruction in the leading military powers that their discharge will have catastrophic consequences.[7]

When he starts to examine the alternative to the genetically determined armament logic, the peace movement, Thompson at the same time changes his model of explanation: it is teleologic now. The collective activity of the peace movement is explained by its objective, its attempt to prevent the onset of exterminism. The activity of the armament movement can be explained in the same way. As a matter of fact, these two goal-directed social movements are constantly and, we could say, dialectically interdependent. In addition, 'peace' and 'security' conflict as value-rational goals. According to the peace movement, peace means security; the armament movement, in its turn, considers that security based on arms means peace. This difference in priorities leads to a profoundly different view on the content of security policy. It can naturally be seen in choice of means of the two movements, but even more clearly in their goals. The demand of the peace movement for disarmament also aims at political liberation, whereas the importance given to security based on arms by the armament movement implicates that security is also seen as order and control of social activities.

These differences in the means of security policy and its goals, in particular, seem to derive from a different idea of power. We can try to solve this problem by using the conceptual analysis made by Arendt (1970, pp. 43–56). In this analysis the definition of power deviates from the usual view of power as an ability to control others' activities for one's own benefit. The efficiency of this control is usually increased by different kinds of dictatorial military and economic means. Power can, however, be defined in a positive way, too, and not only as an ability to deny other actors certain values or resources. According to Arendt, power can be defined as the ability of a collective to reach goals set by co-operation (in this case power approaches the concept of competence). Violence can also serve as a way to materialize to set goals. It is primarily instrumental by nature and it resorts to arms to increase the strength of the actor. Strength, as Arendt uses the concept, approaches that of capacity, which means that military capacity is a method that can be used as an instrument of both power and violence.

For Arendt, power is the prerequisite for all forms of control and not so much a goal. A collective can hardly create a political strategy combining means and goals without certain power. Power need not be justified as long as the prerequisite is legitimate. In Arendt's opinion, the use of violence can be justified in self-defence, for example, but due to its instrumental nature it can never be legitimate as such. By using violence it is possible to create obedience among citizens and destroy the ability of a collective to co-operate in order to reach goals. However, the use of violence and its instruments can never create legitimate power.

This conceptual starting point leads us to the conclusion that military power and its use, although perhaps justified in certain situations, can never be legitimate as such. Power as competence and ability to co-operate is of a primary nature. It is through power that a community realizes itself when promoting set goals. The means of violence, weapons systems, may hinder this self-realization. As a matter of fact, Arendt's idea of power can be materialized most truly when the instruments of violence have been removed. From this angle, the increase of power requires that arms be demolished, not that their quantity be increased. The acquisition of power means liberation from the hierarchical control and decision-making created by technological weapons systems.

The means of violence can be resisted under certain circumstances and within certain limits with non-violent social defence. As a matter of fact, the legitimacy of social order and its social stability, i.e. power in Arendt's view, is the prerequisite for all defence and, in particular, non-violent defence. However, responding to violence with power only works up to a certain point. Power comes from people, violence from technology. Those who respond to violence with power 'notice that they do not face people but artefacts of technology created by people' (Arendt, 1970, p. 53). As a consequence, arms can only be accepted as the means of defence of legitimate power. Correspondingly, they cannot be accepted on grounds aiming, in addition to defence, at various social subsidiary goals, such as control and order. In that case military power turns against the legitimate use of power emerging from civil society.

The validity of the above examination is restricted to conventional arms. The ethical and practical political problems connected with the use of military power increase severalfold when we move from conventional arms to nuclear weapons. Arendt's point of view justifies the use of military power for defensive purposes. As is well known, self-defence is, however, a flexible and ambiguous concept in international relations. It is particularly problematic in the age of nuclear weapons, the typical feature of which is a lack of proportionality between means and goals. How big does the threat directed against different security values have to be so that defending them with nuclear weapons would be justified?

The rational relation between means and goals has ruptured in the era of nuclear weapons. For this reason applied strategic theories and military doctrines based on the use of nuclear weapons are politically irrational compared with mere deterrence grounded on retaliatory capacity.[8]

Nuclear weapons and deterrence

Research on deterrence policy has increased considerably in the 1980s. Instead of the former conceptual analysis this research has been, to a great extent, empirical. In practice, the research has been primarily directed either to deterrence policy before the pre-nuclear era or to the conventional deterrence in the shade of nuclear weapons. In its new incarnation research on deterrence had been interdisciplinary. However, the problem has been that the effects of nuclear deterrence cannot be analysed empirically. They cannot be separated from the other structural or process factors of international politics. This has divided the research into two tendencies: on the one hand, the application of counterfactual reasoning, and, on the other hand, discussion on the ethical problems of using nuclear weapons. The reason for the proliferation of deterrence research is undoubtedly the changes that have taken place since the 1970s in the nature of the nuclear weapons doctrines of the major powers.

Caspar Weinberger (1984), the former US Secretary of Defense, has brought up the concept of a protracted nuclear war. According to the concept, the Soviet Union must never have a greater nuclear weapon capacity than the United States. Deterrence policy must go on even during a nuclear war (intra-war deterrence). This idea is shared by the Harvard Nuclear Study Group (1983): 'nuclear strategy will not end when nuclear war begins'. It is believed that the deterrence policy pursued during a nuclear war is able to control the way the opponent uses its nuclear weapons, and, in particular, to prevent the opponent from escalating the war (escalation control). And finally, it is believed that nuclear weapons can help to contribute to the termination of war. The reason for the inclusion of nuclear strategy in warfare is the desire to supplement the traditional tasks of nuclear weapons deterrence, i.e. to prevent a nuclear weapon attack against the home territory of the United States (basic deterrence) or its allies and to repel a conventional attack against the allies (extended deterrence).

The role of nuclear (intra-war) deterrence is based on pure speculation and is not traceable to any deterrence theory. One of the central problems of nuclear deterrence is the gap between deterrence theory and deterrence policy (George and Smoke, 1974, pp. 503–8). This gap is especially deep in the internal deterrence of a nuclear war as there is no applied strategic theory as a guideline. This gap concerns, however, deterrence policy in general. Deterrence theory can only partly describe and explain reality and therefore the prescriptive value of the theory is also limited. On the other hand, it is obvious that nuclear deterrence has restrained the activities of governments in crisis situations and has prevented the escalation of these crises into wars. Nuclear weapons, together with the bipolarity of the international system, have made nuclear powers more interested in controlling and solving crises.[9] However, this development is hardly due to the size and composition of the nuclear weapons arsenals of the great powers; rather, the development follows from the 'existential deterrence' created by nuclear weapons. A stabilizing effect deriving from this kind of deterrence can be accomplished with a nuclear weapons arsenal which is considerably smaller than the present one, i.e. a so-called minimum deterrence, which is based on the mutual vulnerability produced by a small number of offensive missiles (Jervis, 1985, pp. 45–9; Rotschild, 1985, pp. 85–106).

The supporters of nuclear deterrence can actually be divided into two groups. One regards nuclear weapons as a basis for international order; anarchy and the various reasons for war connected with it would break loose without them.[10] The other group, in its turn, considers nuclear weapons politically and militarily feasible when one aims at reaching national goals. Justified arguments can be produced against both these views. The argument about nuclear weapons as producers of order may, however, be partially true. It in a way already follows from the fundamental notion of deterrence, the purpose of which is to prevent any actions contrary to the preferences of the subject.

Two problems emerge, however, in this respect; one is linked with the domain of the deterrence theory, and the other with its content. The domain of this theory is narrow: it only covers—in a static way—a part of the reality of international politics. Deterrence policy regulates military competition and presumably increases, although it does not guarantee, its stability. However, relatively few cases of international conflict are connected with armament. In this respect ideological dissensions, economic inequality, states' internal instability and the incompatibility of interests, in general, are considerably more important catalyst of military confrontation. All these phenomena are of a dynamical nature and indicate the complexity of the international system.[11] Hence, due to its partial and static nature, deterrence theory cannot provide a basis for an integrated policy of regulating conflicts. In other words, deterrence theory is adequate for neither a descriptive nor a normative theory of international politics.

Due to its static nature, military deterrence can maintain order only by preventing change. It is true, though, that the different forms of deterrence are probably affected in different ways in this respect. In the world of nuclear weapons retaliatory deterrence is not activated until the other party has used nuclear weapons. On the other hand, anticipatory deterrence means that states are also ready to be the first to use nuclear weapons when social or military values are being threatened.[12] In retaliatory deterrence the possibility of using nuclear weapons is clearly defined, and nuclear weapons are not actually meant to be used as instruments of the politics of order. As far as this model of deterrence is concerned, international order has to be guaranteed in some way other than collective security or the organization of intergovernmental interdependencies. Anticipatory deterrence can, in principle, be used for preventing a change, although resorting to nuclear weapons in a purpose like this is a policy filled with risks. In practice, anticipatory deterrence does not work as the politics of order, neither is it ethically justified.[13]

The above discussion leads us to observe that general or existential deterrence has, when evaluated counterfactually, decreased the likelihood of a war between nuclear powers. In this respect, politics based on deterrence theory has partially worked. When again evaluated counterfactually, deterrence theory and policy has not been able essentially to direct change in international relations. The international system would hardly be essentially different were nuclear weapons never invented or brought into use. In other words, the impact and explanatory power of nuclear weapons and the deterrence theory based on them have been limited.

Nuclear weapons can be and have been used as political instruments. In that case the objective is not only to influence the opponent but also to increase the credibility of deterrence by showing that the commitment to use nuclear weapons can also be redeemed. As a matter of fact, one also attempts to create a political effect with the strategic theory based on the opportunity to use nuclear deterrence and nuclear weapons. The strategic debate between nuclear powers includes, in fact, a constant intention to have a political effect. This effect is founded on the political statements derived from the strategic theory concerning the circumstances and requirements for using nuclear weapons. In point of fact, the reality created by this kind of strategic theory and, on the other hand, the political reality resemble each other only to a minor extent. In other words, the general model of deterrence, with its definitions, formalizations and political instructions, does not normally correspond to or anticipate the special political reality in which deterrence theory has to be applied.

Practical politics is rational only to a limited extent, and, due to the psychological, ideological and bureaucratic factors influencing it, differs from the mechanical rationality created by the strategic theory. One normally wants to turn the strategic theory based on deterrence into a general model that would fit all antagonistic situations. This kind of aspiration to generalization is, however, fallacious. In this case the area of the theory's application is left undefined, and so is its relevance in different situations; in other words, the context-dependency of deterrence is forgotten. Deterrence may certainly work, it is not a question of that, but it only works under certain circumstances and on certain terms (Craig and George, 1983, pp. 172–88). The validity of this observation is also proved by empirical studies. To take an example, a study dealing with 54 cases of extended deterrence showed that deterrence had worked successfully in 31 cases and failed in 23 cases. The success of deterrence was best explained by the local military superiority of the actor that had applied deterrence as well as by the close economic and military relations with the actor that was being defended. On the other hand, the fact that a state owns nuclear weapons only had a marginal effect on the functioning of deterrence in practice (Huth and Russett, 1985, pp. 496–526).

Notes

1. An adequate example of treatises that are based on the technological imperative and that are naive as far as their conception of politics is concerned, is provided by Bereanu (1983, pp. 49–57).

2. This approach is reflected, among others, by Ruhala's (1977, p. 30) comment: 'The study of security policy has most clearly to be based on the same factors as the decisions concerning it. The content of politics cannot be plausibly explained without advancing more or less from the starting points of the decision-maker.'
3. For more about these models of explanation, see, for example, Niiniluoto (1983, pp. 153–63).
4. The discussion of these themes has been analysed, among others, by McKenzie (1983).
5. I have attempted to apply this kind of interpretation when explaining the nuclear arms race between the United States and the Soviet Union (Väyrynen, 1983).
6. This section has been particularly influenced by Wolfers (1952), and Fischer (1984, pp. 42–6).
7. Thompson's (1982, pp. 64–6) analysis leads, of course, straight to the question of the relationship between technology and politics. He does not attempt to specify this relationship very systematically, although it is, of course, absolutely essential from the point of view of armament. Lewis Mumford expressed in his days a view, according to which technologies can be divided into democratic and authoritarian as far as their social nature is concerned. Nuclear weapons and energy are usually authoritarian in that their production is concentrated and their control is strictly hierarchical. In today's world we can hardly think of a form of technology that requires more concentrated decision-making than nuclear weapons. Langdon Winner thinks that the nature of nuclear weapons technology requires a concentrated and hierarchical organization and strict authoritarian relations. The other alternative is that some technology is consistent with a certain social order, in which case this order may also result from other reasons than technology, from political and cultural reasons, for example; see Winner (1980, pp. 121–36). Thompson's view seems to be that nuclear weapons technology creates a social and international order that will destroy itself. In this respect it influences capitalist and socialist social systems in the same way. Nuclear weapons form, from the point of view of their ultimate nature, political technology, in such a way that they create similar authoritarian and submissive relations regardless of the social system.
8. For an analysis of various deterrence doctrines, see Jervis (1984).
9. See Gaddis (1986, pp. 120–3). For an opposite view, see Mueller (1988).
10. This view is shared among others by Gaddis (1986), and Osgood and Tucker (1967).
11. See Osgood & Tucker (1967, pp. 21–4). A similar analysis has been made by Buzan (1983), who stresses that international insecurity is caused by two analytical independent dilemmas: armament (defence dilemma) and power competition (power-security dilemma).
12. For more about these conceptions, see, for example, Shue (1985).
13. The ethical questions connected with nuclear weapons and nuclear deterrence have been analysed from different angles by Kenny (1985) and Nye (1986).

Bibliography

Arendt, Hannah, 1970. *On Violence*. San Diego, CA: Harcourt Brace Jovanovich.

Bereanu, Bernard, 1983. 'Self-Activation of the World Nuclear Weapons System', *Journal of Peace Research*, vol. 20, no. 1.

Bull, Hedley, 1981. 'Force in International Relations. The Experience of the 1970s and Prospects for the 1980s' in Robert O'Neill and D.M. Horner (eds), *New Directions in Strategic Thinking*. London: George Allen & Unwin.

Buzan, Barry, 1983. *People, States and Fear. The National Security Problem in International Relations*. Guildford: Wheatsheaf Books.

Craig, Gordon A. and A.L. George, 1983. *Force and Statecraft. Diplomatic Problems of Our Time*. Oxford: Oxford University Press.

Eskola, Antti, 1987. 'Human Consciousness and Violence' in Raimo Väyrynen, Christian Schmidt and Dieter Senghaas (eds), *The Quest for Peace*. London: Sage.

Fischer, Dietrich, 1984. *Preventing War in the Nuclear Age*. Totowa, NJ: Roman & Allenheld.

Freedman, Lawrence, 1985. 'Strategic Studies' in Steve Smith (ed.), *International Relations. British and American Experiences*. Oxford: Basil Blackwell.

Gaddis, John Lewis, 1986. 'The Long Peace. Elements of Stability in the Postwar International System', *International Security*, vol. 11, no. 4.

George, Alexander L. and Richard Smoke, 1974. *Deterrence in American Foreign Policy*. New York: Columbia University Press.

Gray, Colin, 1982a. *Strategic Studies and Public Policy. The American Experience*. Lexington: University Press of Kentucky.

Gray, Colin, 1982b. *Strategic Studies. A Critical Assessment*. Westport, CT: Greenwood Press.

Harvard Nuclear Study Group, 1983. *Living with Nuclear Weapons*. New York: Banton Books.

Huth, Paul and Bruce M. Russett, 1985. 'What Makes Deterrence Work? Cases from 1900 to 1980', *World Politics*, vol. 36, no. 4.

Jervis, Robert, 1984. *The Illogic of American Nuclear Strategy*, Ithaca, NY: Cornell University Press.

Jervis, Robert, 1985. 'MAD is the Best Possible Deterrent', *Bulletin of the Atomic Scientists*, vol. 41, no. 3.

Kaldor, Mary 1986. 'The Weapons Succession Process', *World Politics*, vol. 38, no. 4, pp. 577–95.

Kenny, Anthony, 1985. *The Logic of Deterrence*, Chicago: The University of Chicago Press.

Kurth, James A., 1973. 'Why We Buy the Weapons We Do', *Foreign Policy*, no. 11, pp. 33–56.

Lawrence, Philip K. 1985. 'Nuclear Strategy and Political Theory: A Critical Assessment', *Review of International Studies*, vol. 11, no. 2, pp. 105–21.

McKenzie, Donald, 1983. 'Militarism and Socialist Theory', *Capital and Class*, no. 19, pp. 36–50.

Mueller, John, 1988. 'The Essential Irrelevance of Nuclear Weapons: Stability in the Postwar World', *International Security*, vol. 13, no. 2, pp. 55–79.

Niiniluoto, Ilkka, 1983. *Tieteellinen päättely ja selittäminen*. Keuruu: Otava.

Nye, Joseph S., 1986. *Nuclear Ethics*. New York: Free Press.

Osgood, Robert E. and Robert W. Tucker, 1967. *Force, Order and Justice*. Baltimore, MD: The Johns Hopkins University Press.

Rapoport, Anatol, 1964. *Strategy and Conscience*. New York: Harper & Row.

Rotschild, Emma, 1985. 'Common Security and Deterrence' in Raimo Väyrynen (ed.), *Policies for Common Security*, London: Taylor & Francis/SIPRI.

Ruhala, Kalevi, 1977. *Turvallisuuspolitiikka. Ulkopolitiikan ja strategian peruslinjat ydinaseiden aikakaudella*. Helsinki: Finnish Institute of International Affairs.

Senghaas, Dieter, 1969. *Abscreckung und Frieden. Studien zur Kritik organisierter Friedlosigkeit*. Frankfurt am Main: Europäische Verlagsanstalt.

Senghaas, Dieter, 1972. *Rüstung und Militarismus*. Frankfurt am Main: Europäische Verlagsanstalt.

Shue, Henry, 1985. 'Conflicting Conceptions of Deterrence', *Social Philosophy and Policy*, vol. 3, no. 1, pp. 43–73.

Snidal, Duncan, 1985. 'The Game Theory of International Politics', *World Politics*, vol. 38, no. 1, pp. 25–57.

Thompson, E.P., 1982. 'Notes on Exterminism, the Last Stage of Civilization' in E.P. Thompson, *Zero Option*. London: Merlin Press.

Väyrynen, Raimo, 1983. *Ydinaseet ja suurvaltapolitiikka*. Helsinki: Tammi.

Väyrynen, Raimo, 1984. 'Ydinaseet, politiikka ja toiminnan teoria', *Sosialistinen politiikka*, vol. 13, no. 2, pp. 22–35.

Weinberger, Caspar W., 1983. *Department of Defense Annual Report to the Congress: Fiscal Year 1984*. Washington, DC: United States Government Printing Office.

Winner, Langdon, 1980. 'Do Artifacts Have Politics?', *Daedalus*, vol. 109, no. 1, pp. 121–36.

Wolfers, Arnold, 1952. 'National Security as an Ambiguous Symbol', *Political Science Quarterly*, vol. 67, no. 4.

3 Process and Progress in Disarmament: Some Lessons of History

Dick Richardson

'Disarmament' is an infuriating word, much abused by politicians and political scientists for their own ends. In recent years, it has come to mean all things to all people. For some, it represents the supreme aim of an ideal world society. To others, it symbolizes the pursuit of unreality. Many use the word without really understanding it. Others do not even make the attempt. Yet any understanding of progress and process in disarmament necessitates coming to terms with terminology.

During the first 'Golden Age' of disarmament theory and practice— the 1920s and early 1930s—there was general consensus as to what should be understood by 'disarmament'. Politicians, interest groups, diplomats, political scientists all agreed: 'disarmament' was the word used to describe the limitation of armaments by international agreement. All aspects of all armaments were covered: acquisition, deployment and use, direct or indirect. Restrictions might be quantitative or qualitative, land, sea or air. They might concern renouncing first use of weapons, or demilitarized zones, verification or confidence-building measures. Whatever the area of armaments under discussion, the term used was the same: 'disarmament'.

Using the term in this way had many advantages. It could, for example, be used as an adjective as well as a noun. (It was easy to talk of a 'disarmament convention', less easy to talk of a 'limitation of armaments convention'!) Similarly, as a noun it could easily be qualified to indicate the issues, problems or type of convention under discussion: quantitative disarmament, indirect disarmament, land disarmament, chemical disarmament. Qualified by the word 'unilateral', it could be used to signify measures of disarmament carried out voluntarily by a single power. Most important, however, its meaning was clearly understood by all concerned, from Prime Ministers to the proverbial man and woman in the street. 'Disarmament' was the term used in the press (informed and uninformed) and on the radio; it was the term used in government documents and academic journals; the term used by contemporary historians. The so-called 'Conference for the Reduction and Limitation of Armaments' held at Geneva in 1932–4 was always referred to as 'the Disarmament Conference', and still is to this day.

Given this definition of disarmament, it is clear that a disarmament convention might not involve a reduction of armaments. In fact, an agreement to limit armaments might involve an increase in armaments, since the most important principle involved is that of limitation of armaments, not the level of limitation. This, too, was recognized in the 1920s and 1930s. Both the London Naval Treaty of 1930 and the Anglo-German Naval Agreement of 1935 permitted increases in armaments; yet both are referred to as disarmament agreements by modern-day historians and political scientists as well as contemporary observers (Morgenthau and Thompson, 1985, pp. 423–4, 433–5; Iriye, 1987, pp. 5–6).

The inter-war consensus on terminology broke down after 1945, when political scientists began to adopt 'arms control' as the generic term for negotiations rather than 'disarmament'; 'disarmament' was redefined as 'the reduction or abolition of armaments' (Bull, 1961, p. ix). The intention, in part, was to clarify matters and to distinguish between what is practicable and what is not in international negotiations. Certainly there is a slight incongruity in disarmament agreements leading to increases in armaments. But the main impetus behind the change in terminology was the desire of a number of political scientists to counter the advocates of 'general and complete' disarmament such as Philip Noel-Baker. The idea was that 'arms control' should be construed as attainable but that 'disarmament' should not. Hedley Bull (1961) was a leading advocate of this line (see also O'Neill and Schwartz, 1987).

The result of this attempted change in terminology has been unfortunate. Not all political scientists have adopted the term 'arms control' as a generic term. Some continue to use the term 'disarmament' in its wider sense. Others use both items interchangeably. Some see disarmament and arms control as incompatible. Others see 'arms control' as a step towards more general 'disarmament'. Two leading thinkers, Hans J. Morgenthau and K.W. Thompson, simply become confused. They define 'disarmament' in the new way, while continuing to use it in the old, and later contradict their own definition (Morgenthau and Thompson, 1985, ch. 23)! Similarly, outside the ivory towers of academe, the media and pressure groups have tended to continue with the old terminology while diplomatic and military bureaucracies tend to use the new. Politicians give every impression of being schizophrenic on the subject, using whatever term suits their purposes at any given time.

Historians find themselves in a difficult position. Not only are they faced with the post-1945 conflict over the definition of 'disarmament', they can point to the term 'control' being used in a very different way in the 1920s and 1930s. At that time, mainly due to a rather slipshod interpretation of the French word *contrôle*, it was used to mean verification. Overall, they have tended to use the term 'disarmament' in the old (generic) way. There is much sense in this. Historically, it is more accurate; politically, because it is easier to understand, it is more likely to give rise to consensus both inside and outside academe. More generally, but no less importantly, it impedes the manipulation of terminology by self-seeking politicians and sardonic political scientists. It is for these reasons that the term is used in its generic sense in this chapter.

The discipline of history is all too often ignored by political scientists in drawing up their theories of disarmament and arms control. Yet it is only through the analysis of a spectrum of international negotiations over an extended period of time that a true appreciation of process and progress in disarmament can be achieved. It is not good enough to fit a small number of historical examples into preconceived theories; disarmament theory should arise out of historical practice. It is important also in this respect to integrate three levels of investigation: the individual, the state and the international system. Hitherto, political scientists have concentrated on the state and the international system at the expense of the individual. It is necessary to redress that balance.

One of the consequences of the emphasis on the state and the international system has been the general assumption that arms negotiations are pursued in good faith. Failures are usually put down to 'technical difficulties', ideological differences, conflicting strategies and the pitching of demands at too high a level on the part of 'opponents'. This may be true in specific circumstances. But a full understanding of the reasons for success and failure necessitates an evaluation of the inner convictions of the individuals charged with policy-making and negotiation. Do they believe in disarmament or not? Some would suggest that individual attitudes to disarmament are unimportant; that individuals act only in accordance with the national interest as drawn up in governmental memoranda, briefs and instructions (Tate, 1942, ch. 18). But in reality, interpretations of the national interest by delegates in the light of their inner convictions can make or break a set of negotiations, or at least give rise to a reassessment of responsibility in the event of a failure of negotiations. Such, for example, was the case at the Geneva Naval Conference of 1927, when Viscount Cecil's resignation led to the general (and correct) acceptance that responsibility for failure lay chiefly with the British Conservative government (Richardson, 1989, chs 9–10).

At the level of the individual, there is a direct connection between a lack of belief in disarmament and the failure of disarmament negotiations. The same can be said of governments, which represent collectivities of individuals. At the same time, a mere belief in disarmament does not necessarily lead to success. Other facts have to be taken into account, notably political leadership, political will, an understanding of the technical side of disarmament, and an appreciation of the same problem as seen through the eyes of other parties to the negotiations. Only when all five factors are present will negotiations normally be successful. By looking at various sets of negotiations over the past 90 years, both successes and failures, the intricacies of the disarmament process and the importance of the individual within that process will become clear. The aim is to promote a better understanding of both process and progress.

Disarmament negotiations before 1914

The Hague Peace Conference of 1899, the first major disarmament conference in the modern era, has often been seen as a breakthrough in the international acceptance of the desirability of arms limitation from a political point of view (Hale, 1971, p. 20; Tate, 1942, pp. 292–3). This may be true, but only in the most formal sense. The great powers accepted the Tsar's invitation to the conference not from a love of peace, but from a desire to avoid offending the Tsar; not from a wish to discuss disarmament, but from the fear of being held responsible for not discussing it. The German Kaiser, Wilhell II, talked of 'the young Tsar's humanitarian nonsense' while his Foreign Minister, Bernhard von Bülow, made it clear that he, too, was opposed to disarmament as such—only in rather more diplomatic language (Mendelsohn-Bartholdy, 1922, vol. 15, document 4219; Bülow, 1931, vol. 1, p. 275). Count Goluchowski, the Austro-Hungarian Foreign Minister, adopted a similar attitude to his German counterpart and effectively suggested that the proposed conference did not discuss disarmament at all (Gooch and Temperley, 1927, vol. 1, document 265). The Prime Minister and Foreign Secretary of the United Kingdom, the Marquess of Salisbury, expressed considerable scepticism of the Tsar's scheme and held that the 'perfection' of instruments of war acted as a deterrent to war—perhaps the first official usage of the term 'deterrence' in modern history (Gooch and Temperley, 1927, vol. 1, document 269). The French Foreign Minister, Théophile Delcassé, thought similarly, and expressed himself vigorously to the German ambassador in Paris:

In this conference we have entirely the same interest as you. You will not limit your forces at this moment nor agree to proposals of disarmament, we are in the same position. On both sides we wish to spare the Tsar and to find a formula to circumvent this question (Mendelsohn-Bartholdy, 1922, vol. 15, document 4253).

It was easy enough for the powers to pour scorn on the Tsar's proposal when it was couched in the general terms of his initial Rescript. It was more difficult to oppose the discussion of disarmament once the concept of a peace conference had been accepted, however, reluctantly. Nevertheless, they were forced to do so once the agenda for the conference was formulated in the so-called Muraviev circular of 11 January 1899 (for the text, see Dupuy and Hammermann, 1973, pp. 50–2). This was a truly prescient document. In it, the Russian Foreign Minister, Count Muraviev, set out the agenda not only for the Hague Conference, but, indirectly, for almost every disarmament conference in the twentieth century. Itemized for discussion were: the limitation of effectives; the quantitative and qualitative (vertical and horizontal) limitation of matériel; budgetary limitation; the prohibition of agreed categories of weapon; and the concept of 'no first use'. There were also proposals for a discussion of confidence-building measures, arbitration, mediation and the conduct of war. The only significant exceptions were demilitarized zones (deliberately excluded on the basis that they were a 'political' question) and the problem of verification. In other words, the issues of disarmament were well-enough known last century; the problem has been the inability and, as often, the unwillingness of statesmen to resolve them.

The reaction of the powers to the Muraviev circular underlines the fundamentally duplicitous approach of the leaders of the powers towards disarmament at the time, which, in a more sophisticated form, has become integral to the arms control process today. Basically, the powers did not want to agree on arms limitation. Salisbury described the Muraviev scheme as *pas sérieux* and would commit the United Kingdom to nothing in the way of limitation (Mendelsohn-Bartholdy, 1922, vol. 15, document 4237). In his initial instructions to the chief British delegate at the conference, Sir Julian Pauncefote, Salisbury deliberately excluded any detailed reference to disarmament save for two vitriolic memoranda from the Admiralty and War Office which opposed all disarmament. His idea was 'to deflect discussion onto other topics' (Gooch and Temperley, 1927, vol. 1, document 274–6).

Salisbury's dismissal of disarmament was reinforced by his choice of delegates, more especially the naval delegate, the militaristic Admiral Sir John Fisher, who upheld the notion that 'Might is Right' and described the whole proceedings as 'nonsense' (Mendelsohn-Bartholdy, 1922, vol. 15, documents 4274, 4351). The disarmament policy of the United Kingdom at the Hague Conference, therefore, was one of rationalization based on the idea that arms limitation was impossible.

British policy was not unique in this respect—the United States followed a very similar line. In his instructions to the American delegates, Secretary of State John Hay declared that disarmament was 'inapplicable' to the United States and that 'the question of limitation could not profitably be discussed' (Dupuy and Hammerman, 1973, p. 53; also Gooch and Temperley, 1927, vol. 1, document 282). He had a particular objection to qualitative disarmament; his statement that 'The expediency of restraining the inventive genius of our people in the direction of devising means of defence is by no means clear' is no different from President Reagan's defence of the SDI programme. Similarly, his choice of naval delegate fell upon Captain A.T. Mahan, who rivalled Fisher in his defence of armaments. According to the First Delegate, Ambassador Andrew D. White (1905, vol. 2, p. 347), Mahan had 'very little, if any, sympathy with the main purposes of the conference' and his views 'prevented any lapse into sentimentality'.

German policy was similar. In line with the Kaiser and Bülow's predetermined views, the policy of the Imperial government was to 'leave others to oppose impossible demands, so that Germany could not be reproached for having hindered by her conduct a great humanitarian work' (Brandenburg, 1933, p. 130). The ruse might have succeeded, or caused difficulties to the other powers, if the instructions had been carried out. Instead the German military delegate, Colonel Gross von Schwarzhoff took a militant line and intimated that Germany would under no circumstances be party to a limitation, still less a reduction, of armaments (Gooch and Temperley, 1927, vol. 1, document 282). It was a gaffe which effectively ended the consideration of disarmament as such at the Hague, and enabled the other great powers to escape their own (and, with the exception of Russia) equal responsibility for the breakdown.

At least Schwarzhoff's policy had the virtue of being honest. He was opposed to disarmament and said as much. So, too, did his colleague at the Hague, Baron Karl von Stengel, author of *Der Ewige Friede*, which glorified war as a God-given institution and declared that attempts at arms limitation were absurd (Tate, 1942, pp. 229–30, 350). In future years, statesmen would not be nearly so honest. It can be suggested that one of the major accomplishments of the first Hague Conference was to bequeath a considerable element of duplicity into the arms control process. This, however, was the logical and inevitable consequence of the principle being accepted that armaments could be a matter for international discussion; there was no other way forward for opponents of disarmament than a policy of deception.

The first Hague Conference is a classic case of the five factors necessary for the successful conclusion of a disarmament convention being absent. The position barely changed down to the Great War in 1914. On the surface, it appeared that the British Liberal government from December 1905 onwards undertook the leadership of the disarmament cause. A proposal for a reduction of naval expenditure was mooted for presentation at the second Hague Conference in 1907, and, when it became clear that it would be rejected, a proposal for exchange of information was substituted (Gooch and Temperley, 1927, vol. 6, document 1). But it was voted down, as the British knew it would be, by the other powers under German leadership (Gooch and Temperley, 1927, vol. 6, document 206; Woodward, 1964, ch. 8). In reality, the motives of the British were somewhat less than altruistic. The implication of the British proposal for naval limitation was that the other powers (but primarily Germany) should recognize British maritime supremacy for the foreseeable future at a time when Britain had accomplished a major technological breakthrough with the launching of HMS *Dreadnought* on 10 February 1906. In this respect, the British government's position at the second Hague Conference can be compared with that of the American government at the time of the Baruch Plan of 14 June 1946.

A further factor in the Liberal government's advocacy of naval limitation, not only at the second Hague Conference but during bilateral discussions with Germany over the next six years, was the pressure exerted by the small but vociferous radical wing of the party. The idea was that money saved on naval expenditure could be used for social reform at home. The Foreign Secretary, Sir Edward Grey, and successive Prime Ministers, Sir Henry Campbell-Bannerman and H.H. Asquith, wanted to ensure that priority was given to maintaining the lead in naval armaments over Germany, but they were forced to recognize the political importance of the 'disarmament lobby'. They therefore pursued negotiations with Germany in apparent good faith and claimed that it was German intransigence that caused the failure of negotiations. (That the Germans were similarly intransigent is irrelevant.) Two further precedents had been set. First, the concept was established that 'peace groups' could be sidestepped more easily by entering into negotiations rather than resisting them. Second, the practice was inaugurated of statesment declaring after failed disarmament negotiations that 'there is no ground for reproaching my country with having failed to do her utmost to promote world disarmament'. The British Foreign Secretary during the years 1931–5, Sir John Simon (1952, p. 186), was to use those very words concerning the breakdown of the Geneva Disarmament Conference of 1932–4. The theory of disarmament was accepted; the practice was not.

Of course, armaments and disarmament agreements are only one aspect of power—and power management—in international relations. Security agreements are the other major factor. This, too, was realized by the powers at an early stage. At various stages of the Anglo-German naval talks, the Germans tried to interest the United Kingdom in a neutrality agreement in return for concessions on the German naval programme. The idea was not so much to secure a disarmament agreement, rather to tempt the United Kingdom with such an agreement in order to secure a free hand on the Continent—in effect, to dominate Europe. The manoeuvre was so transparent that the British did not fall for it (Gooch and Temperley, 1927, vol. 6, document 174), but again, it acted as a precedent for similar attempts in the future. At no point in the pre-1914 period did the factors necessary for a major disarmament agreement exist.

Disarmament negotiations 1919–34

The overt or thinly-disguised militarism, the almost unthinking reliance on armaments for security of the period before 1914, was to be severely shaken by the Great War of 1914–18. Many leading statesmen came to believe that it was the arms race of the pre-war years which had precipitated the outbreak of conflict. Most famous, probably, was Woodrow Wilson, but perhaps the most influential was Sir Edward Grey, whose memoirs have so often been quoted on the subject: 'The enormous growth of armaments in Europe, the sense of insecurity and fear caused by them—it was these that made war inevitable' (Grey, 1928, vol. 1, 162, vol. 2, 265–7). Grey's thesis that arms races cause war was challenged in public by only a very few individuals in the decade and a half following the Treaty of Versailles, at least in the English-speaking world. The desirability of disarmament was enshrined in the Covenant of the League of Nations (Article 8), and in the preamble to Part V of the Treaty of Versailles, where it was declared that the enforced disarmament of Germany after the Great War was 'to render possible the initiation of a general limitation of armaments of all nations'. For fifteen years, members of the League of

Nations, with the co-operation of the United States and Soviet Union, endeavoured to redeem the pledge of general disarmament.

Or did they? The outstanding achievement in the field of arms control in the inter-war period was the Washington Naval Treaty of 6 February 1922. Yet this was the product of an American initiative, not the League of Nations. The Washington Treaty is indicative that all five factors necessary for the successful conclusion of an arms control agreement were present. First and foremost, there was a belief in disarmament; there was a common assumption among the victor powers of the Great War that the naval race in which they had engaged—to some extent unwittingly as a result of wartime plans— was fruitless and counterproductive when they had no common enemy. Political leadership was apparent, too, in that, on this occasion, the United States acted as the 'Gentle Knight' of international relations (Louis J. Halle's (1984, ch. 11) phrase) using its undoubted power and moral authority to prescribe the parameters of an agreement acceptable to the five great naval powers—the United States, the United Kingdom, Japan, France and Italy. The leaders of the powers also displayed a political will in overcoming the objections of the 'hawks' to an agreement. At the same time, the victory of the proponents of agreement was hardly total. In accepting parity with Italy in capital ships and aircraft carriers, Briand, the French Prime Minister, was forced to capitulate to the demands of his military leaders that land and air disarmament should not be discussed. Similarly, the militarists (or should it be navalists?) within the British Admiralty managed to limit the quantitative restrictions on vessels to capital ships (which the more forward-looking strategists of the days were already beginning to regard as obsolescent) and aircraft-carriers. They succeeded in their efforts to exempt cruisers and destroyers from limitation, except for a tonnage and gun-calibre limitation for cruisers which they themselves put forward (Chatfield, 1942, vol. 1, 195–7; Chalmers, 1951, pp. 365, 369–70). The fourth and fifth factors necessary for the conclusion of a convention were also present. The political leaders had a sound enough understanding of the technical problems connected with restricting the classes of vessel limited. More important, they were able to appreciate the genuine concerns of the other parties to the negotiation. In this respect, the British and Americans accepted a Japanese proposal to retain the status quo in naval bases in an agreed agrea of the Pacific, in return for Japan accepting an inferiority of 1:3.5 in the proportion of permitted capital ships and carriers.

In recent years, the Washington Treaty has come under attack from British and American historians and political scientists on the grounds that Japan was left 'supreme' in the western Pacific and able to follow a path of imperial expansion in the later 1930s (see, for example, Halle, 1984, pp. 95, 99; Gray, 1976, pp. 17–18). But such an argument is primarily a rationalization based on hindsight. Apart from the fact that it assumes that British and American imperialist activities in the Far East were 'good' and the Japanese 'bad', it misinterprets both the historical situation and the nature of the disarmament process. In many respects, the Washington Treaty represented a defeat for Japanese interests. The Tokyo government agreed to withdraw its forces from Siberia, to restore Chinese sovereignty over Shantung and to drop the alliance with the United Kingdom—in addition to accepting inferiority in naval armaments. At the strategic level, the most relevant factor was no longer sea power, it was air power, as indicated by the Virginia coast experiments of 1921. It was Japan's proximity to the Asian mainlaind, control over Korea, position in Manchuria and potential string of air bases in the western Pacific which guaranteed her supremacy in the area—not her battleships. Further, the attack on the Washington Treaty is based on the premise that disarmament agreements are unchanging and meant to uphold a given status quo. This, however, is true only as far as the actual stipulations of a treaty are concerned and for the length of time specified. Political, social, economic and ideological factors which impinge on armaments treaties are constantly changing, and there is a continuing need to update arms treaties to bring them into line with the realities that surround them. The disarmament process should be seen as dynamic, not static. The Washington Treaty should not be blamed for the Far Eastern War of 1937–45.

The Washington Treaty was one of several disarmament treaties concluded in the aftermath of the Great War. Others included the Geneva Gas Protocol of 17 June 1925, basically a no-first-use convention regarding chemical and bacteriological weapons; the London Naval Treaty of 22 April 1930; and the Anglo-German naval agreement of 18 June 1935. But the main objective of the advocates of disarmament, the negotiations of a general armaments convention under the auspices of the League of Nations—in other words the halting of the central arms race—was not achieved. The task was never likely to be easy, because of the complicated nature of the questions involved and the fact that the questions themselves touched raw nerves of national power and national security. Many problems were resolved. There was general agreement on the technical side as to what was achievable; there was a reasonable understanding of the needs of the powers concerned, and in particular that a favourable issue depended on reconciling the German claim for equality of rights in armaments—not equality of armaments—with the French demand for 'security'. What was lacking was political will, political leadership, and a belief in disarmament itself. For fifteen years, a battle waged in every country between the proponents and opponents and disarmament. The opponents won.

Most commentators on the Geneva negotiations, whether or not they consider the whole proceedings futile, have blamed the failure of the negotiations on an intransigent France or, more usually, an aggressive Hitler. This is a misconception. Although there were many opponents of disarmament in France, most French governments took the view that disarmament was not impossible. The symbols of this were the policies of Aristide Briand at the Ministry of Foreign Affairs throughout the later 1920s and the work of Joseph Paul-Boncour as delegate at the League and later as Prime and Foreign Minister on a number of occasions down to 1934. Despite their fear of a revived Germany, French leaders tended to take the view that it was better to move towards accepting the German claim to equality than to face the alternative of a renewed arms race and the increased likelihood of war. They believed that any German rearmament over the levels specified by Versailles could be controlled by means of an international convention. Their price was an effective organ of verification and increased security guarantees, the extent and nature of which would depend on what was conceded to Germany on the armaments side of the equation. Even after Hitler had withdrawn Germany from the Disarmament Conference on 14 October 1933, the French, under Paul-Boncour, continued to negotiate. It was only after the formation of the National Government of Gaston Doumergue on 9 February 1934 that France took a dramatic lurch towards the policy of the 'hawks', with André Tardieu, Marshal Pétain, Louis Barthou and the formerly liberal but by now almost fanatically anti-German Herriot in the Cabinet (Vaisse, 1981).

If it was in the French interest to negotiate a disarmament convention, so, too, was it in Germany's interest. One can hardly suggest that there was a specific belief in disarmament *per se*, even before Hitler came to power. Germany remained, in essence, a militaristic power, even though her military capacity had been drastically curtailed by Versailles. The continuity in German foreign policy from Bethmann-Hollweg and the September memorandum of 1914, through Stresemann and his successors (in chastened international circumstances) to Hitler is uncanny. In some ways, indeed, the policy of Hitler's conservative predecessors was rather more aggressive than Hitler's in the period down to 1934. There was far less reason for Papen and Neurath (Chancellor and Foreign Minister, respectively) to withdraw Germany from the Geneva Disarmament Conference in July 1932 than for

Hitler to do so in October 1934. They could only complain of the slowness of a conference that had been in existence for five months; Hitler could complain, justifiably, that the western powers had gone back on their word. The British, in March 1933, had proposed a disarmament scheme which would have granted Germany considerable equality in armaments (not just equality of rights) within five years; and this had been accepted as the basis of negotiations. But over the summer of 1933, the United Kingdom had come together with France, Italy and the United States to try to force on Germany an eight-year convention whereby the building up of German armaments towards the French level would not only be delayed but would be made conditional on the satisfactory institution of an 'automatic and continuous' control regime over an initial four-year period. It was not so much the control regime itself to which Hitler objected (he had, in fact, already agreed to it), it was the fact that, after the four-year *période d'épreuve*, there was no assurance that the western powers would agree to consider it 'satisfactory' (UK Foreign Office, 1947, series 2, vol. 5, document 434; UK Foreign Office, 1957, series C, vol. 1, documents 479, 499).

Essentially, a resolution of the Franco-German disarmament problem in the inter-war years depended on the policy followed by the United Kingdom. The French demanded greater security in return for reducing their military advantage over Germany. A full alliance with the United Kingdom would have provided this, although for many years the French would have accepted less. For example, under the so-called Paul-Boncour Plan of 14 November 1932 they demanded of the United Kingdom only a reaffirmation of existing commitments under the Covenant of the League of Nations, more specifically Article 16, the sanctions article (Dupuy and Hammerman, 1973, pp. 213–20). Germany, for her part, was ready to accept increased British commitments to France as the price of equality. As late as February 1934, Hitler said he would not take exception to an Anglo-French alliance (UK Foreign Office, 1947, series 2, vol. 6, documents 302–6; UK Foreign Office, 1957, series C, vol. 2, documents 270–1, 273, 276; Avon, 1962, p. 63). So why was the United Kingdom, the accepted mediator, unable to bridge the gap between the two continental powers? The answer is simple. British governments, with the significant exceptions of the Labour administrations of 1924 and 1929–31, neither understood nor accepted the five factors upon which the success of disarmament negotiations is built.

The main culprits in this respect were the Baldwin government of 1924–9 and the 'National' (in reality Conservative) government of 1931–5, together with the politico-military bureaucracy which surrounded them. The reason is not hard to find. With few exceptions, notably Viscount Cecil of Chelwood, Chancellor of the Duchy of Lancaster in the years 1924–7, members of both governments and bureaucracy were sceptical of, or completely opposed to, the concept of disarmament itself. This is not the usual view. British politicians and historians like to give the impression that the United Kingdom carried her arms reductions in the years following the Treaty of Versailles much further than any other power—an example other powers should have followed but did not (see Londonderry, 1943, ch. 2, pp. 3–5). Nothing could be further from the truth. British arms reductions after 1919 had nothing to do with a quest for disarmament; they were practical measures taken only after careful examination of the circumstances of the time and with due regard to political, economic and strategic circumstances. In fact, after reaching a low point in 1923, the defence estimates were to rise under the Baldwin government to a steady £113–118 million per annum, which represented some 14 per cent of government expenditure and 3.2 per cent of national income. These figures compared favourably with those of 1913, when, faced with the German menace and naval race, the United Kingdom had spent only an extra 0.4 per cent of national income on defence, that is 3.6 per cent. On the basis of expenditure per head of population, in the mid-1920s, the United Kingdom spent some one-and-three-quarter times that of France, over twice that of the United States, two-and-a-half times that of Italy, three-and-a-half times that of Japan, five times that of Germany and six times that of the Soviet Union (Higham, 1962, pp. 325–7; Jakobsen, 1927; Coates, 1928, p. 82).

In the intellectual and international climate of the 1920s and early 1930s, it was difficult for British leaders to come out openly against disarmament. But behind the scenes and in private writings the true thoughts of British leaders are clear. Baldwin, Prime Minister during 1924–9 and effective leader behind the shadow of Ramsey MacDonald in the years 1931–5, while not lacking in protestations of goodwill, held strongly that disarmament was visionary (Richardson, 1989, pp. 20, 199). W.C. Bridgeman, First Lord of the Admiralty in 1924–9 and Baldwin's chief confidant at the time, had a complete belief in the Royal Navy and consistently supported the demarcation of an extensive naval programme. He held that 'so long as the Disarmament Conference continues ... so long will friction and misunderstanding prevail' (Bridgeman, 1928, p. 167). His successor from 1931, Sir Bolton Eyres-Monsell, remarked to the British delegation at Geneva: 'The sooner your bloody conference is wound up, the better for all concerned' (Noel-Baker, 1979, p. 105). MacDonald had shown himself a true friend of disarmament in years gone by, but from 1931 he was no more than a figurehead, a prisoner at the mercy of the Conservative/National majority of 497 in the House of Commons. He was also beginning to lose his faculties—he broke down during a speech to the Geneva conference in March 1933—and was never able to get to grips with the problems of general disarmament as he had with naval disarmament at the time of the London Naval Treaty of 1930. Far from accepting that Britain needed to mediate between France and Germany in order to bring them together, he deliberately rejected it: his idea was to ask the French and Germans 'to put their demands in such a way that Britain could say that she supported both sides' (UK Foreign Office, 1947, series 2, vol. 4, document 211).

Similarly, there was no real understanding of the disarmament problem by the Foreign Secretaries, Sir Austen Chamberlain (1924–9) and Sir John Simon (1931–5). Chamberlain always distrusted what he called 'grandiose schemes which were to be applied everywhere logically and simultaneously', though he came to co-operate amicably with Viscount Cecil over the Geneva negotiations by 1927 (Richardson, 1989, pp. 21, 199). For his part, Sir John Simon has gained the reputation of being the most disastrous Foreign Secretary in the twentieth century. The reputation is not undeserved. He was weak and pliable, easy meat for the hawks within the Cabinet on the disarmament issue. He was no match, for example, for the Minister for Air, the Marquess of Londonderry, who fought a long battle in the Cabinet against air disarmament. The latter regarded the Disarmament Conference as 'highly dangerous and insincere' and was fond of saying that he had 'saved the R.A.F. from the disarmers' (Londonderry, 1943, pp. 71ff.; see also Noel-Baker, 1979, pp. 61, 105, 124).

This is only the tip of the iceberg. Numerous other examples of the inner feelings of important Cabinet members opposed to disarmament could be cited, including Churchill's oft-repeated 'zoo allegory' (Gilbert, 1976, p. 305). It could be shown how the hawks, led by Churchill, Lord Birkenhead and Admiral Beatty managed to break up the Geneva Naval Conference of 1927 (Richardson, 1989, ch. 9). It could be shown how some of the more important members of the government bureaucracy, notably Sir Eyre Crowe (Permanent Secretary at the Foreign Office, 1920–5), Sir Robert Vansittart (Permanent Secretary, 1931–8), Sir Maurice Hankey (Secretary to the Cabinet, 1919–38) and most of the military leaders added their weight to the anti-disarmament cause and delayed matters over the years (Richardson, 1989, ch. 3). There is no need. The inbuilt inner obstacles of the personnel involved ensured that the United Kingdom in practice—as distinct from theory and rhetoric—became the leading opponent of disarmament in the interwar years. At the World Disarmament Conference of 1932–4, the culmination of the disarmament discussions, a settlement depended on a British initiative; the other powers appealed to the United Kingdom to play the 'Gentle Knight'. The government refused. The United Kingdom did not present a disarmament plan to the conference until March 1933, by which time the conference had been sitting for over thirteen months and Hitler had come to power!

Even then, the initiative was not the Cabinet's; it was that of the British delegate in Geneva, Anthony Eden, in conjunction with his Foreign Office and military advisers, Alexander Cadogan and A.C. Temperley. MacDonald, after whom the plan is (most inappropriately) named, launched it at Geneva not in any hope that it might be successful, but in an effort to ensure that Germany would be held responsible for the failure of the conference (UK Foreign Office, 1947, series 2, vol. 4, document 290). His lack of faith in the plan was such that, within two days of submitting it, he was in Rome negotiating with Mussolini for a four-power pact.

In effect, therefore, it was the United Kingdom that killed the general disarmament negotiations of 1919–34. The efforts of such personalities as Viscount Cecil, Philip Noel-Baker, Anthony Eden and Arthur Henderson (Foreign Secretary in the Labour government of 1929–31 and President of the Disarmament Conference, 1932–4) were in vain. It was not so much a victory of Right over Left. After all, Cecil and Eden were prominent members of the political Right. It was a case of the hawks defeating the doves (Temperley, 1938).

Disarmament negotiations since 1945

A brief look at post-war negotiations tells the same story. Disarmament agreements have been negotiated only when there has been political will, political leadership, technical understanding, an ability to appreciate the other parties' case; and only then when a belief in disarmament has existed. Basically, there were no major agreements between 1945 and 1960 because the Americans never genuinely believed in disarmament. They tried to use their supposed desire for disarmament first as a means of maintaining military advantage (the Baruch plan of June 1946) and then as propaganda (support of the Anglo-French memorandum of 11 June 1954); but their bluff was called by the Soviet memorandum of 10 May 1955. The Soviet memorandum itself might have been a bluff—but the only way to call it was to negotiate. Instead, the Western powers withdrew their proposals and exposed their own insincerity. It was only the Cuban missile crisis of October 1962 which pushed the Americans into negotiating seriously.

Whether or not the Soviets negotiated seriously during the period 1945–60 is a matter of conjecture. Their position at the various disarmament talks is in many ways reminiscent of that of the Germans in the early 1930s. There may have been little belief in disarmament *per se*, but it was in their interest to negotiate seriously as the Americans had such a superiority in atomic and nuclear weapons. Certainly they reciprocated American willingness in the 1960s and early 1970s—a period which can now be viewed almost as a second 'Golden Age' in disarmament theory and practice.

The era of agreement in the 1960s and 1970s further substantiates the case that disarmament is not simply the prerogative of the Left. One could hardly term Lyndon Johnson or Richard Nixon, more especially in the light of their policies in South-East Asia, 'woolly-headed idealists'! They each, however, came to accept that disarmament agreements could strengthen international stability while maintaining, if not improving, the national security of both the United States and Soviet Union. Jimmy Carter followed the same path, too, though with rather less political will—in this case a euphemism for vacillation—much less technical understanding and a flawed appreciation of the motives and interests of the Soviet Union. As a result, the opponents of agreement were able to marshal their forces, delay the negotiation of a SALT II accord and bring about an anti-disarmament consensus in the United States.

Steps in the process included the Jackson–Perle memorandum of February 1976 (which opposed agreement on the basis of the Vladivostok accords of November 1974) and the formation, also in 1976, of the so-called Committee on the Present Danger, a hard-line anti-Soviet group whose leading personality was Paul Nitze of NSC-68 infamy. In the new climate of opinion, Ronald Reagan was elected President of the United States on a programme of rejecting the SALT II treaty and inaugurating on a new arms race.

Throughout most of his period of office, Reagan rigidly maintained an anti-disarmament course. He launched the most massive and costly arms programme in world history. He rejected the possibility of a comprehensive test ban—perhaps the most important and far-reaching arms control agreement that is readily attainable. He appointed Nitze as his chief arms control adviser, although in the new climate of opinion Nitze is termed a 'moderate'! He broke the (admittedly unratified) SALT II treaty. At the Reykjavik summit in October 1986, he rejected a comprehensive arms limitation settlement because of his obsession with the doubtful, destabilizing and hideously expensive SDI programme. And he all but formally adopted the so-called 'wider' interpretation of the 1972 AMB treaty, in effect abrogating the treaty.

So why did the United States and the Soviet Union sign a treaty on intermediate-range nuclear weapons (INF) at the Washington summit on 8 December 1987? Part of the answer can be found in a feature of the disarmament process which has been apparent since the first Hague Conference of 1899: the fact that, whatever the motives for being involved in negotiations in the first place, once negotiations have started the negotiators themselves have a better appreciation of the fears and hopes of other parties to the discussion, a better understanding of the technical problems involved, and an increased awareness of the methods by which the questions under discussion can be resolved.

Sir Julian Pauncefote noted this in his report to Lord Salisbury on the first Hague Conference (Gooch and Temperley, 1927, vol. 1, document 283). Bridgeman came under the influence of Cecil and supported an agreement at the Geneva Naval Conference of 1927 (Richardson, 1989, ch. 9). Nitze came close to accepting an agreement over theatre nuclear forces during his famous 'walk in the woods' with the Soviet arms negotiator Yuli Kvitsinsky on 16 July 1982 (*The Guardian*, 13 and 21 January 1984). Reagan seems to have been initiated into the process at the Reykjavik summit.

A second aspect of the disarmament process was also involved. Part of the 'great game' of international arms negotiations is to put forward proposals which appear eminently reasonable yet are unacceptable to opponents. In the case of the INF negotiations, Reagan's initial offer of the so-called 'zero option' on 18 November 1981 was a bluff. It was put forward in the knowledge that it was unacceptable to the then Soviet Leader, Yuri Andropov; and its aim was not to promote disarmament, rather, as later admitted by General Bernard Rogers, Supreme NATO Commander, Europe, to spike the guns of the 'freeze' movement in the United States and the 'peace movement' in Europe (Talbott, 1984; *Guardian*, 3 March 1987). The American ploy had considerable initial success, but on 28 February 1987 the new Soviet leader, Mikhail Gorbachev, turned the tables on the American President by calling his bluff and accept the 'zero option'. The United States tried to backtrack, linking the 'zero option' with increased demands on shorter-range weapons and verification; and at one time a link with conventional arms and chemical weapons was canvassed (*Guardian*, 3 and 4 March 1987). But to no avail. The increasingly weak internal position of the President in the aftermath of 'Irangate' ensured that the treaty would be signed.

The INF agreement further illustrates the importance of the five factors mentioned above in ensuring the success of negotiations. On this occasion, the political leadership was supplied by Gorbachev. Since becoming Soviet leader in 1985, he has effectively set the agenda for international arms negotiations—with initiatives on comprehensive limitation, chemical arms, strategic arms, the test ban and verification. It was his intervention on 28 February 1987 which effectively made the breakthrough at the INF talks. He assembled a formidable team of arms negotiators, whose understanding of the technical side of disarmament was second to none; and he showed considerable strength of will in piloting the proposals through the Soviet hierarchy and refusing to be deflected from his major goals by either internal or external forces. In public at least, he championed the cause of disarmament.

On the American side of the equation, the five factors were not present to the same extent; but circumstances combined to produce an enhanced presence at an appropriate time. Reagan may not have believed in disarmament *per se*, but political realism in the wake of the Iran/Contra affair convinced him of the benefits to be gained by signing an agreement, or rather the dangers of not signing an agreement. Certainly he gained an understanding of the Soviet position at the Reykjavik summit, and he possessed an excellent negotiator in Nitze, whose knowledge of the technicalities of disarmament matched that of his Soviet counterparts. In the background, of course, the SDI programme marches on . . .

The full implications of the INF Treaty are not yet apparent. Optimists see the treaty as a stepping-stone towards a strategic arms reduction treaty. Super-optimists look even further towards an agreement on short-range nuclear weapons. Pessimists see the agreement as a political sham and a military irrelevance. Its provisions are already being circumvented in American and Soviet plans to deploy large numbers of air- and sea-launched cruise missiles, and land-based missiles within the treaty limits. But then, the disarmament process runs parallel to the armament process; and the process is as infuriating as the word itself.

Bibliography

Avon, Earl of, 1962. *The Eden Memoirs: Facing the Dictators*. London: Cassell.

Brandenburg, E., 1933. *From Bismarck to the World War*. London: Oxford University Press.

Bridgeman, W.C., 1928. 'Note of December 11, "Political Notes" ', *Bridgeman Papers*, Vol. 2. Shrewsbury: Salop County Record Office.

Bull, H., 1961. *The Control of the Arms Race*. London: Weidenfeld and Nicolson/IISS.

Bülow, B. von, 1931. *Memoirs*. Boston: Putnam.

Chalmers, W.S., 1951. *The Life and Letters of David, Earl Beatty*. London: Hodder and Stoughton.

Chatfield, Lord, 1942. *The Navy and Defence*. London: Heinemann.

Coates, W.P., 1928. *USSR and Disarmament*. London: Anglo-Russian Parliamentary Committee.

Dupuy, T.N. and Hammerman, G.M. (eds), 1973. *A Documentary History of Arms Control and Disarmament*. Dunn Loring: Dupuy Associates.

Gilbert, M., 1976. *Winston S. Churchill*, Vol. 5. London: Heinemann.

Gooch, G.P. and Temperley, H., 1927. *British Documents on the Origins of the War 1898–1914*. London: HMSO.

Gray, C.S., 1976. *The Soviet-American Arms Race*. Farnborough: Saxon House.

Grey of Fallodon, Viscount, 1928. *Twenty-Five Years*. London: Hodder and Stoughton.

Hale, O.J., 1971. *The Great Illusion, 1900–1914*. New York: Harper.

Halle, L.J., 1984. *The Elements of International Strategy*. Lanham: UPA.

Higham, R., 1962. *Armed Forces in Peacetime*. London: Foulis.

Iriye, A., 1987. *The Origins of the Second World War in Asia and the Pacific*. London: Longman.

Jakobsen, M., 1927. 'Memorandum of March 26', *Viscount Cecil of Chelwood Papers*. British Museum Additional Manuscripts, 51099.

Londonderry, Marquess of, 1943. *Wings of Destiny*. London: Macmillan.

Mendelsohn-Bartholdy, A. *et al.* eds, 1922. *Die grosse Politik der europaischen Kabinette*. Berlin: Deutsche Verlag für Politik und Geschichte.

Morgenthau, H.J. and Thompson, K.W., 1985. *Politics among Nations*, 6th ed. New York: Knopf.

Noel-Baker, P.J., 1979. *The First World Disarmament Conference, 1932–33*. Oxford: Pergamon.

O'Neill, R. and Schwartz, D. (eds), 1987. *Hedley Bull on Arms Control*. London: Macmillan/IISS.

Richardson, Dick, 1989. *The Evolution of British Disarmament Policy in the 1920s*. London: Pinter.

Simon, Sir John, 1952. *Retrospect*. London: Hutchinson.

Talbott, S., 1984. *Deadly Gambits*. New York: Knopf.

Tate, M., 1942. *The Disarmament Illusion*. New York: Russell & Russell.

Temperley, A.C., 1938. *The Whispering Gallery of Europe*. London: Collins.

UK Foreign Office, 1947. *Documents on British Foreign Policy, 1919–1939*, Series 2. London: HMSO.

UK Foreign Office, 1957 et seq. *Documents on German Foreign Policy, 1918–1945*, Series C. London: HMSO.

Vaisse, M., 1981. *Securité d'abord*. Paris: Pédone.

White, A.D., 1905. *Autobiography*. London: Appleton-Century.

Woodward, E.L., 1964. *Great Britain and the German Navy*, London: Cass.

4 Political Consequences of Nuclear Disarmament in Europe: The Loss of US Forces

Simon Duke

Both superpowers have committed themselves to the long-term goal of ridding the world of nuclear weapons, or at least creating a world where nuclear weapons can serve no role. The INF Treaty, which was signed in December 1987 and approved by the Senate in May 1988, has opened up the very real possibility of further cuts within Europe and maybe globally. The progress of the INF talks and those currently being held covering different weapon types (the START talks at the strategic level, the CD talks in Geneva, and the CSCE process comprising the 35-member CSCE discussions on Confidence and Security Building Measures (CSBMs) and the 23-member talks on Conventional Forces in Europe (CFE) are largely due to the emergence of a new conciliatory Soviet leadership. It follows that much of the progress of the various talks and future arms control initiatives depends upon the success of the efforts at economic restructuring and internal political reforms within the Soviet Union.

The atmosphere within which arms control initiatives and the ensuing negotiations take place is remarkably different from that of the Brezhnev era, due largely to the high political and economic significance that arms control has been given by both superpowers. Under the Reagan administration both leaders of the superpowers differed over the question of the utility of nuclear weapons—both probably with an eye on respective versions of *Realpolitik*. Reagan's vision was never a nuclear-free world *per se* but a world in which a shield against nuclear attack would render the nuclear weapons 'impotent and obsolete' and thus remove any point in possessing them. Gorbachev, in contrast, called for the complete elimination of all nuclear weapons by the year 2000 before the CPSU Central Committee on 15 January 1986; he has since repeated that call on several other occasions. The two 'visions' are sufficiently different to pose fundamental problems in any attempt to reduce the level of nuclear weapons possessed by the rival alliances—quite apart from questions of doctrine, technology, industry and bureaucracy. President George Bush's stance on the utility of nuclear weapons is harder to ascertain. The NATO summit of May 1989 would seem to indicate a willingness to consider real reductions in the superpower nuclear arsenals; but the rhetoric emanating from the White House is still reminiscent of that of the Reagan era.

It is also worth observing at this stage that disarmament is quite different to arms control. Disarmament tends to deny the existence of many fundamental differences between the alliances by proposing cuts (and, more often than not, failing to create a safer world in the process, merely altering the number of weapons while maintaining the unequal ratios which are the reasons for feelings of insecurity, threat and eventually conflict) which deny the existence of asymmetries which, even if there are no weapons, will not be removed. Arms control does necessarily imply a reduction in the number of any given weapon systems but an attempt to regulate military competition. The SALT agreements and the ABM Treaty serve as examples of the latter. To characterize the utopianist ideals of the Kremlin and the White House as being more inclined to disarmament and arms control, respectively, is not entirely unfair. The discussion also serves to illustrate that while it may be may seem an obvious statement that a nuclear-free Europe (and world) would be a safer place, the case is by no means clear-cut as long as there is a failure to halt the proliferation of nuclear weapons on a global scale. In this sense Europe, which hosts many of the world's nuclear weapons, serves as a particularly interesting case. While the nuclear arsenals are traditionally seen in terms of super-power politics, the 'knock-on' effects of these weapons for the Middle East, to take one example, are not clearly understood. The mesmeric effect of nuclear weapons has also left many blind to the rapid advances in conventional weapons technology that also makes conventional war in Europe potentially devastating. They, too, have become weapons of mass destruction. Any notion that the removal of nuclear weapons may expose Europeans to a greater likelihood of conventional war, but that this is not as devastating, must be strongly resisted.

Nuclear disarmament is only one of the options that faces Europe for the future and certainly the current level of nuclear weapons in Europe is unsupportable, if only for the practical reasons of obsolescence and the cost of developing new systems which many are increasingly loth to pay. Until we understand the role of nuclear weapons in Europe it is impossible wholeheartedly to advocate disarmament or a continuation of the status quo allowing for the retirement of a few systems here and a few new ones elsewhere. Since the vast majority of US overseas nuclear deployments are made with the European theatre in mind this chapter will aim to clarify, not answer, the main debating points surrounding the US nuclear presence in Europe.

The nuclear arsenal in Europe

Before considering the political consequences of nuclear disarmament in Europe and, more specifically in the context of this brief present-ation, those US nuclear systems in Western Europe, we should be aware of roughly how many nuclear warheads there are deployed in Europe as a whole. NATO controls between 6,000 and 8,000 nuclear warheads and over 7,000 delivery systems and it also has 541 land-based surface-to-surface missiles with ranges from 110 to 2,500 km—this will, most probably, be modified as the withdrawals start in compliance with the INF Treaty. There are approximately 366 SLCM/SLBMs and 443 air-to-surface missiles in NATO's nuclear arsenal. Many of these weapons are concentrated in the Federal Republic of Germany where, aside from the LRINFs and SRINFs, there are around 4,000 nuclear-capable artillery guns with a range of about 30 km. In addition, there are the nuclear capable aircraft with a range of between 1,600 and 4,700 km. There are approximately 2,500 of these aircraft capable of carrying about 1,800 nuclear bombs.[1] The propor-tional distribution of the warheads is shown in Table 4.1.

Table 4.1. *The distribution of all nuclear warheads located in European NATO area* (per cent)

Aircraft-borne	40
Nuclear artillery	26
Sea-based	14
Surface-to-air	7
INF	5
Atomic Demolition Munitions	4
Battlefield tac.	3
SRINF	1

Source: Based on author's estimates and Sweedler (1982, p. 2)

Precise figures for the Warsaw Pact are less readily available but most sources suggest a range of between 8,000 and 10,000 nuclear warheads for use in Europe. There are 382 INF missiles, between 75 and 97 SRINF and 1,240 battlefield or tactical nuclear missiles which together can carry over 2,000 warheads. The Soviet Union also has single-warhead SCLM/SLBMs targeted on Europe amounting to 470 missiles.[2] A breakdown of the Warsaw Pact ratios (Table 4.2) shows some interesting variances with the NATO deployments.

Table 4.2.   The distribution of all nuclear warheads located in European
Warsaw Pact area (per cent)

Aircraft-borne	53
Nuclear artillery	11
Battlefield nucs	15
INF	11
Sea-based	6
SRINF	4

Source: as Table 4.1

The total number of US nuclear warheads in Europe is difficult to estimate exactly. Catherine Kelleher (1987, p. 448) estimates 5,924 US warheads in Europe with another 2,013 reserved for US use in Europe in 1985. McNamara (1986, p. 30) stated that there were (also in 1985) 4,808 US nuclear warheads in Europe, while another publication lists 4,350 US and NATO nuclear weapons in Europe excluding the British and French forces (if we add on the British and French forces there are 64 missiles deployed on four British Polaris SLBMs.) The French deploy 80 missiles on five M-20 SLBMs and 16 missiles on the M-4 SLBM (*Arms Control Today*, May 1987, p. 7). The final figure does not appear to include the 400 SLBMs which are integral to NATO's general strike plan or the A-6 and A-7 carried-based aircraft normally on station in the Mediterranean. The estimates for the Soviet nuclear-capable systems are also difficult to pin down precisely. If we take the figures for Soviet nuclear-capable aircraft alone, estimates vary between 6,000 and 2,000 (IISS, 1987, p. 208). A third source (US Dept of Defense, 1987, p. 77) cites a figure of 5,200 for the total tactical air force of the Soviet Union, where approximately one-third are assigned to Europe and the western Soviet Union.

The current nuclear arsenal in Western Europe is primarily American. These weapons comprise those reserved for exclusive US use and those for use by the NATO allies but held under the custody of US units. Based on figures compiled in 1984, 64 per cent of the non-strategic nuclear force warheads in Europe (3,447 from a total of 5,357) are reserved for exclusive US use (Table 4.3)

The operational control of these weapons in peacetime remains mainly under the aegis of an American commander and only those weapons reserved for quick reaction alert (QRA) are under joint control with an ally. The bulk of these weapons are either for tactical air missions or for short-range 'battlefield' artillery.[3] The number of US nuclear warheads in Europe has fluctuated significantly since the

Table 4.3. The distribution of American nuclear weapons in Europe between exclusive US use and NATO use

Weapon/warhead	US use (%)	NATO use (%)	Total
Bombs/B-28, B-43, B-57, B-61	82	18	1735
Depth bombs/B-57	68	32	190
Lance/W-70	47	53	695
8 inch artillery/W-33, W-79	54	46	935
155 mm artillery/W-48	81	19	732
Honest John/W-31	0	100	200
Nike-Hercules/W-31	22	78	500
ADMs/W-45, W-54	100	0	370
Total	64	36	5357

Source: Calculated from Arkin *et al.* (1984).
Note: Data pertaining to INF weapons still deployed in Europe but due for removal under the INF Treaty have been omitted. Sea-based weapons are likewise omitted.

1960s, when, to use Former Secretary of Defense Robert McNamara's enigmatic 1967 phrase, there were 'around 7,000 warheads in Europe'. His successor, Clark M. Clifford, affirmed the gist of the figure when he stated scarcely a year later that there were 7,200 warheads in Europe. In May 1965 there were 5,945 warheads, and by December 1981 the figure had increased slightly to 6,032. The abolition of Atomic Demolition Munitions (ADMs), Honest John and Sergeant missiles saw a drop in the number of warheads to 4,636 by December 1986. If we assume there is no progress in arms control, apart from the INF Treaty, we could expect to see 2,813 US warheads in Western Europe by 1995 (*SIPRI Yearbook 1987*, p. 12).

The INF Treaty was widely heralded as paving the way towards a safer nuclear-free world that would be brought about by the stage-by-stage elimination of nuclear weapons. While it is not the author's intention to detract from the considerable achievement that the INF Treaty undoubtedly represents, the impact of the treaty, as a step along the road to a denuclearized Europe, has already been eroded. Within NATO circles there is already pressure for nuclear moderniz-ation (a follow-on Lance missile with a vastly improved range) and in other quarters there have been active measures to compensate for the loss of the INF missiles, or at least the threat engendered by their absence. The best example of such an active measure is the British government's acceptance of an extra 50 F-111 bombers to complement the 150 already available. The new bombers, designated F-111Gs, will be equipped with air-launched cruise missiles, according to General William Kirk, Commander-in-Chief of US Air Forces in Europe (*The Independent*, 29 June 1988). NATOs High Level Group (HLG) has also discussed, at various times since 1988, the possibility of deploying cruise-missile-carrying B-52s on rotational tours to Europe as well as putting US sea-launched cruise missiles in Atlantic waters under NATO command. In short, while the INF agreement is politically significant, these discussions make it clear that the ability to substitute for the cuts is straightforward, at least in the military sphere. The will actually to live with a real reduction in the level of nuclear weapons in Europe, without allowing for the possibility of supplementation, has yet to be demonstrated.

The role of US nuclear weapons in Europe has been presented to Western Europeans in various guises and most notably in its 'coupling' form; namely that US nuclear weapons deployed in Western Europe serve to symbolize the links (political and other) between European allies and the United States but also as a 'sign of multilateral participation in nuclear-use planning and decision-making, the most important of alliance functions' (Kelleher, 1987, p. 449). The fluctuation in the number of US warheads and, for that matter, troops in Europe, tends to suggest that the numbers are not sacrosanct in the military sense but are more important in political and psychological terms. The numbers changed due in part to the upheavals within NATO (and, in particular, the transition from a strategy of massive retaliation to one of flexible response) but also because of purely domestic considerations; various political and fiscal decisions within the United States have led to the reduction of the number of nuclear weapons in Europe in spite of the American exhortations for their European allies to do more for their defence. Thus, the level of US forces in Europe, both nuclear and conventional, does not necessarily match the tone or content of the messages emanating from Congress regarding any perceived threat.

The first significant change to come about specifically as the result of a concerted attempt to reduce the number of nuclear warheads in Europe as a whole was the 1979 dual-track decision which, somewhat paradoxically, committed the United States to introducing new missiles but also to an arms control process that might limit them. Arguably, the INF agreement has made politically symbolic gestures towards reduction in the levels of the nuclear arsenals in Europe, but in the military area its significance is far less apparent. Indeed, as suggested above, the 'success' of the INF deal will be qualified or negated by plans to modernize existing nuclear forces. While it might be the case that the military significance of the INF agreement is indeed limited, there are other changes that have gone largely unremarked upon. In response to alliance concerns about the controllability and usability of nuclear weapons in Europe the North Atlantic Council made the decision at Montebello in October 1983 to cut 1,400 warheads from the stockpile by 1986, leaving just over 4,500 warheads; it should be observed, however, that the cuts were to be balanced by modernization and the introduction of a new generation of weapons. The cuts were mainly made to the Pershing 1As, the Nike-Hercules, the eight-inch (W-33) shells, the 155 mm (W-48) shells and the ADMs. These cuts, unfortunately, were not prompted by any munificence or aspiration to nuclear disarmament. Some systems were withdrawn because better alternatives were available (including conventional alternatives) and others (like the ADMs) were gladly given up because the precise operational plans for their use had long concerned NATO officials. A significant reduction was also made in the nuclear element of 'dual-capable' systems. Some of America's NATO allies have also used nuclear systems deployed on their soil as bargaining chips to reduce the number of nuclear systems and thus the threat that was implied in hosting these forces. The Dutch bargaining, under the leadership of Ruud Lubbers of the GLCM deployment is typical; the Dutch eventually agreed to accept the GLCMs but only on the condition that the Dutch F-16s would drop their nuclear role and the P-3 Orions their nuclear ASW role. In fairness, it should also be pointed out that European nations have also requested nuclear protection, or an extension of the US nuclear umbrella, as was the case with the initial request of West Germany under Chancellor Schmidt for the INF missiles.

Growing public opposition to nuclear weapons in Europe that leads to changes in government policy could also have an effect on the number and distribution of weapons systems—a recent example of this being the Danish Social Democrats' motion of April 1988 (which passed by 75 votes to 58) effectively to ask for a positive denial or confirmation of the existence of nuclear weapons on board vessels entering their territorial waters. This not only prompted a debate within NATO and snap general elections in Denmark but flew in the face of the United States' traditional 'neither confirm nor deny' policy. The decision of the Spanish government in January 1988 to demand the removal of the 401st US Fighter Wing from Torrejón, near Madrid, as a condition for the renewal of the basing agreement, was also symptomatic of a general reassessment of the utility of certain US facilities in Europe, particularly since the United States is in a position to give less aid in return for basing access.

The figures and facts above are meant to give a feel for the scale of nuclear weapons in Europe and the considerable problems that would be encountered in any possible disarmament forum. It should, however, be pointed out that consideration of the political consequences of nuclear disarmament in Europe cannot solely be confined to nuclear weapons since the weapons are an integral part of the general armed forces in Europe and those deployed outside the European theatre. The nuclear disarmament of Europe must be considered within the context of the general security equation which includes conventional and CBWs. The central concern is that in disarming Europe in the nuclear sense we might merely exchange one form of deterrence for another equally nebulous one. The distinction that is often made between weapons of mass destruction (i.e. nuclear and chemical weapons) and conventional weapons is no longer justifiable, given the vastly improved accuracy and firepower of today's conventional weapons compared to their Second World War counterparts. A non-nuclear war would be comparable in its destructive effects to a nuclear one (Westing and Molski, 1989). Efforts to denuclearize Europe with only passing regard for other forms of equally important reductions may well endanger the security of Europe.

Some thoughts on the general consequences of US nuclear disarmament in Europe

Why nuclear weapons in Europe?

Nuclear weapons were from an early stage part of the post-war security systems and have remained so. The fact that they have remained as a central part of the picture is hardly surprising since the United States lacked the massive conventional forces in the immediate post-war period, due to very rapid demobilization, which meant that the guarantee to Europe had to be nuclear for two reasons. First, due to the short range of the delivery systems in the period 1945–50 (until the development of the B-36, the first bomber with intercontinental range) the United States had no option but to deploy her few nuclear weapons from overseas bases. Without access to overseas bases the United States could not have utilized the deterrent effect of these weapons—a fact which meant as much for US security as for those the United States was purporting to defend. Second, the commitment to Western Europe, which was initially viewed as temporary, had to be seen to be that of a superpower—in this sense the symbolism was unmistakeable. As early as 1947 special 'loading pits' suitable for the Fat Man type bomb had been prepared in the United Kingdom and the

Marianas; NATO merely gave this presence a political context and allowed the United States to pose as a magnanimous defender of liberty.

The associated question of why the United States felt obliged to defend a war-shattered Europe has no single answer but a mixture of ideological, pragmatic and economic considerations. Perhaps the most compelling is that the United States simply did not have an option as it did after the 1914–18 war. A retreat into splendid isolation, although feared by some in Europe like Ernest Bevin, Attlee's Foreign Secretary, was never seriously entertained as an option. The experience of fighting two world wars on other people's soil also reinforced the US faith in the wisdom of 'forward defence' (that is, on someone else's soil) or, to give it its European name, extended deterrence.

The utility of nuclear weapons

The basing of US nuclear weapons in Europe is long-standing, dating from 1954 when the Mace and Matador systems were deployed in West Germany (although these were actually pre-dated by nuclear-capable B-29s which rotated to the United Kingdom but were not officially based there). It has, however, become increasingly controversial on both sides of the Atlantic over the course of four decades. The early US nuclear weapons were seen as effective manpower substitutes that would keep down the cost of expensive overseas personnel deployments; in reality the United States had no choice but to rely upon its nuclear superiority for as long as possible when the conventional force disparities became obvious once the United States and Western Europe started their rapid post-war demobilization. The same recognition of conventional weakness led to a rejection of a no-first-use policy at an early stage when NSC-68 was adopted in September 1950. Since then, the US conventional force deployments to Europe have always been thought of in tandem with the nuclear deployments and as part of NATO's flexible response strategy adopted in 1967, which reserves the right to escalate a conflict, assuming a hostile attack, from a conventional to various nuclear forms of exchange, until the aggression ceases.

The central problem confronted by those who have to plan for and, in time of war, use nuclear weapons is that of credibility. Nuclear weapons have little value as weapons but the threat that they might be used is what actually gives them a role and thus some credibility. According to NATO strategy the alliance reserves the right to use nuclear weapons first if attempts to stop an attack at the conventional level have failed. Since there is a widely perceived conventional force superiority of the Warsaw Pact forces over the NATO conventional forces, exacerbated by demographic problems in West Germany, the chances of NATO having to resort to the use of nuclear weapons at an early stage would appear to be high. But, if all they can do is destroy vast tracts of land and habitation for man and creature alike, is their use as a weapon credible except in a denial role (which perversely also denies the initial occupant the fruits of land)? The dilemma is not new but it is one that has not been adequately addressed. Attempts to circumvent the central credibility problem by adopting doctrines such as the Follow-on-Forces-Attack merely open up new problems; for instance, the high reliance put on dual-capable systems in their conventional guise which, if lost, would rapidly reduce the number of nuclear options available and thus would tend to encourage the choice of a nuclear option at a fairly early stage. This, in turn, would probably encourage a nuclear exchange at an early stage of a conflict. The wisdom of the hosting of nuclear weapons in non-US NATO countries has further been challenged by historical developments. Historically the presence of nuclear weapons in Europe was accepted as a cheap NATO substitute for the superior manpower of the Soviet forces. However, Soviet parity, and in some cases superiority, in nuclear systems from strategic to battlefield level has reduced the belief that a Warsaw Pact invasion of Europe would be met by the measured responses envisaged in NATO strategy. The notion of confining or limiting a war, let alone a nuclear exchange, by the Queensburyesque notion of flexible response is at best naive.

The reason for the credibility problem that NATO (and the Warsaw Pact) face, as outlined above, is associated with the huge numbers of nuclear weapons in the European theatre. Deterrence works so long as the threat of damage or the inflicting of pain can be made in the knowledge that any retaliation is of lesser consequence. This is not the case in Europe. There are simply too many nuclear weapons systems for there to be any general deterrent to war. Indeed the very existence of such preposterous levels of nuclear armaments which makes their very use incredible could actually encourage lower-level conflict. Furthermore, the most effective deterrent, deterrence after all being a psychological state where risks and gains are balanced, is one that is highly mobile (so that its position is unknown) or invulnerable (so that it cannot be denied). The argument that hundreds of short-range battlefield systems that are delivered by gun, missile or aircraft are effective deterrents is unconvincing since their operating locations are known and, because of their range, they tend to be highly dangerous for the users or friendly forces operating in the vicinity. The proliferation of nuclear forces into all types of range and delivery platform has not increased the deterrent effect of nuclear weapons, which is the only function for which they are suited. The deterrent function could far better be served by removing most, if not all, of the land-based nuclear missiles, and relying on the sea-based deterrent force of the United States (backed up by the British and French independent deterrents) assigned to SACEUR. These forces are by far the best suited to the deterrent role because of all delivery systems they are the most difficult to track and thus their whereabouts at any one time are not exactly known.

Nuclear surgery without side-effects?

There has been peace in Europe for 40 years. This could be because of the existence of nuclear weapons in Europe from 1949 onwards, alternatively, peace could have reigned in spite of nuclear weapons. This dilemma is at the foundation of any discussion of the future role of nuclear weapons in Europe. The argument cannot satisfactorily be proven either way. To come to grips with the political consequences of nuclear disarmament we must, within the confines of this peace, examine the currently perceived role of US nuclear weapons in Europe and the likely results of their removal. The consequences could be viewed under the following general arguments.

First, it is impossible accurately to predict the political consequences of a US nuclear withdrawal from Europe without detailed information about the background to such a scenario. Did the disarmament come about as the result of a superpower agreement or an intra-alliance arrangement? Are other forces involved in any way (i.e. chemical or strategic nuclear forces)? What is meant by 'disarmament'; is it actual destruction of warheads or missiles (and if so, is it unlikely that the Soviet Union would agree to such asymmetrical reductions) or merely relocation or storage out of the European theatre?

Second, without a clear indication of what happens to other parts of the US nuclear arsenal, it is similarly difficult to ascertain the results of a nuclear withdrawal. The theoretical linkage between conventional battlefield, tactical and strategic systems is well understood in NATO's flexible response strategy—although a nuclear-disarmed Europe would mean the end of the strategy anyway. Simply to remove a rung with no guidance as to what happened elsewhere could be foolhardy at worst and, at best, it could be a gamble. In order to be a truly denuclearized region there has to be an absence of nuclear weapons as well as the inability of other surrounding areas to strike targets within the region with nuclear weapons. For this reason progress on conventional or short-range systems reductions must be thought of in the context of a more general reduction which includes the strategic systems and the START talks.

Third, the US nuclear and conventional force commitment to Europe has traditionally been regarded as symbolic of common interest and aims. This linkage, particularly in its political context, is still seen by some allies as important but there are serious disagreements among the European NATO members focusing on whether there should be nuclear weapons in Europe and, if so, how many and where they should be. Indeed, a minority of European nations have borne the brunt of the nuclear burden—the Federal Republic of Germany, Italy and the United Kingdom being the main ones, while others like Iceland, Spain and Norway prohibit the presence of nuclear weapons on their soil. There is an open question about the extent to which the latter group may have benefited, or otherwise, from the decision of a few to take the weapons. The issue of spreading the nuclear load among the different countries is a sensitive issue and one that the West Germans feel most acutely. The insistence of Helmut Schmidt on the principle of 'non-singularization' at the time of the 1979 dual-track decision was simply the expression that the risks, and any perceived benefits, had to be carried by more than one and ideally by all.

If we postulate that, for some reason, these weapons are removed (for example, a third zero) it is unlikely that the United States would feel inclined to continue with its conventional force presence in Europe at the current level of around 326,000; many of these forces directly or indirectly support the nuclear missions. There is also the problem that many of the systems capable of deploying nuclear warheads, like tactical fighters or artillery pieces, are in fact dual-capable, or even triple-capable if we add the chemical element. Hence, any posited reduction in nuclear forces has two options. The first option is to concentrate on reducing the number of warheads. This form of reduction is the most difficult to implement, partly for technical reasons, since destroying warheads is difficult, but also because the removal of nuclear warheads (and their destruction) would require highly intrusive inspection that would be far in excess of that needed to implement the INF agreement. The second option is the removal of the launchers. This would *ipso facto* require substantial cutbacks in other fields since many systems are dual-capable; thus a cut in the number of launchers would necessarily mean cuts in other fields that could weaken respective defence postures to an unacceptably low level. Special problems are also associated with tactical fighters which are highly mobile and, barring the destruction of the aircraft or the bases from which they operate, any practical reductions will be very difficult to implement.

The nuclear disarmament of Europe could entail far more than just ridding Europe of nuclear weapons—obviously much of the political (and military) significance of such an act would depend upon what 'threat perceptions' remained within Europe and the importance attached to the current force balance in Europe.[4]

Fourth, plans for nuclear disarmament exist in various guises— various proposals have been forwarded advocating nuclear weapon-free zones (NWFZ) and denuclearized zones in central Europe, northern Europe and the Balkans.[5] Interest in nuclear arms reductions has been expressed, with varying degrees of sincerity, in other fora. The super-powers do not have the monopoly on such plans either; Poland's forwarding of the Rapacki Plan and later the Jaruzelski proposals, which proposed nuclear-free zones and concentrated upon the reduction of weapons and equipment and not specifically manpower, unlike many other plans, serve as examples. While it is indeed conceivable that there could be some type of breakthrough leading to a significant reduction in the superpower nuclear arsenals in Europe, there are some countries who currently appear unwilling to entertain the notion of a nuclear-free Europe. France, in particular, would be unlikely to surrender her nuclear forces *in toto*. Having effectively starved its conventional forces to modernize its nuclear forces, it would presumably be very reluctant to reduce its nuclear forces. As with France, the British possession of an independent nuclear deterrent is intimately bound up with national defence postures as well as with national pride and self-image. In the event that the Soviet Union insisted that the French and British forces be included in discussions, or, if not directly included, be used as an offset, problems could also be encountered with the United Kingdom, particularly in view of Mrs Thatcher's visit to Moscow when, on 31 March 1987, she declared that she was not prepared to accept the denuclearization of Europe. The Soviet negoti-ators have thus far agreed to exclude the two European independent nuclear deterrents from the arms control process although, if one takes the avowed aim of the superpowers' leaders to rid the world of nuclear weapons seriously, these forces will have to be included eventually. No doubt the French and British leaders are also aware that the longer these forces are excluded from the arms control process the greater their significance and influence will be in the light of the other European missile reductions.

Fifth, verification is an obvious area of concern particularly since information about the precise number and whereabouts of the Soviet warheads is scarce. The INF Memorandum of Understanding does,

however, provide some encouragement on this point, with both sides
having openly declared information pertaining to INFs and their
whereabouts. But although the INF agreement should not be belittled,
the verification problems associated with that agreement are minor
compared to those of the shorter-range systems. Verification implies
that there is enough political acumen to judge whether the various
means of monitoring agreements reveals enough. Existent national
means of verification, the normal jargon for satellites and intelligence,
would in all likelihood be inadequate for verifying a nuclear disarmament in Europe. There would have to be some form of highly intrusive
inspection scheme that would involve the inspection of hundreds of
different locations. However, the tasks associated with verification of
any disarmament measure need not be overwhelming, as Thomas
Hirschfeld (1987, p. 102) suggests:

nuclear warheads are moved according to standard procedures in which the
troops moving them are trained. Retraining troops and relocating weapons
take time and effort; destandardization of movement and storage, while
perhaps useful for fooling intelligence, raises the risk of accident or unintended
use. Monitoring these procedures over time would presumably enhance
confidence about when nuclear-capable units were reinforced with nuclear
weapons in many, but not all, instances. Therefore, the separation of launchers
from storage sites helps monitoring. In the case of forward-deployed, short-
range launchers like artillery, this separation could theoretically be done by
removing all storage sites from some defined forward area; also, collocation of
planes and warheads could be discontinued.

However, concerns about verification are not necessarily foremost in
the minds of the politicians who advocate substantial reductions in the
nuclear arsenal. Alfred Dregger, chairman of Helmut Kohl's party
faction in the Bundestag, recently advocated scrapping all NATO
nuclear artillery pieces—thus also reflecting an understandable
German preoccupation with short-range systems which are predominantly deployed upon West German soil (*Washington Post*, 6 May 1988,
p. 28). His argument was based on the premise that most nuclear
artillery pieces are in the Federal Republic of Germany and that
their use in war would inevitably include NATO soldiers as well as
West German civilians. Significantly, verification provisions were not
mentioned.
    Negotiating a reduction in or the elimination of nuclear weapons
from Europe will not be straightforward, due in part to the reasons
outlined above, but also because we have not yet conceived of a viable
alternative to nuclear deployments. Attitudes towards US nuclear
deployments in Europe would appear to be quite contradictory. On the

one hand, there would appear to be a demand for enhanced deterrence (seen in the demands for post-INF nuclear modernization), which would theoretically reduce the likelihood of nuclear war, accompanied by demands that more be done with reduced resources. The same confusion as in the public arena can be seen in the arms control forum. For instance, the MBFR (Vienna) negotiations had a nuclear component from the mid-1970s until the end of the decade. NATO offered during these negotiations to withdraw 54 nuclear-capable F-4s, 36 Pershing 1As and 1,000 warheads and in return the expectation was that the Soviet Union would withdraw a tank army. The Soviet Union declined the offer and NATO unilaterally withdrew 1,000 obsolete warheads—a gesture which was not reciprocated. Those who argue that a unilateral cut in the NATO nuclear arsenal would lead to a reciprocal reduction on the opposing side have to note that historical experience tends to disprove this; unilateral cuts tend to be just what they say they are. The nuclear component of the MBFR negotiations fell into disarray with NATOs 1979 LRTNF modernization decision—the dual-track decision. The lessons to be learnt from the MBFR negotiations indicate that any reductions leading to disarmament must be reciprocal. The Conference on Disarmament in Europe (CDE) probably offers a more fruitful forum for negotiation since the geographical scope of the negotiations encompasses the area from the Atlantic to the Urals. Within this forum the neutral and non-aligned nations have a significant role to play which could be resented by larger actors who would be carrying out major adjustments in their policy subject to the approval (or disapproval) of smaller states. The CDE would also have to have its mandate extended to include discussion of nuclear forces since it is currently limited to conventional force discussions. It could be that the various arms control fora are simply not the venues to make such decisions and that unilateral reductions (the force of example) have a role to play in the light of the fundamental changes taking place under Gorbachev's guidance, although while both sides are engaged in negotiations any such reductions, be they conventional or nuclear, are highly unlikely.

Political consequences of US nuclear disarmament in Europe

Political consequences, as distinct from other consequences, are in reality difficult to distinguish. The main concern here is with the changes to the structure and cohesiveness of the NATO alliance that the removal of some or all of the US nuclear weapons could engender. The US nuclear contribution has, largely because of the nature of the weapons systems, been the most visible contribution to European defence. It is not necessarily the most important, though. From a Eurocentric perspective the conventional commitment does more to bind the United States to the defence of its European allies. A reduction in the US conventional commitment to Europe, in particular that to West Germany where over 70 per cent of the US forces in Europe are deployed, would severely damage the moral of the alliance and, in military terms, would certainly make things difficult, but not impossible. A reduction in the nuclear role of the US forces would give the United States the choice of converting those previously engaged in manning and maintaining those nuclear systems to other tasks within Europe or continental United States. If the option of redeployment to the United States were selected the effect on the morale of the European allies could also be serious. However, without a considerable amount of collateral information that explains how and why nuclear disarmament took place it is difficult to say anything beyond the merely speculative. Some general trends, and they are no more, can be ascertained in the light of the INF debate and the reaction to the treaty. Thus, if we fly against the stated policy of NATO and the United States, which respectively advocates full implementation of the Montebello agreement and the continuing presence of US nuclear weapons and strong conventional forces in Europe, and assume that some form of nuclear disengagement is under way in Europe, several political consequences can be ascertained.

The first consequence, and the most extreme one, is that the removal of nuclear forces from Europe and, as I have argued, of a large proportion of the US conventional presence in Europe, may lead to the unravelling of the two alliance blocs. It is not the nuclear weapons *per se* that are the cement of the alliance but the US forces in general, given that no single European power, or group of powers, has yet demonstrated the necessary political acumen and resolve to take over the leadership of a European defence effort. This might in turn lead to the resurgence of many old problems within Europe—the Balkan question, the traditional animosity between Greece and Turkey, and the German reunification question. The anti-nuclear lobby make the argument that ridding Europe of this most obvious and noxious form of superpower dominance would *ipso facto* unite Europe and lead to a common house of Europe. History, unfortunately, does not bear this out: prior to the superpower hegemony of the post-war era, two world wars had as their catalyst essentially intra-European problems. It is also worth noting that Russia was not the instigator in either case. Many of the problems have not actually been solved but are for various reasons suppressed, largely due to the presence of the two superpowers in Europe arising from the post-1945 world. Too much can be made of the historical examples but they do tend to give a rather discouraging picture for Europe's post-nuclear future unless necessary political and economic infrastructure exists to bring together European nations prior to any dramatic disarmament.

We should also consider closely what we understand by nuclear disarmament in Europe. Just because Europe is disarmed in the nuclear sense does not imply that nuclear weapons have no role to play in European politics or security. Nuclear weapons will still continue to carry a considerable influence in European thinking and planning if they continue to be deployed elsewhere. Indeed, an argument could be made that in this case nuclear weapons would actually have an increased profile in European political consciousness; their very absence could increase the feelings of threat that might emanate from the various threshold countries which could yield increased influence in European affairs.

Second, nuclear disarmament in Europe raises several possibilities for Europe that span the political and military spectrum. The Europeans could accept superpower influence over their affairs which, although not as intense as before, would nevertheless be prevalent. Particular problems would be presented for Western Europe which, for reasons of geographical asymmetries in its position between the superpowers, would face a greater Soviet influence than the US could exert on Eastern Europe should it wish to—in the event of a crisis any US forces being redeployed to Europe would have to travel around 6,000 kms while Soviet forces would have to come only 650 kms from behind the Urals to the central front. This option of what could politely be termed 'acquiescence' has been decisively rejected by France and the United Kingdom, which rely on their own nuclear systems to resist Soviet pressure. Unless we are prepared to talk about wider disarmament (in other words strategic systems as well) it is inconceivable that the United Kingdom and France would surrender their independent nuclear deterrents. The presence of two nuclear powers in Europe (which would make complete Soviet nuclear disarmament in Europe unlikely) would not provide a guarantee for non-nuclear Western European countries—a kind of 'Euro-bomb'. Several reasons can be forwarded to support this assertion. The requirement for an 'umbrella' of some form existed long before the two independent nuclear arsenals. The British and French deterrents were designed specifically with their own defence in mind and not that of anybody else. While there is no ambiguity about this in the French case there could be some doubt about the United Kingdom which, under the conditions of the 1962 Nassau Agreement, is required to assign her forces to NATO but, in case of emergency, can use them for purely national contingencies. There is no reason why NATO allies should trust a British/French nuclear guarantee any more than a US one. Nor would a British/French nuclear force generate the same degree of uncertainty in the Soviet eyes as that generated by the substantial US presence. There are few signs that the French or British are ever prepared to entertain the idea of a combined Euro-deterrent. This idea, ironically, has gained little support in the two countries but gained most enthusiasm from Yuri Andropov, who tried to link the number of SS-20 warheads in Europe to those of the British and French nuclear forces during the INF talks which, in turn, illustrated a fundamental misunderstanding of the role of the independent deterrents. The West Germans, in particular, would justifiably feel uncomfortable with the swap of a US nuclear guarantee for a possible Franco-British one.

The third main consequence of nuclear disarmament in Europe derives from the perceived function of US nuclear weapons in Western Europe. Given that nobody has actually advocated a satisfactory or meaningful way in which to utilize nuclear weapons in war without unacceptable losses, we must turn to their main role, that of symbol. US nuclear weapons have since the 1950s been seen as a sign of linkage between the United States and its Western European colleagues as well as between the strategic forces and the theatre nuclear forces. Soviet forces in Eastern Europe have correspondingly been used to serve as a reminder of who is the hegemon in that bloc. The 326,000 US service personnel in Europe are also part of this symbolic commitment and, in the event of nuclear disarmament, it is unlikely that they would remain, partly because they are intimately linked with many of the nuclear tasks but also because the nuclear presence is seen as protecting their conventional forces as well as the indigenous forces. In the event of their withdrawal much of the linkage would be lost, which need not necessarily be disastrous. Certainly the symbolism argument alone is not strong enough to justify the continued presence of US nuclear weapons in Europe when faced with the military reality that there is now no obvious need for European bases. An additional problem confronted with the coupling or linkage argument is that the components required to achieve this symbiosis are no longer readily identifiable because of an increasingly fluid political situation. This point is particularly borne out in the attitudes of Gorbachev to Europe and the consequent reduction of tensions in Europe. Gorbachev (1987, p. 229) has also advanced a fifteen-year programme providing for the 'stage-by-stage' elimination of nuclear weapons by the end of the twentieth century. The United States can no longer count on its generous military support for Western Europe to provide political hegemony, as was the case in the two post-war decades. The 1980 grain embargo and the 1982 gas pipeline embargo are interesting cases in point; in both cases, the Western Europeans decided that trade wars were not in their interest and the embargoes were thus lifted shortly after they were imposed.

The removal of US military forces, or at least the bulk thereof, would remove an important if rather diffuse political link in European–US relations. The apparent US dominance in European affairs cannot wholly be explained by US military munificence. A large portion of the explanation must rest on the fact that there is no obvious leadership in Europe. The removal of nuclear forces from Europe could provide the impetus for more pan-European initiatives or alternatively it could be divisive. There may also be indeterminate economic effects where the United States might feel less inclined to invest in what it perceives as a less stable environment. The results of Soviet nuclear disarmament in Eastern Europe are equally difficult to predict, although the reasons for having nuclear weapons in Eastern Europe serve less of an overt political function and are aguably more military symbols.

If we confine ourselves to conjecture on the future of a nuclear-free Western Europe, much depends on which country or group of countries assumes the hegemonic mantle. There is no obvious alternative to Pax Americana but it is true, as Helmut Schmidt has argued, that Europe has much potential which is largely underutilized because of a lack of leadership within Western Europe itself. Schmidt (1985, p. 64) wrote that the necessary leadership, towards co-operation, could come 'from a group of nations or from a single country—or from an outstanding individual . . . I have already advised Americans not to be impatient'. There are signs, admittedly nascent strugglings, that Western Europe is making fresh moves towards some kind of European defence entity based on the WEU or a European pillar within NATO. However, there are no appreciable signs of a significant change in thinking that appear conducive to pan-European unity in the defence field. Such attempts at co-operation, like the Franco-German brigade, are encouraging but thus far largely cosmetic.

The fourth and final point refers to the current role of nuclear weapons in Europe. Truistically, it follows that to understand the impact of the removal of these weapons we must understand their current role. The role of nuclear weapons in Europe has, in the past, been left extremely vague—largely through default but also by design. The logic behind this situation on the NATO side is that deterrence is primarily a pyschological phenomenon, thus the maximum amount of uncertainty about the deployment of and plans for the use of nuclear weapons against an enemy would effectively deter an adversary because there would be an inherent ambiguity about when and where a nuclear response might fall. This ambiguity has unwittingly also obscured the precise function of the weapons. It has been claimed that nuclear weapons have made a more peaceful world and Europe is often touted as proof of this, there having been no European war for 40 years; this peace presumably is accounted for by the value of nuclear weapons for extended deterrence. There may be a grain of truth in the argument but it has not stopped losses of US or Soviet troops elsewhere, often killed with weapons supplied by one or the other superpower. It could also be argued that the very presence of nuclear weapons has encouraged, and will continue to encourage, sub-nuclear (i.e. conventional) violence because the threat to use nuclear weapons is seen as incredible—this has not been the case in Europe, where there are substantial conventional forces that are *in situ*. Nuclear weapons are in many people's minds synonymous with war and terror and thus if we rid ourselves of these weapons we are safer. This cannot be proven while the role of nuclear weapons is so imprecise and badly understood but it should not engender a false security that somehow makes the threat or act of conventional war somehow acceptable. Given our current level of expertise and arms production any war, be it nuclear or conventional, is unacceptable. Europe needs no reminder of this.

Conclusions

The future role, composition and size of US nuclear systems in Europe is unclear. Some believe that the INF agreement has opened up the possibility of a de-nuclearized Europe. This position overemphasizes the significance of the agreement since in military terms it represents a small adjustment in NATO's posture. Indeed, more drastic adjustments in the number of nuclear weapons in Europe have been carried out unilaterally. What is significant, and encouraging, about the INF agreement is that it shows that an agreement is possible where there is the will to adjust the force levels and rid Europe of some of the nuclear weapons. However, the agreement also showed how important it is to have a verifiable treaty and, given the relatively small number of nuclear weapons involved in the INF Treaty, the complexity of negotiating a reduction in the number of battlefield systems will be considerable. The current level of nuclear weapons in Europe is becoming increasingly unacceptable to many of its citizens, while the high cost of maintaining US forces overseas irks many US taxpayers. Public pressures emanating from both sides of the Atlantic will tend to encourage reductions in the excessive nuclear arsenal in Europe.

There are still those in the military forces of NATO countries who see the INF agreement as dangerously destabilizing and who maintain, incorrectly, that the agreement has put additional emphasis on the numerically superior Warsaw Pact conventional forces. The agreement has not 'exposed' NATO to a new threat; the forces were there anyway and they pre-date NATO's INF deployments. Pershings and GLCMs were put there to address a quite different problem in the form of what was perceived to be in the late 1970s a destabilizing Soviet advantage in theatre nuclear weapons heralded by rapid deployment of SS-20s. In reality, the point of having nuclear weapons has seldom, if ever, been justifiable on military grounds. The rationale for nuclear deployments in Europe is primarily political. If they are justified in public in terms of the 'threat' and act (somehow) as a manpower multiplier then the current emphasis within the alliance on the Conventional Defence Initiative (CDI) should actually weaken the case for maintaining the current level of nuclear weapons in Europe.

Nuclear disarmament cannot be neatly compartmentalized; even if the negotiations deal only with nuclear systems the effects are not necessarily confined to nuclear systems. The presence of a considerable number of dual-capable systems in Europe will complicate negotiations and will mean that any agreement on nuclear systems will also mean a reduction in conventional systems. Nor can nuclear disarmament be compartmentalized in the sense that genuine nuclear disarmament in Europe would actually mean much more than expelling those systems in Europe. For comprehensive disarmament strategic systems would have to be reduced (particularly submarine-borne missiles) as well as the independent deterrents of France and the United Kingdom.

So long as strong opposition to nuclear weapons exists, accompanied by a process of *détente* and confidence-building measures, the political and military rationale for keeping US, and other, nuclear forces in Europe becomes harder to maintain. Above all, the hypocrisy of maintaining that nuclear weapons keep the peace, while at the same time warning that a nuclear conflict will spell disaster for all is a central paradox of European security. Nuclear weapons in the security context do not guarantee peace, but this is not to say that they do not have any function. The function of US nuclear weapons within the alliance was traditionally that of providing cohesiveness (although it was over the credibility of the US nuclear umbrella that de Gaulle chose to withdraw France from the NATO Integrated Military Command in 1966) and, to the possessor, hegemony. The economic resurgence of Europe since 1945, the gradual evolution of a Western European security entity, the open questioning of US leadership over several issues and the pursuit of *détente* policies by several governments has led to a reassessment of East–West relations. Whatever the outcome of the reassessment, inspired by Gorbachev's *glasnost* as much as anything else, any move towards nuclear disarmament in Europe will mean a diminution of influence for the United States over European security and other policies. The reduction, or even abolition, of nuclear weapons in Western Europe may well affect the future of the US ground forces in Europe as well and the loss of their nuclear component may lead to their withdrawal. Even if this did not come about the remaining conventional forces, although still highly symbolic, would simply not entitle the United States to the same leadership because, as a proportion of NATO's conventional forces, US forces are far less impressive and influential than the nuclear contribution, which is almost wholly American. Indeed, the entire NATO command structure is designed around the fact that the United States is the nuclear power in the alliance—without the nuclear role there would be no justification for SACEUR always being an American. Of course, the nuclear disarmament of NATO would also entail a new strategy for the alliance as well as posing problems for the superpowers over their strategic nuclear weapons and in what context they might use them.

The most dangerous trap of all for those who think about creating a nuclear-free Europe, by various means like arms control, disarmament of the unilateral or multilateral variety or the creation of nuclear-free zones, is that the weapons tend to have a mesmeric effect. A nuclear-free Europe would not necessarily be a safe and non-violent Europe. The advances in conventional weaponry have been so vast, compared to their Second World War vintage counterparts, that a nuclear-free Europe could blind us to the very real dangers of these weapons. The emphasis and the political initiative should be aimed at achieving reductions in categories of weapons including conventional, chemical and nuclear projectiles. It is only on this basis that we can stand any chance of creating a safer Europe with political consequences that we could all live with.

Notes

1. Figures compiled from *SIPRI Yearbook 1988*, pp. 39–39; IISS (1986, pp. 207–11); US Dept of Defense (1987, pp. 39–43, 77–9).
2. Figures compiled from *SIPRI Yearbook 1988*, pp. 40–1; IISS (1986, pp. 207–9); US Dept of Defense (1987, pp. 39–43).
3. Either eight-inch or 155 mm artillery rounds.
4. The failure to agree on common counting rules and thus common force levels has held up many of the arms control talks although Soviet data

have been promised on several occasions. For an example of the current NATO assessment of the military balance of conventional forces in Europe (which covers many of the dual-capable systems) see NATO Press Service (Brussels, 1987).

5.　One such proposal was made by Soviet Ambassador, Yuri Kashlev, at an informal meeting of the group of 23 states in Vienna on 22 June 1987. In accordance with the Budapest Appeal he called for a limit on all weapons integral to NATO and Warsaw Pact air and ground forces deployed between the Atlantic and the Urals. The most famous proposal along these lines was the Jaruzelski proposal of May 1987 which set up a forum of thirteen nations—the MBFR participants plus Denmark and Hungary— to negotiate limitations on nuclear and other armaments in this corridor.

Bibliography

Arkin, W.M., Cochran, T.B. and Hoenig, M.M., 1984. 'Resource Paper on the U.S. Nuclear Arsenal', *Bulletin of Atomic Scientists*, August–September.

Gorbachev, M., 1987. *Perestroika: New Thinking for Our Country and the World*. New York: Harper and Row.

Hirschfield, T.S., 1987. 'Tactical Nuclear Weapons in Europe', *Washington Quarterly*, Winter.

International Institute for Strategic Studies, 1986. *The Military Balance 1986–1987*. London: IISS.

International Institute for Strategic Studies, 1987. *The Military Balance 1987–1988*. London: IISS.

Kelleher, C., 1987. 'Nato Nuclear Options' in A.B. Carter, J.D. Steinbrunner and C.A. Zraket (eds). *Managing Nuclear Operations*. Washington, DC: The Brookings Institution.

NATO Press Service, 1987. *Conventional Forces in Europe: The Facts*. Brussels.

McNamara, R.S., 1986. *Blundering Into Disaster*. New York: Partheon.

Schmidt, H., 1985. *A Grand Strategy for the West*. New Haven, CT: Yale University Press.

Sweedler, A., 1987. 'Nuclear Weapons in Europe', paper prepared for the Center for International Security and Arms Control, Stanford University.

US Department of Defense, 1987. *Soviet Military Power*. Washington, DC: US Government Printing Office.

Westing, A. and Molski, B.A. (eds), 1989. *Battlefield Europe: Conventional War and the Human Environment*. London: Sage.

5 NATO and the Political Consequences of Nuclear Disarmament in Europe

Pekka Sivonen

The public discussion on European security is likely to be affected in many different ways by the INF agreement and the prospect of further steps towards nuclear, conventional and chemical disarmament. This chapter concentrates on the relationship of politics and nuclear disarmament within NATO.

We are witnessing at least the following politically relevant developments. First, the logic behind the nuclear arms race has been maintained by the realities created during the Cold War years, and has contributed to the petrification of that setting. On the other hand, the policy aiming to establish rules for real (even if partial) disarmament creates in the long run rules for mutual *management* of security. It is obvious that the growth of anti-nuclear sentiments since the Cold War has made that kind of mutual responsibility between East and West a necessity. When change is unavoidable, prudence and realism require statesmen to reorientate their policies according to the new realities.

Second, in the West, the debates on the ethics of nuclear deterrence have been closely bound up with the question of social ethics in rival political systems. The value of freedom has been successfully presented as a factor strong enough to neutralize any doubts about the justification of nuclear build-up.

This situation has now changed. The stabilization of the arms race can no longer be 'officially' acceptable. Consequently, there will be a further growth of anti-nuclear sentiments.

Third, disarmament is gaining ground as one of the most important criteria for successful arms control. The INF Treaty and negotiations in progress are in this respect most influential in creating a *process*, a pressure to stay on this course.

Arms control and *détente*

Many liberal and leftist political analysts in the West used to regard *détente* as a precondition for meaningful disarmament agreements. It was held that disarmament must be preceded by new political relations between American and Soviet leaders, so that they could trust in each others' sincerity and peaceful intentions at the negotiating table.

The weaknesses of this line of reasoning have been clearly revealed by recent developments. Attitudes towards *détente* cannot be the standard for evaluating Western politicians in disarmament issues. Otherwise Ronald Reagan would never have signed a disarmament agreement.

When *détente* fell into disgrace in the United States in the late 1970s, it became obvious that arms control had to be protected against political fluctuations in American–Soviet relations. In the United States it was widely held that the Soviets had benefited much more from *détente*. So, in the face of the realities, the scholars and politicians who were in favour of arms control realized that it had to be somehow separated from the concept of *détente*—otherwise arms control would remain captive to the political relations between the big two. Would it not be possible to achieve some progress in arms control even without *détente*? Would such a situation not be preferable to a combination of *détente* and no lasting arms control process?

There were many pragmatic arms control specialists in the United States, liberals and conservatives, who favoured this kind of reasoning, and several programmes were formulated on this basis (for example, Nye, 1982). The role of arms control as an instrument of *détente* was thought to be diminished by introducing a practice of informal understandings and agreements instead of public diplomacy. Strict verification procedures had to be included in formal agreements.

But those who believed in the possibility of arms control after *détente* were modest in their expectations on *disarmament*. The general tendency was to emphasize the necessity of stabilizing the nuclear 'regime' whatever the international political atmosphere. This would be an urgent goal, yet modest enough to be attained even during tense American–Soviet relations.

The Reagan administration combined very different elements in its arms control policy. Its willingness to negotiate arms control agreements that were not founded on political *détente* was parallel with the reasoning of pragmatic arms control specialists; its willingness to effect mutual deep cuts in nuclear weapon arsenals was parallel with the main demand of independent Western peace movements; and its desire to keep SDI at any price was parallel with one of the main objectives of the 'hard-liners'. Yet the administration's policy was not consistent in any of these mental frameworks. This is not to say that the policy was inconsistent: it was logical if it is evaluated by some other criteria.

This orientation came under growing pressure from the establish-ment of strategic analysis. Their message was: return to more traditional arms control and security policy by scaling down the SDI effort, by setting out clear objectives for nuclear disarmament, and by dropping the anti-nuclear rhetoric. This kind of reorientation has been advocated above all by the Atlanticists, who are concerned about the future of NATO. The present Bush administration seems to be influenced by this criticism.

The changing role of nuclear weapons in Europe

The Soviet Union deployed its SS-20 missiles in the 1970s for reasons concerning arms race dynamics, on the one hand, and European political objectives, on the other. As regards the arms race dynamics, SS-20 was a result of the technical failure to develop a solid-fuel strategic missile which in the West was named SS-16. Its third phase was removed, and the new version was MIRVed and made mobile (Hagelin, 1984).

The political motives behind the SS-20 programme arose from the Soviet interpretation of the road to *détente* of the 1970s. As the Soviet leaders believed they had forced the United States into accepting *détente* through nuclear parity, they presumably also believed it would be possible to create a new relationship *vis-à-vis* Western Europe through nuclear build-up. The Soviet Union tried to establish a separate nuclear balance in Europe. The Soviet medium-range nuclear weaponry would balance American, French and British nuclear forces deployed in Europe and capable of hitting targets on Soviet soil.

The Soviet intentions cannot be solely explained in military terms, though. Moscow hardly had any illusions about the military usability of the SS-20s, whether for nuclear attack or nuclear coercion. Rather, the idea was to turn nuclear build-up into a mutual political discourse about the management of security and armament issues between the Soviet Union and Western European nuclear powers. However, France and the United Kingdom were not willing to tie their independent nuclear forces into East–West politics.

But it was not until 1987 that the Soviets realized that the concept of nuclear balance is not going to be accepted in the West as a description of the European situation. In early 1987 Gorbachev dropped the Soviet demand that an INF agreement must involve simultaneous cuts in French and British nuclear forces, but still insisted that these forces had to be frozen in the event of a Russian–American agreement. And in spring 1987 he finally gave up even this demand and opened the way for disarmament.

Refusing to put their own weaponry on the table, the French and British countered Soviet policies on Europe with their own alliance policy. The Soviets responded with their own: the deployment of SS-12/22 and SS-23 missiles in East Germany and Czechoslovakia made it clear that the whole of Eastern Europe would be affected by the controversy.

In a similar way, the Soviet willingness to dismantle INF and SRINF is motivated by political reasons. The new Soviet leaders do not want to let this sad affair hinder the development of more constructive East-West relations in Europe, which they need for both economic and political reasons: to strengthen the economies of the Comecon countries, to maintain political stability in Eastern Europe, and to multipolarize their foreign policy in order to reduce its dependency on superpower relations.

In any event it is clear that the Soviets are willing to de-emphasize the role of nuclear weapons in their policy on the continent. They have not scored any political victories in Europe which could be explained by nuclear build-up. The political risks involved in nuclear disarmament in Europe are greater for the Americans than for the Russians; after all, the continuity of Soviet political power in Eastern Europe is communicated by its conventional military presence in the area, not so much by its nuclear presence. Indeed, even in ideological terms it is problematic for the Soviet Union to be perceived as a military superpower without comparable vitality in other respects. 'Peace' and 'nuclear disarmament' have been Soviet catchwords since the Khrushchev period, and giving some real new content to them must be seen as an attempt to establish some kind of ideological appeal in the West.

But the role of nuclear weapons in Europe is not only declining; it is also acquiring a more *national* character. Even through the WEU or some other arrangement, it is unlikely that the French and British nuclear weapons will ever gain such a guarantor status as American missiles on European soil. The Americans could replace their ground-based missiles with comparable systems deployed on American vessels cruising the northern seas, or on American bombers operating from bases in the United States, but these arrangements would leave no role for the European allies to play. As a purely American move, this could not communicate the same political meanings and symbolism as the GLCMs and Pershing 2s deployed in European NATO countries.

As has been said, the Soviet nuclear deployments in Eastern Europe do not have a predominantly alliance-oriented rationale; they mainly serve Soviet national interests. This is why the removal of SRINF from Eastern Europe contributes to a mood of expanding national sovereignty on security issues in the area.

There are still thousands of battlefield nuclear weapons in place on both sides of the inter-German border, and these are controlled by the superpowers. But we may be witnessing a process of nuclear withdrawal, in which INF and SRINF disarmament merely represents the first phase.

The growing importance of public opinion

In the West it is generally felt that nuclear weapons form part of the current security problematic rather than part of the solution. Accordingly, the majority of the Western European public is of the opinion that the constant nuclear build-up represents a greater threat to their personal security than the Soviet Union as a political entity (Flynn and Rattinger, 1985, pp. 372–3). The decline of the ideological warfare has no doubt contributed to this: although harsh rhetoric is still being used to describe the ideological motives behind the expansionist policies of the rival military-political bloc, fewer and fewer people in the West believe that the Soviet Union has immediate expansionist objectives in Europe. Public images of threat have also been affected by the repeated political losses of Western European communist parties, together with their withering ideological fervour. One of the most important developments in Western Europe has been the *simultaneous* growth of anti-nuclear sentiments and a seemingly final disillusionment with communist ideology. No serious political force in Western Europe can identify anti-nuclear activism with pro-Soviet attitudes. Although it appreciates the new Soviet realism in arms control issues, the public is not exactly fascinated by the Soviet system or ideology. *Glasnost* and *perestroika* are not enough to change this current.

In 1955 only just over one-quarter of the Americans believed that nuclear war would lead to the annihilation of the human race; today four in five Americans believe this. The Americans mention the nuclear arms race as one of their foremost concerns three times more often than they did in the 1970s (Yankelovitch and Doble, 1984).

In Western Europe the worries about nuclear confrontation have reduced the willingness to fight against a military attack; the high probability of nuclear escalation has brought the perspective of total destruction too close. In this situation, what course can a prudent and realistic statesman take?

In a poll conducted in 1981 it was found that one in five Britons, one in four West Germans and Dutchmen, one in three Italians and two in every five Frenchmen were opposed to all use of military force, even in response to an attack by the Soviet Union. The first use of nuclear weapons, even as a last resort to prevent a military defeat, enjoyed even less popular support (Rielly, 1984, p. 103).

A NATO-wide public opinion poll conducted in 1984 revealed a marked difference between the Europeans and the Americans in this respect. According to the poll, 43 per cent of NATO Europeans were willing to fight for their country in an unavoidable war compared with 71 per cent of Americans (Hofmann, 1987, p. 12). Images of devastation caused by wars fought on European soil are familiar and frightening to the Europeans. But who would attack the American homeland? In the United States, 'to fight for your country' stands for willingness to fight outside the continental United States. It is striking to watch an Independence Day parade in any American city and see a banner with 'Veterans of Foreign Wars' written on it, followed by uniformed GIs.

The one and only possible way for anyone to attack the American mainland is through a large-scale nuclear attack. This is why a willingness to fight for 'your country' means, on this level, a willingness to take nuclear revenge against the aggressor. The question of using American nuclear weapons on American soil is not raised. The whole issue of nuclear weapons is perceived as a matter of peace versus holocaust, not as a matter of any citizen's personal responsibility to reduce the suffering that a war would cause to his/her countrymen.

Again, things are different in Europe. In a 1980 opinion poll 53 per cent of West German citizens accepted the use of conventional weapons on West German soil for defence against an attack. However, only 15 per cent favoured defence 'if nuclear weapons have to be used on the soil of the Federal Republic'.

What can the present polarization mean for the future of NATO?

In this situation it is only natural that questions of national security become politically divisive issues in domestic debates. In many European NATO countries this polarization has been apparent both in social activism (peace movements and reactions to them) and within the party system.

The cost-effectiveness of defence against an armoured offensive has been considerably improved by recent technological developments. In particular, the progress made in terminal guidance technologies has provoked speculation about the possibility of adopting purely defensive (non-provocative) military doctrines for NATO in Europe, and to rebuild the military forces accordingly.

For most of the 1980s, party polarization in defence issues was more serious in European NATO countries than ever before since the early years of the alliance. Now this polarization is alleviating. The British Labour Party has retreated from its earlier, strongly anti-nuclear position. The Social Democratic parties in West Germany, the Netherlands, Belgium, and Denmark never went that far in their own nuclear criticism in the first place. On the other hand, the conservative and centre-to-right parties are not unanimously supporting the traditional orientation in defence issues anymore. The most important deserter from the ranks is the West German Christian Democratic Union (CDU). In spite of the new uneasiness on nuclear defence, the public is against *unilateral* nuclear disarmament. Together these sentiments pull the major parties from the left and the right towards the centre in defence issues.

There has been a vigorous debate on the feasibility of 'non-provocative defence' scenarios. Military feasibility notwithstanding, it is hard to see how this kind of defence posture could be adopted unilaterally. Would it not be politically impossible to carry out a unilateral doctrinal shift into area defence in densely populated central Europe? How can you base defence on geographical depth if the other side maintains an offensive conventional military posture? The human costs of defence would be too high to be politically acceptable.

Understandably, the West German Social Democrats have been more reluctant to accept area defence scenarios than British socialists. But what is 'non-provocative defence' without area defence principles? Do they not belong together?

Mutuality can offer a solution, in the long run. If NATO and the Warsaw Pact could agree on the mutual adoption of measures intended to reach 'non-provocative defence' postures, these fears would be alleviated.

Nuclear weaponry will remain the main concern in the Western European debate on security. It would be naive idealism to count on the ability of national decision-makers to limit the use of nuclear devices to a 'manageable' level if a war broke out. A prudent statesman perceives the current emphasis on nuclear weapons as too dangerous a course to be followed for ever.

But why should a nuclear-free world be the only alternative? The current risks could be considerably reduced by transforming the existing purposes of nuclear weaponry. The present war-winning nuclear strategies have kept the nuclear arms race going and lowered nuclear thresholds. If nuclear weapons were deployed and maintained only for purposes of minimum deterrence, it might be possible to reverse these trends. Barry Buzan (1987, pp. 269 ff) has pointed out how the fashionable concept of 'common security' can be seen as complementary to the logic of minimum deterrence. This is because interdependence of the military securities of states, together with the necessity to slow down the arms race, is acknowledged by both.

How can NATO adapt to the changing environment in Europe: anti-nuclear sentiments in Western Europe, the growing expectations concerning disarmament and the renewal of European security structures, and a potential polarization of parliamentary politics on security issues in its European member states? Adapt it must, otherwise these trends will turn against NATO itself, which enjoys considerable support among its members.

In the central and northern European NATO countries public support for membership has remained steady and high: around 60–80 per cent of those polled are pro-NATO, and the figures have declined only slightly over time (see, for example, Treverton, 1985, pp. 74–5). It is interesting to note that this support for NATO cannot be explained by the current threat perceptions *vis-à-vis* the Soviet Union.

The Soviet political system and ideology are as disliked in Western Europe as ever. In fact, the decline of Western European communist parties can be partially explained by this disillusionment, which seems not to be affected by the present Gorbachev reforms. But perceptions of Soviet foreign policy have mellowed quite a lot in two decades. The Soviet Union is seen as a more 'normal' power than it was during the Cold War years: as a superpower conducting power politics as usual, not as an expansionist, revolutionary state. Consequently, even the much increased Soviet military power of today is seen as a much lesser threat to the security of Western Europe than was the case three or four decades ago (Flynn and Rattinger, 1985, pp. 369–71).

Attitudes towards the Soviet Union have ceased to be a sharply divisive issue in the Western European domestic debate, and this has created room for growing doubts concerning armed security. The connection between support for nuclear build-up decisions and attitudes towards the Soviet Union has broken down.

Obviously NATO is not perceived in its member countries as a traditional military alliance, which would require a serious external military danger to motivate its own prolonged existence. NATO is accepted as a political symbol and reality. This does not guarantee any automatic support among the public for the armament projects it may undertake.

In American post-war planning, NATO and the Marshall plan were initially meant to put allied Western Europe on its feet. For the Americans, this aim has been achieved only too well. In the post-war years, the American economy and foreign policy offered to allied Western European countries leadership and an example to follow. This was especially true for West Germany, where a whole new pro-American political generation was raised or re-educated.

All the NATO European countries have now come politically of age, become economically successful and integrated, militarily stronger than ever. Even if the Americans were able to offer true political leadership, that would not make a great difference. The present situation favours a more Europeanist NATO, and has brought up a new political generation. This new generational gap can endanger the traditional support for NATO. Atlanticism is becoming more like a pragmatic choice, instead of remaining such an ideology as it has hitherto been.

This mental sea change is especially strong among the best educated. In a 1981 poll among university-educated Britons, West Germans, Italians, Dutchmen and Norwegians, 5–14 per cent of those over fifty years old favoured neutrality over membership of NATO for their own country, compared with 27–39 per cent of those in the 18–34 age group (Szabo, 1983, p. 172). Anti-NATO sentiments among the young generation have not been this strong since the very first years of the alliance. But will this situation persist? Is this merely a reflection of generational tensions, or will the young adults maintain their views as they grow older?

If reliance on nuclear weaponry is the primary cause for this growing neutralism among the educated young adults, NATO could reverse the trend by de-emphasizing nuclear deterrence. But according to the surveys the dissatisfaction is deeper. In fact, a choice between *neutralism* and membership of NATO is at issue. There is much more in this than just a dissatisfaction over nuclear weapons. Favouring neutralism over NATO membership means, first and foremost, being against military co-operation between Western Europe and North America. It is not neutrality *per se*, but opting out of superpower confrontation (Hakovirta, 1986).

In Western Europe, the reputation of American foreign policy has declined in the 1980s to an all-time low in the post-war period. This is due to the basic differences in style and substance which separate American foreign policy from the policies of its European allies.

This means that no military reorientation is enough to re-establish the popularity of NATO among the demographic groups where it has suffered most. If there exists a solution at all to this situation, it is a political and not a military one. But it would seem that there is no solution. The relatively small neutralist minority cannot be appeased, because that would require a far-reaching political reorientation on both sides of the Atlantic. On the other hand, this minority is hardly growing fast enough to endanger the alliance for many years. NATO can live with this opposition; it is rather the issue of deterrent versus defensive alliance which has the potential seriously to divide NATO in the coming years.

As to NATO's internal cohesion, there is no panacea

One obvious way to enhance security in the current situation is mutuality in adopting measures which limit the capability of the military alliances to conduct large-scale strategic offensive operations in Europe. This capability can be reduced by conventional and nuclear build-down, chemical disarmament, increased observability of military forces, and structural changes limiting offensive weaponry. Practically all of these available alternatives are interdependent. An obvious precondition for dismantling tactical nuclear weapons is curtailing the opponent's ability to carry out armoured breakthroughs in wartime conditions.

In short, neither nuclear disarmament nor purely non-provocative defence are in themselves adequate solutions. The only realistic alternative is to find a new European balance of power through mutual disarmament and management of the change taking place in the existing security system. But even a development towards a conventional defence posture for NATO, not to speak of the *purely* non-provocative characteristics discussed, raises many doubts about its political compatibility with the American commitment to NATO.

First, the Americans say they want to keep their troops in Western Europe in order to raise the nuclear threshold. In this domestic rationale we see a link with the European battlefield and the personal security of the Americans: following a NATO first use of nuclear weapons the Soviet Union would retaliate with a counterstrike against the American continent. If all American nuclear weapons on European soil were dismantled, it would be much harder to motivate American voters to support a military presence in Europe. In wartime these troops would be fighting for European NATO countries, not so much for American security. In this it is supposed that the United States would have to give up the doctrine of first use of nuclear weapons if all American battlefield nuclear devices were withdrawn from Europe.

Second, the staying power of NATO can largely be explained by its peculiar characteristics as a nuclear alliance. Relying on nuclear weapons, it has not had to build up its conventional force to the same extent as the Warsaw Pact. In the present political circumstances it would be virtually impossible for the European NATO countries to win public approval for a costly conventional build-up, let alone for a replacement of American troops on top of that. So the question is: can NATO adjust to the changing conditions, or will it cease to exist in its present form?

Wallace Thies (1987) has argued that the theory of collective goods is applicable to NATO, but not to military alliances in general. He explains this by the combination of American power and its nuclear policy of extended deterrence. Disproportionately divided costs of military security do not threaten the existence of NATO, as they would in the case of a purely defensive (as opposed to deterrent) alliance—like one based on conventional forces. Nuclear weaponry makes the difference.

However, over time NATO has evolved towards a more equal burden-sharing arrangement and consciously de-emphasized the role of its nuclear weapons in actual operational planning. The capability of its conventional forces has improved steadily since the 1950s *vis-à-vis* Warsaw Pact forces. With these developments, NATO has lost something of its uniqueness as a nuclear alliance in favour of features characteristic of a traditional military coalition. By reducing Western European fears of a Soviet surprise attack, the relaxation of international tension has also contributed to this development.

But there is no panacea for the problem of internal cohesion within NATO. The traditional security dilemma of European NATO countries, the fear of being abandoned or trapped depending on the state of superpower relations (see, for example, Sharp, 1987), is intimately bound up with NATO's character as a nuclear alliance. A defensively oriented NATO, where American nuclear weapons no longer have their traditional guarantor role, would raise different fears.

First, as I have pointed out, it would be harder to sell the American military presence in Europe to the American public. Why keep 324,000 soldiers in Europe and use as much as 45 per cent of the country's total military expenditures to meet the obligations of NATO (Ravenal, 1985, p. 1026), if these sacrifices are not directly related to the primary objective of national survival? Any kind of denuclearization of NATO's military posture in Europe would raise the issue of Soviet advantages. This would happen even under a relative military balance in Europe, because the American reinforcements would have to cross the Atlantic. Would the European NATO allies be willing to field military forces capable of responding—together with the American forces located in Europe—to any conceivable conventional military threat? If not, then the American public would have to fear the possibility of US forces being trapped on the losing side of a European war.

This means that with a denuclearized military posture Western European fears of abandonment would be aroused during superpower confrontation rather than during superpower co-operation. A perception of increasing danger would raise the fears of entrapment in the United States. During superpower co-operation there would be less anxiety among the American public, and also fewer demands for withdrawal from Europe. Fears about abandonment would not spread among the European NATO countries. There would no longer be a Cold War-type strategy around to retreat from. Rather, the Europeans would fear losing some of their say in issues of European politics and security: the Americans and the Soviets could strike deals over the heads of the Europeans. Western European fears of 'condominium' between the big two might come back—there was speculation about such a possibility in the *détente* years of the early 1970s.

The logical relations described above can be typologized as shown in Table 5.1.

Table 5.1.   NATO doctrinal orientation and superpower relations: main negative effects on public opinion within NATO, deterrence-reassurance - dimension

US–USSR cooperation

Defensively oriented NATO*	FEARS OF 'CONDOMINIUM' IN EUROPEAN NATO —call for a better alliance cohesion	FEARS OF 'ABANDONMENT' IN EUROPEAN NATO —call for American military reassurances	Deterrently oriented NATO†
	FEARS OF 'ENTRAPMENT' IN THE UNITED STATES —call for European military reassurances	FEARS OF 'ENTRAPMENT' IN EUROPEAN NATO —call for a more equal relationship within NATO	

US–USSR confrontation

* A doctrine of 'no first use'; nuclear disengagement in Central Europe; a conventional balance created through NATO reinforcements, or East–West agreement; development towards a non-provocative defence posture.
† The traditional characteristics of NATO doctrinal orientation and force composition maintained.

An issue of politics and strategy: how can NATO replace INF?

The deployment of Pershing 2s and GLCMs in European NATO countries was motivated by politico-strategic considerations, in addition to the familiar intentions related to alliance cohesion and strictly military logic. The American tactical and theatre nuclear weaponry deployed in Europe was seen to convey the wrong message, because of the very short ranges of most of these devices. NATO was prepared to use American battlefield nuclear weapons to stop a Warsaw Pact attack which could otherwise be lost to the aggressor. The collateral nuclear damage caused by this would be mainly suffered by the central and east central European population.

Since the Carter years, the development of officially accepted deterrence theory and practice in the United States has emphasized the threat of punishment. A mere nuclear denial was not considered a sufficiently credible deterrent threat. Zbigniew Brzezinski underlined the necessity to target ethnic Russians, as the guidelines of American nuclear targeting were under development in the Carter administration (Pringle and Arkin, 1983, p. 146).

At the same time the Soviet Union launched its SS-20 missile programme, which would considerably enhance its technical ability to escalate nuclear warfare to the theatre level anywhere in NATO European territory. This gave further impetus to the arguments within NATO for the deployment of long-range tactical nuclear missiles, a position already well articulated. Obvious politico-strategic advantages were seen to result from such a change in the American tactical nuclear inventory: the fears of self-afflicted nuclear damage on West German territory would be alleviated, and the Soviet homeland itself could be threatened.

The latter objective reflected the more offensive and politically active principles of nuclear deterrence that have been in favour within NATO since the late 1970s. Eastern Europe is seen as a reluctant ally of the Soviets, who should carry virtually the whole responsibility in case of a Pact attack on Western Europe. In this situation a politically active deterrent should threaten Soviet territory with nuclear revenge. Long-range tactical nuclear missiles could provide such a capability, while battlefield nuclear weapons would have to be detonated in the central European area.

Consequently, 1,000 American battlefield nuclear weapons were removed from stockpiles in Europe while NATO prepared to carry out the dual-track decision on INF. During the deployment of Pershing 2s and GLCMs, an additional 1,400 warheads were removed. By the time the INF agreement was reached in 1987, the number of American land-based nuclear weapons in Europe had decreased by about two thousand warheads. This agreement will nullify the hitherto accomplished structural reorganization of this arsenal.

This restructuring effort has not received very much attention. NATO has not made the doctrine of politically active deterrence official, let alone public. NATO's Nuclear Planning Group approved the *General Political Guidelines* for nuclear deployments and doctrinal development in October 1986 at Gleneagles, Scotland. According to these guidelines, NATO nuclear deployments and operational nuclear planning should deter the Warsaw Pact by threatening its territory with devastation (Arkin, 1987, p. 6). The range of battlefield nuclear weapons is generally not long enough to sustain this posture.

The long-range tactical nuclear forces (LRTNF) were renamed in 1982 intermediate nuclear forces (INF), in order to separate these weapons from other tactical nuclear devices. Pershing 2s and GLCMs were presented by NATO as merely a balancing force to the SS-20s—a role that never was the only one. But now the issue of politics has surfaced even more. The West Germans are reluctant to modernize the American tactical nuclear weapons located on their soil, and have become more responsive to proposals for a 'third zero'. A 'double zero' raises the perspective of limiting the possible damages of a European tactical nuclear confrontation virtually to the area of the two Germanies.

Within NATO, the doctrine of politically active deterrence was probably seen as a good policy towards Eastern Europe as well. To some extent the events which followed within the Pact confirmed this evaluation. To counter the political objectives put forth by the Western nuclear reorientation, the Soviet Union deployed SRINF in Eastern Europe. This caused a rift in Soviet–Eastern European relations. East German protests at having to locate these missiles on its soil were possibly one of the main reasons for the several postponements of Erich Honecker's visit to West Germany, which was originally scheduled for 1983 but did not occur until 1987.

The crucial question at the moment is how NATO is going to compensate for the dismantling of Pershing 2s, GLCMs and Pershing 1As. If NATO is still willing to maintain its special characteristics as a nuclear alliance, the replacements should be nuclear. ·

French and British nuclear arsenals are going to increase severalfold by the turn of the century. In addition to this, France and the United Kingdom are looking into the possibility of a new co-ordination in issues of nuclear deterrence. Furthermore, France and West Germany are establishing new means of military co-operation. This is, of course, mainly in the field of conventional forces: French troops take limited responsibility for the defence of West Germany. Nevertheless it is also possible that certain French nuclear weapons (such as new air-to-ground nuclear missiles) will be integrated into these arrangements.

And there also is the WEU, as well as Western European co-operation in producing a dual-capable long-range fighter-bomber (the Tornado). All this taken together, both the Western European nuclear capability and nuclear-related military co-operation are increasing considerably. In strictly material terms this would easily compensate for the dismantling of American missiles with a range of 500–5,500 km on European soil. But politically Western European nuclear forces cannot replace American forces.

Three possibilities seem to arise for compensating for the removal of the coupling effect of American INF and SRINF. All of these are based on the introduction of new American nuclear weapons in Western Europe. This means nuclear build-up.

First, instead of heading towards a 'third zero', American battlefield nuclear weapons deployed mainly in West Germany could be modernized. The Pentagon is strongly in favour of this solution, while the West Germans have their well-known doubts. Just a few years ago there were not many analysts who took seriously the idea of modernizing this equipment; on the contrary, it was generally expected that the ageing and strongly escalatory low-nuclear-threshold weapons would be replaced by longer-range capabilities. This did not succeed, because nuclear disarmament was started from the wrong end, so to speak. Now battlefield nuclear weapons are burdened with some of the political symbolism originally intended for INF and SRINF.

The modernization of battlefield nuclear weapons faces major political obstacles, though—especially if the number of these devices increases in the process. The situation varies from one weapons systems to another. The systems with the shortest range are the most unpopular. Atomic Demolition Munitions, for instance, are due for withdrawal. Eight-inch and 155 mm nuclear artillery can be modernized only by going through a politically costly fight with West German public opinion, and this is probably not considered worth the effort. Most likely it is a dead issue.

In this situation it seems that efforts will be concentrated on the modernization of longer-range battlefield nuclear weapons. One of the motives behind INF deployment—the structural reorganization of the tactical nuclear weapons inventory in order to raise the nuclear threshold—can now be found in the level of battlefield weaponry. Some of the shortest-range weapons are being withdrawn, as longer-range systems are introduced. The foremost candidate for modernization is a replacement for the Lance missile. This replacement could have a range of over 250 km. As for now, the greatest obstacle hindering or delaying this modernization is West German public opinion, reflected in the stands taken by all the major political parties in the country.

A second possibility for replacing INF relies on nuclear or dual-capable aircraft, carrying gravity bombs or air-to-surface missiles. The new aircraft required will be available within a few years: F-16, Tornado, and F-15E. Also FB-111A bombers will be available, as these are replaced by Stealth bombers in the 1990s (Arkin, 1987).

This solution would meet the requirement of increasing the number of long-range delivery systems in the American tactical nuclear weapons inventory in Europe. On the other hand, the aircraft specified for nuclear missions would not be available for conventional purposes, which obviously complicates planning for conventional warfare. Nevertheless, this alternative is the most probable candidate for replacing INF in the years to come. People are less suspicious of aircraft than they are of missiles. No wonder that Senator Sam Nunn, among many others, has proposed air-to-ground missiles fitted to fighter-bomber aircraft as a solution to the 'modernization problem', together with a follow-up to the Lance missile (*International Herald Tribune*, 15 February 1988).

But the replacement of Pershing 2s and GLCMs by new aircraft equipped with standoff missiles could cause serious political problems as well. It is commonplace to regard aircraft as not particularly suitable for first-strike missions, mainly because of their vulnerability to defensive measures. However, the situation is very different if the aircraft are transformed into launching platforms for long-range tactical missiles, which are able to penetrate air defences as easily as GLCMs.

Fighter-bombers and medium-range bombers deployed on Western European territory and equipped with American standoff nuclear missiles are in political and military terms comparable to GLCMs, more so than any other conceivable INF replacement solution. Obviously, this is one way to nullify a great deal of what was achieved by the INF agreement. However, at the moment it seems possible to equip new nuclear-capable aircraft only with short-range air-to-surface missiles (with ranges under 500 km) and nuclear gravity bombs. This is not the most provocative alternative. But it would be a most unfortunate step anyway, endangering further progress in European nuclear disarmament.

The third main possibility for replacing INF is to utilize the sea areas around the European continent. As to range and vulnerability, the sea-launched Tomahawk cruise missiles would meet the requirements mentioned above. On the other hand, they would not carry the political symbolism which is possessed by weapons deployed on allied territory. In addition, sea-based deployments would face definite institutional and political problems. The US Navy is determined to maintain its own deployment doctrine. This consists of strategic nuclear and tactical nuclear components, the latter being related to specific naval threat perceptions on open seas and in coastal areas.

The whole concept of a functional replacement of INF by new American deployments in Europe tends to undermine the disarmament process now under way. As far as nuclear disarmament in Europe is concerned, the most logical next step would be the elimination of battlefield nuclear weaponry. Both politically and militarily, that would certainly make most sense: the 'use them or lose them' problematic would be solved, nuclear disarmament would develop into real disengagement, and preparations for nuclear defence would not disproportionately threaten German territory.

The choices have to be made soon. For quite some time the ageing American battlefield nuclear weapons in West Germany have been widely considered merely as bargaining chips, to be removed by a mutual agreement with the Soviet Union. The option of maintaining the present weaponry is hardly conceivable; the only real alternatives are to modernize or to dismantle.

The fate of battlefield nuclear weapons can only be solved in close connection with the issue of conventional offensive capabilities of the military alliances in central Europe. The removal of battlefield nuclear weapons would require limitations in offensive conventional armaments, which are the prime targets of short-range nuclear devices. It is obvious that such a comprehensive solution cannot be attained easily. NATO cannot accept a mutual dismantling of battlefield nuclear weapons if the numerical superiority of the Pact in conventional weaponry is not reduced simultaneously. Otherwise that kind of nuclear disarmament would directly threaten the American commitment.

Fortunately, the prospect of reaching a better conventional balance and alleviating Western fears is fairly encouraging. Gorbachev promised in his UN speech of December 1988 to cut Soviet armed forces unilaterally by half a million men, 10,000 tanks, 8,500 artillery pieces and 800 combat aircraft in two years. This would include six armoured Soviet divisions deployed in Eastern Europe. In addition to this, as of March 1989, the NATO and Warsaw Pact countries began talks in Vienna on Conventional Forces in Europe (CFE).

However, the most offensive battlefield nuclear weapons could also be dismantled by a separate agreement. As Dennis Gormley (1988) argues, this could be done regardless of progress in conventional disarmament.

Battlefield nuclear missiles, with ranges below the 500 km threshold specified in the INF and SRINF agreement, can be used most effectively in a strategic offensive. Among their most probable targets are the adversary's airfields. Eighty per cent of the critical targets associated with the air operation of NATO are located within 300–350 km of the inter-German border (Gormley, 1988, p. 18). NATO obviously considers air superiority absolutely essential for mounting a successful defence against Warsaw Pact ground forces. A mutual disarmament of battle-field nuclear missiles alone would eliminate 6,000 Eastern missiles and 700 Western ones. The Soviets have shown some willingness to agree to such a 'triple zero'.

If battlefield nuclear missiles were dismantled, it would be much easier to restrict a build-up in conventional ground-to-ground missiles. The prospect of new conventional deep-strike capabilities represents one of the most troubling applications of advanced technology in force planning.

Within NATO, the concerns of 'decoupling' are presented as a counterargument to this kind of an agreement. However, the removal of battlefield nuclear missiles would still leave thousands of American battlefield nuclear weapons in West Germany. And as Dennis Gormley (1988, p. 20) argues, the removal of the Warsaw Pact's most offensive advantage in the European theatre would alleviate the fears of a surprise attack—the fears that motivate the Western reliance on this equipment in the first place.

The decisions on tactical nuclear weapons modernization, made in NATO's Nuclear Planning Group (NPG) meeting at Montebello, Canada, in October 1983, are still to be put into effect. The INF Treaty has made West German leaders reluctant to commit themselves to a modernization of Lance missiles, as the summit held in Brussels on 2–3 March 1988 made clear.

But if the modernization programme does get off the ground, two significant changes are to be expected in the American tactical nuclear stockpile in Europe. On the one hand, maybe half of the existing 1,600 free-fall nuclear bombs will be replaced by ALCMs in the weaponry for nuclear-capable strike aircraft. These missiles would probably have a range of less than 500 km. Seven NATO countries are negotiating on the joint development of such a weapon, called a Modular Stand-Off Weapon (MSOW) at this stage.

On the other hand, the 125 km range Lance could be replaced by a new missile with a range of 300–400 km. The official NATO estimate is that Lance will become 'obsolete' by the mid-1990s. The replacement of Lance, however, faces more obstacles than the modernization of nuclear-capable aircraft and their weaponry: not only the West Germans, but also the American Congress can eventually prevent these deployments.

However, the plans for modernization must also be perceived in the context of the ongoing and forthcoming disarmament negotiations. Nothing is quite as effective in preventing a unilateral withdrawal of American troops from Europe as the CFE talks in Vienna mentioned earlier. Likewise, there is virtually nothing at the moment that keeps alive the issue of tactical nuclear weapons modernization within NATO but the possibility of negotiating these plans away. The INF Treaty raises expectations in the West of the possibility of trading off even credible *plans* for new nuclear deployments.

The end of nuclearist ideology?

But there is no redeployment solution to the challenges posed to NATO by the INF Treaty, the CFE talks and the Soviet unilateral disarmament steps. Soviet flexibility in the INF issue has created over-optimistic expectations among NATO decision-makers. If a tough negotiating strategy and bargaining chip tactics paid off in the INF negotiations, the logic goes, why will it not work again?

In the context of growing popular expectations and better East–West political relations, this kind of reasoning easily sets a trap for the policy-makers themselves. Western public opinion supports redeployments and an inflexible negotiation strategy only to the extent that it can be convinced of their necessity in achieving ultimate disarmament objectives.

As to the CFE talks, one can expect public impatience with the NATO position that the Warsaw Pact must make reductions in major weapon categories five to six times larger than those of NATO. However, the Soviets seem to be surprisingly conciliatory in this. At the same time the issue of tactical nuclear weapons modernization has become a hotly disputed issue within the alliance, creating a rift between West Germany and the other key member countries.

This is not a problem that NATO can solve without difficulty. As regards the conventional balance in Europe, even Soviet flexibility could be dangerous for the future of NATO. If the numerical superiority of Warsaw Pact military forces were eliminated by disproportional cuts favouring NATO, Western threat perceptions would be greatly affected. Without such an offensive operations potential as the Warsaw Pact's battle tanks and other armoured equipment has represented, it would be much more difficult to legitimize the present NATO policy of first use of nuclear weapons. That policy is motivated by the need to stop a Pact offensive with first use of American tactical nuclear devices. The abandonment of this doctrine would immediately threaten the whole rationale of extended deterrence. If Western public opinion no longer perceived American nuclear weapons as a necessary counterbalance in the European military equation, the whole basis of the Atlantic security community would be called into question.

A perceived military threat is obviously a necessary precondition for a viable policy of deterrence conducted by democracies. Public support for nuclear deployments in Europe is much more dependent on credible threat perceptions than is public support for conventional force improvements.

If the Soviet Union seriously wants to break the nuclear ties connecting Americans with their European allies, there can hardly be a more effective strategy than to deprive the Westerners of their own threat perceptions. This is why NATO is in no hurry to achieve any kind of conventional disarmament agreement with the Warsaw Pact.

NATO has already gone further in reducing theatre nuclear missiles than it originally intended to. One purpose of American GLCMs and Pershing 2s was to increase the probability of nuclear escalation from tactical to strategic level in wartime conditions. By eliminating these weapons, the INF Treaty does not support the deterrent logic which is the backbone of the alliance.

For NATO, all the options available seem to require adaptation to a changing political environment. Efforts to maintain the American nuclear and conventional presence in Europe at a high level would necessitate an unyielding stand in negotiations with the Soviet Union on European disarmament. This in turn would create domestic pressures for more flexibility. Even if NATO were able to contain too far-reaching changes in the international environment, it would still have to deal with the problem of changing domestic circumstances.

The other possibility for NATO is to adapt to the new imperatives in European security: the diminishing importance of military power, growing scepticism of the political and military usability of nuclear weapons, politically more relaxed and economically more interdependent East–West relations in Europe, and the weakening American commitment. From this point of view NATO could actively aim at further disarmament in Europe, and manage the changing situation rather than face inevitable changes after first resisting them.

Richard Falk (1986, pp. 444–5) uses term 'the nuclearist consensus' to describe the thoroughness with which nuclear weapons have been accepted by American security policy decision-makers and advisers.

Indeed, nuclear deterrence has served virtually as an ideology on both sides of the Atlantic: as a dogma of a simple and lasting solution for the security of the alliance.

National interests have contributed to the cracks that have appeared in this nuclearist façade among the American security establishment. US nuclear guarantees to its European allies, or the doctrine of first use of nuclear weapons, met with criticism in the early 1980s on the part of prominent old Atlanticists: George Ball, Henry Kissinger, McGeorge Bundy, George F. Kennan, Robert S. McNamara, and Gerard Smith. After the Soviet Union had reached a nuclear balance *vis-à-vis* the United States, the latter increasingly saw the traditional NATO doctrine of flexible response as anachronistic. An effort to stop a Warsaw Pact attack with American nuclear weapons could lead to a full-scale nuclear war far easier than in the 'nuclear golden age' of the West.

But for the NATO European security policy establishment it was, and still is, much more difficult to accept the changed realities. According to most of the conservative decision-makers in power in the most important NATO European countries, American nuclear presence and nuclear guarantees have to be maintained at the present level because NATO could never match the Soviet Union in conventional forces. This belief in the fool's paradise of the threat of mutual suicide has served as an easy solution to avoid the high costs of building up conventional forces. After Reykjavik, these European governments have tried to tie American hands in the issue of further nuclear disarmament: this objective was especially apparent in the NATO summit held in Brussels in March 1988, where Margaret Thatcher offered leadership—instead of President Reagan.

In addition to this, there is the special fool's paradise case of France. Reliance on a national massive retaliation policy has been a modern version of the Maginot Line. The enormous popularity that this policy has enjoyed over almost the entire political spectrum testifies to the pervasiveness of nuclearism as an ideology. In France nuclear weapons have been loaded with strong political meanings of nationalism, French greatness (*grandeur*), and a do-it-yourself spirit. These are purposes and symbolism which no conceivable amount of conventional build-up could match.

However, in recent years traditional European axioms have been falling apart. The party politicization dealt with earlier is only one indication of that. More enduring and militarily effective changes are the improvements in conventional military capability, those already carried out and those under way. No one in allied Western Europe talks about conventional forces as a 'tripwire' any longer. The relative strength of conventional NATO forces has improved steadily since the early 1970s, and the member states are keeping to this course by such programmes as the conventional defence improvement effort (CDI). NATO is utilizing the new possibilities offered by high technology in armaments development, which have contributed to the adoption of new operational concepts of mobility and deep strikes. The alliance is acquiring a capability to carry out by conventional military means many of the missions traditionally reserved for tactical nuclear weapons.

Acquiring a capability is not, however, the same thing as actually trying to replace nuclear weapons by conventional means. The strong symbolism of American tactical nuclear weapons as a manifestation of American nuclear guarantees remains, the actual usability of these devices notwithstanding. There are two contradictory logics here: the original rationale of tactical nuclear weapons was to compensate for the conventional military weakness of NATO forces in Europe. Improvements of that conventional capability, together with changed perceptions of the military usability of nuclear weapons, should deprive tactical nuclear weapons of this rationale.

But over time the arguments for keeping these devices in Europe have assumed an increasingly political rather than military emphasis. At the time of the first deployments in the 1950s, tactical nuclear weapons were seen as 'just another weapon' among the US Army personnel responsible for operating them (Betts, 1977, p. 110). Now they are perceived as predominantly political weapons, more and more so even among the military.

However, a situation is emerging where improvements in NATO's conventional capability can be seen as a threat to continued American nuclear presence on the soil of its European allies. First, there is the socialist willingness in certain NATO European countries to tie these two aspects together. Second, the present upgrading of conventional forces is taking place in an environment characterized by nuclear disarmament and the CFE talks. Third, the exploitation of advanced weapon technologies by NATO is in any case likely to improve its position *vis-à-vis* the Warsaw pact in the years to come.

All these factors mean that the importance of nuclear weapons is declining: there is a better conventional balance in Europe, and it is also more and more difficult to launch a surprise attack. If a new military balance can be achieved at substantially reduced overall levels, it would be easier for the NATO European countries to lessen their military dependence on the Americans in general. This, of course, is exactly what the Soviets have been trying to do for decades, and this prospect is causing much anxiety among NATO decision-makers (see, for example, Rose, 1987). On the other hand, changes in the European military balance could help to manage the seemingly inevitable reduction of American military presence in NATO Europe. Within NATO, the adverse political consequences of such a reduction can be limited by tying this measure to an East–West disarmament process.

By the turn of the century the European security environment will probably be very different from today. The role of nuclear weapons will change; there will be fewer people than ever before in the nuclear age living in a fool's paradise. The basis of changed European–American relationships within NATO will be a new European willingness to rely on non-nuclear means of defence. A lot of that willingness and the chance to make such a transformation come true depend on France.

France's faith in nuclear deterrence is unrivalled in Europe. However, this ideology may now be changing, as the French are showing a greater willingness to reintegrate their forces and military planning to some extent with NATO Europe. Armaments collaboration among Western European states, the reactivation of the WEU, negotiations between France and the United Kingdom on nuclear operations co-ordination, new Franco-German co-operation in military exercises, and the French units stationed in West Germany all hint in this direction.

With the French participating in Western European defence co-operation, it could be possible to achieve a real conventional balance with a combination of mutual stabilizing force reductions and new Western European unity. In the long run this would allow significant reductions in American military presence in Europe, without raising excessive Western European fears of endangered security.

But is France ready to play that kind of role? The country is extremely suspicious of the agenda for CFE talks in Vienna, for example. The basis of French exceptionalism is the nationalist symbolism of its military. Can European integration change this situation over time?

NATO in an environment between the Cold War and *détente*

In the 1970s political *détente* was still essentially bound up with arms control; arms control was considered inconceivable without preceding and simultaneous good political relations between the superpowers. These good political relations were supposed to be reflected in substantially increased mutual trade, human contacts, cultural relations, summit declarations of mutual interest in managing conflicts around the world, etc. These expectations were soon to be understood as exaggerated, and arms control was thrown away with the bathwater.

Today, arms control enjoys relative independence of political *détente* between the big two. Because of this the current arms control process may be more durable than the process which took place fifteen to twenty years ago. But how does this process contribute to political *détente*? It is certainly too simplistic to divide the complex political dynamics of East–West relations into two alternatives: The Cold War and *détente*. Do we have proper analytical tools to deal with the present situation?

The need to adapt to the changing conditions has, of course, arisen from the fading of the Cold War in the first place. But it could be dangerous for NATO to encourage highly optimistic popular expectations on the development of *détente*. These might begin to erode NATO's popular support. The threat perceptions might cease to be sufficiently threatening. This dilemma points out one of the most detrimental effects of military alliances on modern international relations.

In order to be successful, any disarmament process has to be acceptable to the leaders of the respective countries. In order to be acceptable, the process must be compatible with the perceived national interests. It must support and complement the existing power base of the politicians in charge. These elements are present in the current disarmament process, as well as in its relationship to *détente*.

On the other hand, our culture is continuously being militarized by the existence and vitality of military alliances. Much of the popularity enjoyed by NATO results from its role as the only important institutional arrangement binding North America and most of Western Europe together. To a large extent, NATO represents the political, cultural, historical and economic common heritage and togetherness of this Western community. To be sure, these countries belong to several joint political and economic institutions; but the most important ones do not reach across the Atlantic (EC) or are not limited to the 'North Atlantic area' (OECD, GATT). NATO *symbolizes* transatlantic political unity.

Bibliography

Arkin, William M., 1987. 'Happy Birthday, Flexible Response', *Bulletin of the Atomic Scientists*, vol. 43, no. 10.

Betts, Richard K., 1977. *Soldiers, Statesmen, and Cold War Crises*. Cambridge, MA: Harvard University Press.

Buzan, Barry, 1987. 'Common Security, Non-provocative Defence, and the Future of Western Europe', *Review of International Studies*, vol. 13, no. 4.

Falk, Richard, 1986. 'Nuclear Weapons and the Renewal of Democracy' in Avner Cohen and Steven Lee (eds), *Nuclear Weapons and the Future of Humanity: The Fundamental Questions*. Totowa, NJ: Rowman & Allanheld.

Flynn, Gregory and Rattinger, Hans, 1985. 'The Public and Atlantic Defense' in Gregory Flynn and Hans Rattingers (eds), *The Public and Atlantic Defense*. Totowa, NJ: Rowman & Allanheld.

Gormley, Dennis M., 1988. ' "Triple Zero" and Soviet Military Strategy', *Arms Control Today*, vol. 18, no. 1.

Hagelin, Björn, 1984. 'Swords into Daggers: The Origins of the SS-20 Missiles', *Bulletin of Peace Proposals*, vol. 15, no. 4.

Hakovirta, Harto, 1986. 'European Neutralism in the East–West System Change' in Harto Hakovirta (ed.), *Fragmentation and Integration: Aspects of International System Change*. Ilmajoki: Finnish Political Science Association.

Hofmann, Wilfried A., 1987. 'Whence the Threat? The Successor Generation and the Equidistance Syndrome', *NATO Review*, vol. 35, no. 3.

Nye, Joseph S., 1982. 'ReStarting Arms Control', *Foreign Policy*, no. 47.

Pringle, Peter and Arkin, William, 1983. *SIOP: Nuclear War from the Inside*. London: Sphere.

Ravenal, Earl, 1985. 'Europe without America: The Erosion of NATO', *Foreign Affairs*, vol. 63, no. 5.

Rielly, John E., 1984. 'Sustaining the Consensus' in Joseph Godson (ed.), *Challenges to the Western Alliance*. London: Times Books.

Rose, François de, 1987. 'NATO and Nuclear Weapons', *Strategic Review*, vol. 15, no. 4.

Sharp, Jane M.O., 1987. 'After Reykjavik: Arms Control and the Allies', *International Affairs*, vol. 63, no. 2.

Szabo, Stephen F. (ed.), 1983. *'The Successor Generation': International Perspectives of Postwar Europeans*. London: Butterworth.

Thies, Wallace J., 1987. 'Alliances and Collective Goods: A Reappraisal', *Journal of Conflict Resolution*, vol. 31, no. 2.

Treverton, Gregory F., 1985. *Making the Alliance Work: The United States and Western Europe*. Ithaca, NY: Cornell University Press.

Yankelovich, David and Doble, John, 1984. 'The Public Mood: Nuclear Weapons and the U.S.S.R.', *Foreign Affairs*, vol. 63, no. 1.

6 Alternative Defence in Central European Debate

Pekka Visuri

Discussion of security policy among researchers has included, since the mid-1970s, alternative defence models or strategies in an effort to diminish the risk of outbreak of nuclear war, particularly in central Europe. The disappointment over the fruitlessness of the negotiations on arms control and disarmament has been reflected in proposals to change the direction of the structure and doctrine of armed forces from offensive into strictly defensive. This point of view is still topical in spite of the INF Treaty.

As far as the debates about intermediate range nuclear weapons within NATO are concerned, the proposers of alternative models were still condemned a couple of years ago to the same class with different kinds of alternative political movements. It was said that the proposed models were militarily inefficient and impossible for NATO as an alliance to accept and that Warsaw Pact would not, anyway, abandon its offensive organization and doctrine of armed forces. The situation has essentially changed now that both military alliances have expressed their willingness to negotiate over developing doctrines into a more defensive direction.[1]

Averting the threat of a nuclear war as a starting point

The sharpest alternative to the security and defence policy pursued by states has traditionally been the pacifist view, which would renounce the use of all violence. However, the abandonment of the right to defend oneself has not gained significant support in any country. Also, unarmed defence in the form of the doctrine of so-called social defence (see, for example, Ebert, 1984) cannot be considered a real alternative defence model, though it can be regarded as an alternative to the whole current thinking concerning security policy. It is generally thought, however, that unarmed resistance to the occupying administration may be possible as a last resort when there is no other way left of defending oneself.

The alternatives that have recently been most seriously discussed require that a security-political system based on nation-states, which

93

is approximately similar to the present one, continues to exist. Both military alliances are, however, ready to restrict the ways in which armed forces are used and to agree on new measures concerning mutual crisis management. A common starting point is to try to avert the outbreak of a nuclear war, but otherwise, as far as nuclear weapons are concerned, there are still great differences of opinion.

The development of alternative defence models started from the situation in western central Europe in the mid-1970s. The defeat of the United States in Vietnam and its obvious willingness to cut down its commitments in European defence were background factors. At the same time the political and military power of the Soviet Union seemed to be increasing and spreading globally. The arms race went on in spite of the successful Conference on Security and Co-operation in Europe (CSCE) in Helsinki.

A research group directed by Carl Friedrich von Weizsäcker at the Max Planck Institute in Starnberg studied the opportunities to lessen the risk of outbreak of nuclear war and to limit the effects of the use of nuclear weapons. In *Verteidigung und Frieden* Afheldt (1976), one of the closest assistants of Weizsäcker, presents a model of decentralized area defence appropriate for West Germany.

The following theses, which Afheldt considered his starting points, have offered a basis for many other considerations of alternative models:

1. Temporarily unlimited, successful defence with conventional means is not possible for West Germany.
2. Defensive use of nuclear weapons would lead to such destruction that it cannot be regarded as a rational means.
3. A deterrence strategy carried out in practice without the possibility of defence is not credible (Afheldt, 1976, p. 209).

The solution that Afheldt offered was a combination of *détente*-minded security policy and a defensive system tied to defending own territory. New technology, mainly anti-tank missiles, seemed to provide small, scattered 'technocommandos' on the attacking routes with an opportunity to fight effectively against the armoured troops of the Warsaw Pact. Decentralized defence could not be destroyed by nuclear weapons.

It was hoped that area defence would create a sufficient deterrent in order to prevent an attack without the danger of escalation into a nuclear war.

Afheldt had got material for his model from Mao Zedong's strategy of guerilla war and from Spannocchi doctrine, a model of area defence that was being employed in Austria. The German contribution was chiefly the extensive use of new technology in the fighting of infantry. Afheldt continued, in co-operation with military persons and scientists interested in the plan, to develop his ideas into a defensive system that would be adopted for the territory of West Germany in particular. *'Defensive Verteidigung'* was supported by calculations which showed that reticulate defence, rather like the Swiss-type militia system, could effectively wear down the armoured aggressor (Afheldt, 1983).

Afheldt's colleague, Major-General Jochen Löser (1981), has presented a slightly more conventional model of area defence, *raumdeckende Verteidigung*. In this model the attempt is to keep armoured reserves at a distance of 100–200 km from the border district. The troops capable of attacking should be removed from 'disengagement zones' on both sides of the border. A dispersed defence model concentrated on anti-tank defence and based on both local and mobile 'modules' had also been presented by the Frenchman Guy Brossollet (1975).

A common threat perception in the above-mentioned and many other models recommending a more conventional, defensive use of troops (for example, a 'defence wall' constructed in the border zone with the help of artillery fire—see Hannig, 1988) was a massive invasion by Warsaw Pact forces, quickly heading towards the Atlantic Ocean through Germany. This threat perception of NATO, deriving from the years of the Cold War, also supposes that the permanent aim of the Soviet Union is to occupy Western Europe, whenever an opportunity arises, preferably with a surprise attack and, if needed, supported by tactical nuclear weapons.

In the last few years that model of a massive surprise attack has been slightly moderated and diversified in NATO planning. Moreover, it is not believed that the Soviet Union would easily resort to nuclear weapons in battlefield operations. At the same time a question arises: is it at all reasonable to plan defence only in order to repel a particular kind of offensive model? The alternative defence models that have been presented so far are prone to this criticism (see, for example, Krause, 1988, p. 124).

On the other hand, we can point out that the Follow-on Forces Attack (FOFA) battle doctrine, which was officially accepted as development policy by NATO in 1984, is also based on a one-sided assumption about the possibility of preventing, according to a specific schedule, the advance of Soviet follow-on echelons by directing the attacks at the bottlenecks of the road system.

Another basic assumption connected with the threat perception should be criticized, too. The purpose of decentralizing defence in an extremely large area was to prevent the Soviet Union from using tactical nuclear weapons. When there are no typical nuclear weapons targets available, such as armoured troops massed for attack or infantry placed densely on the defence line, the use of nuclear weapons would lose its meaning. The weakness of this reasoning lies, in the first place, in the fact that fast-moving armoured troops armed with the most modern equipment cannot be considered easy targets for nuclear weapons, even if one did not even take into account the political and strategic restraints linked with nuclear weapons. The image of masses of tanks attacking close together is out of date because conventional anti-tank weapons and artillery compel one to decentralize dislocations. The force of an armoured offensive consists, above all, of the interaction of rapid manoeuvres and the close support of artillery and air forces.

The same rules also apply to the armoured troops used for defence, which means that, from the point of view of combat technique, it is not justified to claim that they form 'tempting' targets for nuclear weapons.

The decentralized defence model of lightly armed troops does not, as we have seen, offer any decisive advantage compared with armoured troops as far as the lessening of any nuclear threat is concerned. On the other hand, among Western researchers and planners there prevails a firm view, according to which the use of nuclear weapons against combat forces is not the most essential feature of the Soviet doctrine.

Discussion in West Germany before the INF Treaty in 1987

The thought of abandoning nuclear deterrence and the majority of offensive-capable major units was, for NATO as well as for most German military persons and politicians, far too radical to be even seriously studied. The ideas of Afheldt and many others who had presented models of area defence or suggested that the share of light infantry be increased, remained, for the most part, topics of discussion among experts in strategy and some representatives of the peace movement until the culmination of the debate over Euromissiles in 1982–3. The then discussion of alternative models was taken up by the West German Bundestag.

The Social Democratic Party (SPD), which had previously strongly supported NATO's official strategy, withdrew its support after it became a member of the opposition in the autumn of 1982. The party then started to show interest in alternative, explicitly defensive models of area defence, instigating an extensive hearing in the Bundestag in 1983–4 (Biehle, 1986). The CDU/CSU, the coalition in power, used its majority to push through a resolution which stated that there were no grounds for making changes in the prevailing NATO doctrine of 'flexible response'. Everyone was, however, unanimous that different models of security-political alternatives should still be studied.

The SPD Party Conference in Nuremberg in August 1986 accepted a defence programme based on the principles of the formation of a nuclear-free zone and of considerably decentralized regional defence. The purpose was to turn the *Bundeswehr* into a force 'structurally incapable of attack' according to a model designed by Andreas von Bülow (1986, pp. 636–46), the SDP's expert on defence.

The defence programme drawn up by the Social Democrats was scathingly criticized by the government and the *Bundeswehr*. In particular, the effects of the programme on relations between the allied states were criticized; it was thought that it would lend justification to US demands for the withdrawal of American troops. On the other hand, the idea of increasing the share of reservists and decreasing dependence on nuclear weapons was not, as such, opposed by *Bundeswehr*. The Bülow model was not, however, considered mature, not, at least, as a measure taken only unilaterally. Critics also drew attention to the fact that the current structure of the *Bundeswehr* had been designed by Social Democrats, and that at that time (in the 1970s) no one claimed that the *Bundeswehr* could attack the Soviet Union (see Bertram, 1986; Domröse 1986).

After the Social Democrats lost the Bundestag elections in winter 1987, the discussion of the defence programme abated. Although the result of the elections was greatly determined by domestic policy, it was fairly generally thought that the new radical defensive thinking certainly did not increase the SPD's share of the vote.

The situation in Western discussion after the INF Treaty

The proposals for abandoning nuclear weapons made by the leaders of the superpowers and, particularly, the INF Treaty (concluded in December 1987) banning land-based intermediate and SRINF missiles have added momentum to the discussion of alternative defence models. Many new factors have come along, especially initiatives concerning disarmament and negotiations taken by WTO. The INF Treaty was confusing for NATO planners in that nuclear disarmament was started, in a way, from the wrong end (see, for example, *Welt am Sonntag*, 26 April 1987), i.e. from the most up-to-date part of the doctrine. The weakest and most dangerous link of NATO nuclear strategy, short-range battlefield weapons, were left untouched to wait for decisions on dismantling or modernization. The scarcely feasible amount of the tactical nuclear armament had been reduced to a half from the top level in the late 1960s (see, for example, Arkin and Fieldhouse, 1985, pp. 102–9).

For militarily and, for the time being, also politically justified reasons, the aim is to develop the *Bundeswehr* further in the spirit of forward defence (*Vorneverteidigung*) and perhaps by applying the forward expansion of the battlefield in accordance with NATO's FOFA doctrine and AirLand Battle (FM 100–5) of the United States. This means, among other things, the acquisition of new longer-range tactical rocket launchers (MLRS), automatic and precision guidance munitions, and new light cruise missiles or RPVs (Reinfried and Schulte, 1987, pp. 210–24). In order to implement the FOFA doctrine, NATO confirmed in the spring of 1986 an extensive programme of conventional defence improvements (CDI) for the years 1987–1992 (Defense Planning Committee, 1986). A similar development programme, 'Bundeswehr 2000' (or *Heerestruktur* 2000) has been drawn up for West Germany. Conventional defence has already strengthened considerably, but it is difficult to find further financing for these programmes (Carrington, 1988, pp.4–5). Budget difficulties may, for their part, increase the pressure to study more inexpensive alternatives (like area defence).

To sum up, the alternative models have not been generally accepted in West Germany, but neither have they been totally rejected. The most vehement attitudes must also be seen as a part of a political power struggle. The view represented by the former general inspector of the *Bundeswehr* and chairman of NATO Military Committee, General Altenburg, which is something of a compromise, is doing very well and will probably get increasing support from all parties. According to Altenburg's proposal, dependence on nuclear weapons would be constantly decreased and the share of reservists increased, but the basic structure of the *Bundeswehr* would not be touched.

The national territorial defence (*Territorialheer*) of West Germany has continued to strengthen in relative terms which partly creates opportunities for a more strictly defensive doctrine.

Hans-Dietrich Genscher, the Minister for Foreign Affairs, has worked purposefully for the banning of short-range nuclear weapons, and Chancellor Kohl has expressed similar ideas. The decision about modernization of Lance missiles and comparable systems has been postponed largely at the Germans' request (see *Europäische Wehrkunde*, no. 11. 1988, p. 619; *Newsweek*, 5 December 1988, p. 19).

If the SPD were to gain power, a shift of emphasis—perhaps not a very radical one—would perhaps occur in the direction of nuclear disarmament and area defence. The reason for this is that within the

SPD there are similar pressures to those in the British Labour Party: it is felt that defence programmes containing unilateral disarmament initiatives that have not proved popular ought to be abandoned, and a stance more favourable for NATO adopted.[2] In spite of heated discussion, there are no irreconcilable differences of opinion between the SPD and the CDU/CSU about the *Bundeswehr*. There are also relatively many proponents of the SPD's ideas among *Bundeswehr* officers. A confusing factor in West German security-political life before the Bundestag elections 1990 would be the populist Greens and republican parties.

We can conclude, on the basis of the discussion in West Germany, that radical models of area defence (such as Horst Afheldt's plan for 'technocommandos' and those of Löser and Bülow) would only be realizable as a part of an extensive European security-political solution. Unilateral proposals for changing the system have not received wide support. For the same reason, it does not seem possible that a nuclear-free 'corridor' could be created in central Europe as a separate act. The most important prerequisite would be a considerable reduction of Soviet armoured troops at least in East Germany and Czechoslovakia, which probably requires that the number of American troops on West German territory be decreased. We have already received signs of the Soviet Union's willingness to withdraw its troops from central and Eastern European countries. I will return later on to the initiatives and measures taken by the Warsaw Pact in adopting a more defensive doctrine.

Disagreements over force comparisons connected with the disengagement and decrease of troops have lessened slightly but have not completely disappeared. In the last few years a fair amount of literature has been published which has presented qualitative bases of calculation instead of the former simple examination concerning numbers only (see, for example, Europaprojektet, 1986; Bülow, 1985; Magenheimer, 1986; 1987; Stratman, 1986; Stützle, 1983). The complexity of the problem concerning force comparisons has also been admitted. The dispute between the alliances about the starting values and weightings of the calculations continues, and so more neutral and verified basic information is needed for mutual use. Both alliances as well as most experts in strategy and politics regard the maintenance of the balance of armed forces as a prerequisite for disarmament decisions. The balance of forces does not, however, guarantee crisis stability as such; rather, even at its best, it is only a part of the whole. No exact figures can be presented that would make attack either possible or impossible. To top it all, the asymmetry of armed forces allows only rough estimates.

Can neutral countries serve as examples?

Johan Galtung has, in the 1980s, spoken many times in favour of non-provocative defence models. He was particularly inspired by the positive results in politics achieved by six neutral European countries. According to Galtung, these countries (Austria, Albania, Finland, Sweden, Switzerland and Yugoslavia) are not threatening peace, but they have secured their safety at a high level. Neutral countries have also often served as examples when considering strategic alternatives suitable for NATO (see, for example, Kaltefleiter, 1987, pp. 431–8; Raven, 1987, pp. 438–44).

Galtung (1984) outlined a programme of four approaches to avoiding war: conflict resolution; balance of power; disarmament; and alternative security policies, which is divided into four subheadings—transarmament, non-alignment, inner strength (the decrease of vulnerability and the increase of invulnerability by mainly social, economic and political means) and outer usefulness, and co-operation for other states' benefit.

Like many other developers of non-provocative defence models, Galtung also emphasized the acquisition of defensive weapons instead of offensive ones. Anti-tank weapons should be acquired instead of MBTs and anti-aircraft weapons instead of fighter-bombers. Transarmament like this has been found, however, to be a difficult approach to discussions. If Switzerland, for example, had 800 MBTs, this would not necessarily mean that neighbouring countries would consider them offensive weapons. This leads us to the question of the significance of the doctrine of armed forces and general organizational features as far as the forces' offensive capability is concerned.

The neutral countries of Europe have not been very delighted with their exemplary role, when more and more new proposals have been made on the frontiers of the military alliances for studying non-offensive doctrines, disarmament and the withdrawal of superpower troops. It is a different thing to implement area defence in small countries subject to the threat of attack for purposes of passage then in 'front line' countries of the alliance such as West Germany or Czechoslovakia. Neutral countries are also afraid of the irksome political consequences that they may have to suffer if tensions arise within the military alliances due to attempts to disengage from the alliance. Do the leading states of the alliance generally allow neutrality to become too alluring? The difficulties ultimately culminate in the discussion of the possible solutions to the German question.

Defence decisions made by neutral countries are primarily based on dissuasive, relative deterrence. The purpose is to show in advance to a potential aggressor that an attempt to occupy the country or to use it as a transit route would cause more losses and waste of time than benefit. Thus, it is a question of deterrence by denial. In distinction to deterrence by retaliation, neutral countries prefer the term 'dissuasion' to 'deterrence'.

The 'high admission fee' strategy has been much studied in Switzerland; this strategy emphasizes demonstrative elements, such as fortifications and impressive peacetime field exercises (Däniker, 1987). In principle, other neutral countries aim for this, too, but their geographical and financial opportunities are weaker. All neutral countries also share a supposition according to which the aggressor would have marginal forces at its disposal against neutral countries, because the troops of the military alliances are almost totally engaged with each other and, on the other hand, a separate attack would cause strong political and military reactions within the opposite alliance.

It is not a simple thing for the member states of the military alliances to apply the principles of area defence used by neutral countries, because the fact that a state belongs to an alliance and perhaps even to its buttresses indicates as such a different starting point.

Keeping these differences of principle and politically delicate viewpoints in mind, the experiences of neutral countries are, however, of great use in research within the military alliances when we think about adopting more defensive doctrines.

The superpowers and alliances have often admitted that the armed forces of neutral countries do not pose a threat to neighbouring countries. Disarmament talks have not dealt with them, either. The leader of the Soviet delegation at the CSCE in Vienna, Ambassador Yuri Kashlev (1987, p. 70) said, for instance:

We know, of course, that the armed forces of neutral and non-aligned countries are of a defensive character. Their reduction is out of question now. But these countries should have the right to take part in decisionmaking concerning European security and at a later stage they could join, on a voluntary basis, the process of practical disarmament. Therefore we prefer to discuss parallelly the further confidence-building measures and steps to reduce armaments and armed forces in Europe by 35 CSCE countries.

Views within the Warsaw Pact

Military doctrine has been understood in the Warsaw Pact as a concept determined by the political leadership dealing with the nature of wars and general principles for war preparations and warfare. Due to the fact that a doctrine had been defined as politically defensive and that strategic-operational matters had been left for armed forces to be solved according to the requirements of the art of war, Western observers saw a striking contradiction in the concept of the Warsaw Pact. The posture of armed forces (structure, dislocation and battle doctrine) by nature, clearly favoured an offensive doctrine (see, for example, Donnelly, 1988, pp. 106–12). This situation also made it impossible to start discussions with Warsaw Pact countries about adopting an explicitly defensive battle doctrine. In addition to this, Western suspicions were strengthened by the fact that within the Warsaw Pact almost all military affairs are kept secret.

'New political thinking' began in the Soviet Union in 1985 by Mikhail Gorbachev also marked a change in attitudes concerning military doctrine. Like economic and domestic policy, it was to be reassessed. The consequence was that an impressive series of disarmament initiatives were taken; the Soviet Union consented, as far as training manoeuvres were concerned, to far-reaching confidence and security-building measures, and showed willingness to discuss the adoption of a clearly defensive military doctrine in practice, too.

The doctrine was characterized by 'reasonable sufficiency', which was explained to mean that the armed forces would be sufficient for defending own territory but not capable of mounting an attack. In the declaration of the new doctrine, given at the Warsaw Pact summit on 29 May 1987, it is stated, however, that armed forces should be kept in preparedness, enabling the repulsion of all attacks and the destruction of a potential aggressor (*Europa-Archiv*, no. 14, 1987, pp. D392–93). The question of dimensioning the capability of counterattack and concretizing defensiveness has recently been the object of many explanations and debates (Møller, 1988, p. 108).

An interesting change took place during 1987 in the definition of the Soviet doctrine. While mainly only the principles of warfare and preparations for war had earlier been discussed, the definitions were now supplemented by mention of the primary nature of the prevention of war. According to the Soviet Minister of Defence, Dimitri Yazov (1987a, p. 28), the current military doctrine of the Soviet Union is 'a system of fundamental views on how to avert war, develop military capabilities and make a country and its armed forces ready to repel aggression. It also explains the method of waging armed struggle in defence of socialism.'[3] Yazov (1987b) deals with the reasons for changing the doctrine.

Many Western observers have found positive the fact that the Soviet Union on the whole started to emphasize defensiveness and the prevention of war as a primary aim. On the other hand, it has been pointed out that in the statements of the leading military persons the stress still lies on the importance of developing offensive tactics; no structural changes had been perceived until the end of 1988 (see Menning, 1988; *Süddeutsche Zeitung*, 3 November 1988).

The tangible proposals for disarmament and arms control made by Warsaw Pact countries concentrated, for a start, mainly on banning the use of nuclear weapons and withdrawing them altogether. Later conventional arms gained a more important position in these proposals. Poland suggested in 1987 that the old plans of Rapacki and Gomułka be continued by establishing a nuclear-free zone in central Europe. In the new proposal troop reductions as well as arms limitations would apply to the territories of nine states (East Germany, Czechoslovakia, Hungary, Poland, West Germany, Belgium, the Netherlands, Luxembourg and Denmark). The measures would be directed at the withdrawal of operational-tactical nuclear weapons; the reduction of troops using conventional arms and of armaments adopted for surprise attacks, in particular; the adoption of strictly defensive military doctrines; and the development and introduction of new confidence- and security-building measures and the development of accurate verification systems. As far as the definition of defensiveness is concerned, one should not attach too much importance to mere figures; rather, a covering analysis should be made about states' offensive and defensive potentials (Prystrom, 1988, pp. 117–18).

The announcement of the reduction of Soviet armed forces made by President Gorbachev in his UN speech on 7 December 1988 indicated the most important step so far on the way to the realization of a defensive doctrine. Especially significant is the promise to withdraw six armoured divisions from East Germany, Czechoslovakia and Hungary by the year 1991. This includes the withdrawal of special units adapted for attack (e.g. airborne and air attack forces and water-crossing units), the reduction of tanks, artillery and fighter-bombers and the conversion of the remaining units into a defensive force. The first Western comments could not help acknowledging the epoch-making nature of the programme (see *Newsweek*, 19 December 1988, pp. 26–27; *Jane's Defence Weekly*, 17 December 1988, pp. 1536–7).

At the time of writing (early 1989), the full extent of Western reaction to Gorbachev's challenge is not yet known. Only one thing is certain—the challenge must be met with tangible counterproposals, because otherwise the credibility of Western security policy will collapse. This situation gives excellent opportunities for the CFE talks connected with the CSCE process.

Michael MccGwire, who has won fame as an expert in Soviet doctrine and armed forces, said as early as spring 1988 that the doctrine of 'sufficiency' indicates an approach in favour of strategic defence that decisively deviates from the previous one. The realization of such a doctrine would result in practice in the inability to launch an attack against Western Europe. Thus the new doctrine also partly corresponds to the outlines of Western defensive doctrines, which have been called 'non-offensive defence'. What is now expected from the West is, above all, the willingness to discuss a new European security regime: 'a new mutual security regime for Europe involving greatly reduced force levels and major constraints on their structure and posture' (MccGwire, 1988, summary in *Military Review*, October 1988, p. 79).

The role of researchers and prospects

The development of European security policy, which has increased in pace in the last few years, has also given cause for discussions about its reasons. It is presumably clear that the situation, which looked very sombre in the early 1980s, but quickly turned towards *détente* and disarmament, was not caused by any single factor—not only by the persistence of Reagan's United States or the new thinking of Gorbachev's Soviet Union. Great underlying forces, such as the terms dictated by technological and economic development and the changes of public opinion, must have been important prerequisites. This time it is justified to refer to the role of researchers, too. This had already been a source of deep disappointment, because and when there was a lot of armament and disarmament research going on which seemed to have no effect whatsoever on control of the arms race.

To begin with, the development of alternative defence models seemed a useless academic occupation, because the military alliances and their member countries paid no attention to them in their official statements. Due to the pressure of technological development and the law of continuity, the doctrines of the alliances became more offensive than ever in the early 1980s. At the same time, however, more research groups interested in alternatives started to appear. Pugwash began to promote research of defensive doctrines in a determined way, which was considered very significant. It was due to this, among other things, that the researchers of the Warsaw Pact countries also grew interested in discussing the research on mutual doctrines and the change of the structure of armed forces, while the political and military leadership continued making verbal attacks on the other party. Researchers got this opportunity to act as reconnoitrers and intermediaries 'between the front lines'.

When the Warsaw Pact began to reassess the general lines of security policy, strategy and doctrine, the terminology and range of models, primarily developed by Western researchers, were already available, starting from the Palme Report (Independent Commission on Disarmament and Security Issues, 1982) and ending in tactical-operational calculations of the effectiveness of defensive weapons against offensive forces. We are now in a situation where the ball is in the politicians' court: they are expected to show courage and take the numerous theoretical models and calculations as the basic material of official negotiations, which means that researchers could offer their services in the critical examination of different proposals and the further development of ideas.

It is true, of course, that not all potential alternative defence models can be further developed or at least officially discussed. Recent developments have also abolished the foundations of certain models. To take an example, it seems that radical models of area defence (as propounded by, for example, Afheldt) are no longer current; rather, the disengagement of roughly balanced troops (maybe by accepting mutual ceilings), and the larger reduction of weapons systems that are clearly considered offensive are more potential solutions. In this respect the proposal made by the Soviet Union on 7 December 1988 is indicative and it automatically excludes certain other approaches.

The special interest of researchers is to press governments to publish statistics about defence policy and other facts connected with armed forces. It is interesting to see that in Warsaw Pact countries, too, some positive proposals have been made particularly in this field. The INF Treaty was an epoch-making step in the whole large field of verification. If nuclear power plants and the production of missile plants can be supervised, there is nothing to prevent one from expanding monitoring of the production of tanks and aircraft. We can probably start from the assumption that the technical and principal problems in an adequately strict control over conventional weapons have been conquered. It is a matter of making political decisions.

As an example of the latest proposals suitable for the current situation put forward by Eastern and central European researchers could be mentioned that by Müller of West Germany and Karkoszka from Poland. Their proposal includes upper limits for the offensive types of weapon of the military alliances in Europe: e.g. nuclear weapons (500 warheads, at most 100 missiles), MBTs (10,000 tanks with a greatest allowed density of 500 per 100 km^2), heavy artillery and rocket launchers, fighter-bombers (500 aircraft) and armoured helicopters (500) (Møller, 1988, pp. 111–12). A similar list supplemented with many measures comprehending mainly exchange of information and observation is included in the proposal presented by a group of researchers (Brie *et al.*, 1988) from East Germany and Poland. Some researchers could see such proposals as too technical or military by nature, but they should naturally be only fragments of a larger security-political concept.

The following list serves as a summary and view on the introduction of markedly defensive doctrines in Europe:

1. Alternative defence models (non-offensive defence, *defensive Verteidigung*, reasonable sufficiency, etc.) are politically and militarily valuable proposals that deserve serious further research.
2. In neutral countries markedly defensive doctrines have already been put into practice largely due to the lack of resources required by more offensive alternatives. The military-political position of neutral countries differs, however, so much from the focal areas of the alliances that the neutrals provide no obvious examples for the alliances.
3. Radical models of area defence (lightly-armed defence dispersed in a large area) or linear defence concentrating on a frontier are not militarily efficient enough to repel manageably attacks carried out with the most modern fighting equipment, nor are they politically viable in the present situation.
4. One should look for solutions mainly on the road leading to the mutual disengagement of offensive troops, the banning of weapons of mass destruction and the reduction of offensive weapons system (see Jochen Löser's proposal).
5. The most important thing is to aim at a general settlement which takes the following factors into consideration: geographical factors, the full adoption of defensive doctrine and structures for the armed forces and the doctrine (the balance for the part of separate weapons systems or the strengths of troops not necessarily being an aim), control and a programme including intermediary goals.
6. One of the aims is to improve crisis stability by means of an extensive programme of measures. Arms control and the reduction of offensive weapons are only a part of it.
7. In the initial phase it is most important to reach an agreement about the release of information concerning military budgets, armaments, organizations and doctrines, about the definition of concepts, the content and schedule of negotiations, and about the studies covering all these areas that will also be made by independent international research groups.

The research of the content and opportunities of defensive doctrines is naturally only a part of the extensive security-political process, and as a separate action it is not of great significance. However, there currently seem to be political opportunities for taking measures that improve crisis stability. If, on the other hand, the situation for some reason grew strained, it would be easier to prevent the crisis in Europe from escalating into an armed conflict or even a major war when the current high preparedness and standard of equipment could already have been lowered in advance. There is general agreement about this, which probably facilitates future negotiations and research into solutions.

Notes

1. The survey of the discussions and views up to mid-1988 is in the special issue ('Alternative Security') of *Current Research on Peace and Violence* (no. 3, 1988).
2. For overall views on the security-political discussion and definitions of SPD policy, see Weiller (1988, pp. 515–28). The Bundestag elections in 1990 may well mean the return of the SPD–FDF coalition. It is also interesting, from the point of view of alternative defence models, that the SPD's leader, Hans-Jochen Vogel, has used Carl Friedrich von Weizsäcker as his security-political adviser and, in matters concerning defence, has followed a policy which is more moderate than that of the former leader, Willy Brandt, and closer to that of Helmut Schmidt.
3. Cf. the definition of 'doctrine' in the military dictionary of the Soviet Union in 1986 (quoted from Donnelly, 1988, p.106): 'A military doctrine is a set of views, accepted in a country at a given time, which covers the aim and character of possible war, the preparations of the country and its armed forces for such war, and the methods of waging it.'

Bibliography

Afheldt, Horst, 1976. *Verteidigung und Frieden. Politik mit militärischen Mitteln*. Munich: DTV.

Afheldt, Horst, 1983. *Defensive Verteidigung*. Reinbek: Rowohlt.

Arkin, William M. and Fieldhouse, Richard W., 1985. *Nuclear Battlefields. Global Links in the Arms Race*. Cambridge, MA: Balliger.

Biehle, Alfred (ed.), 1986. *Alternative Strategien*. Koblenz: Bernard & Graefe.

Bertram, Christoph, 1986. 'Rückkehr zu alten Träumen. Die Sicherheitspolitik der SPD birgt viele Risiken', *Die Zeit*, 9 September.

Bodansky, Yossef, 1987. 'The New Generation of the Soviet High Command', *Jane's Defence Weekly*, 31 October 1987, pp. 1010–12.

Brie, A., Karkoszka, A. Müller, M. and Schirmeister, H, 1988. *Conventional Disarmament in Europe*. Study prepared for the United Nations Institute for Disarmament Research. Potsdam-Babelsberg: Akademie für Staats- und Rechtswissenschaft der DDR.

Brossollet, Guy, 1975. *Essai sur la non Bataille*. Paris: Bélin.

Bülow, Andreas von, 1985. *Die eingebildete Unterlegenheit. Das Kräfteverhältnis West-Ost, wie es wirklich ist*. Munich: Beck.

Bülow, Andreas von, 1986. 'Vorschlag für eine Bundeswehr struktur der 90er Jahre', *Europäische Wehrkunde*, no. 11, pp. 636–46.

Carrington, Lord, 1988. 'East-West Relations: A Time of Far-reaching Change', *NATO Review*, no. 3, pp. 1–6.

Defence Planning Committee Communiqué of the 22nd of May 1986, *NATO Review*, no. 3.

Domröse, Lothar, 1986, 'Die Sicherheitspolitik der SPD und die Thesen des Herrn v. Bülow', *Europäische Wehrkunde*, no. 12.

Donnelly, Christopher, 1988, 'Red Banner. The Soviet Military System in Peace and War', *Jane's 1988*.

Däniker, Gustav, 1987. *Dissuasion. Schweizerische Abhaltestrategie heute und morgen*. Frauenfeld: Hüber.

Ebert, Theodor, 1984. 'Ziviler Widerstand im besetzten Gebiet in Carl Friedrich von Weizsäcker' in *Die Praxis der defensiven Verteidigung*. Hamlin: Sponholtz, pp. 230–63

Europaprojektet, 1986. *Slutrapport. Sammanfattning av genomförda studier av militärstrategiska förhållanden i Centraleuropa*. Stockholm: Öberbefälhavaren.

Europäische Wehrkunde, 1984. 'Zur Lage der Streitkräfte. Interview mit dem Generalinspekteur der Deutschen Bundeswehr', no. 10. pp. 7–10.

FM 100–5 (Operations), 1982. Washington, DC: Department of the Army.

Galtung, Johan, 1984. *There are Alternatives*. Nottingham: Spokesman.

Hannig, Norbert, 1988. *Verteidigen ohne zu bedrohen. Die DEWA-Konzeption als Ersatz der NATO-FOFA*. Mosbach: AFES-PRESS Report, no. 5.

Independent Commission on Disarmament and Security Issues, 1982. *Common Security*. London: Pan.

Kaltefleiter, Werner, 1987. 'Welche Strategie für die NATO? Warten auf den deus ex machina', *Europäische Wehrkunde*, no. 8, pp. 431–8.

Kashlev, Yuri, 1987. 'The Outcome of the Vienna Meeting Depends on the Political Will of the West', *International Affairs*, no. 9. pp. 68–72.

Krause, Christian, 1987. 'Abschreckung vor dem Ende?', *Die Weltwoche*, no. 3.

Krause, Christian, 1988. '"Strukturelle Nichtangriffsfähigkeit"—A Yardstick for Conventional Stability?', *Current Research on Peace and Violence*, vol. 10. no. 3, pp. 121–9.

Löser, Jochen, 1981. *Weder rot noch tot. Überleben ohne Atomkrieg—Eine sicherheitspolitische Alternative*. Munich: Olzog.

Magenheimer, Heinz, 1986. *Die Verteidigung Westeuropas*. Koblenz: Bernard & Graefe.

Magenheimer, Heinz, 1987. 'Zum Kräftestand in Europa-Mitte', *Österreichische Militärische Zeitschrift*, no. 2, pp. 128–38.

MccGwire, Michael, 1988. 'Rethinking War: The Soviets and European Security', *The Brookings Review*, Spring.

Menning, Bruce, 1988. *Soviet Miltary Doctrine: Change and Challenge*, paper for the 5th International AFES-Press Conference, 28–30 October, Mosbach.

Møller, Bjørn, 1988. 'Perspectives of Disarmament in Europe', *Current Research on Peace and Violence*, vol. 11, no. 3.

Nixon, Richard M. and Kissinger, Henry A. 1987. 'Risiken und Chancen eines amerikanisch-sowjetischen Abrüstungs-Abkommens', *Welt am Sonntag*, 26 April.

Prystrom, Janusz, 1988. 'The Problem of Non-offensive Defence—The Case of Poland', *Current Research on Peace and Violence*, vol. 10. no. 3. pp. 115–20.

Raven, Wolfram von, 1987. 'Flucht in den Neutralismus: Ein Lauf der Lemminge, der zum Abgrund führt', *Europäische Wehrkunde*, no. 8. pp. 438–44.

Reinfried, Hubert and Schulte, Ludwig, 1987. *Ausstieg aus der Nuklearstrategie? Chancen und Risiken für die Sicherheit Europas*. Herford: Mittler.

Roth, William and Frinking, Ton, 1988. 'NATO in the 1990s', *NATO Review*, no. 3, pp. 25–9.

Schröder, Hans-Hennig, 1987. 'Gorbatschow und die Generäle. Militärdoktrin, Rüstungspolitik und öffentliche Meinung in der "Perestrojka" ', *Berichte des Bundesinstituts für ostwissenschaftliche und internationale Studien*, no. 45.

Stratman, K.-Peter, 1986. 'Zum Verhältnis konventioneller und nuklearer Rüstung' in Erhard Forndran & Hans Joachim Schmidt (eds), *Konventionelle Rüstung im Ost-West-Vergleich*. Baden-Baden: Nomos.

Stützle, Walther, 1983. *Politik und Kräfteverhältnis*. Herford: Mittler.

Weiller, Matthew A., 1988. 'SPD Security Policy', *Survival*, vol. 30, no. 6, pp. 515–28.

Wettig, Gerhard, 1988. 'Sowjetische Sicherheitspolitik im Zeichen des "neuen Denkens" ', *Osterreichische Militärische Zeitschrift*, no. 1, pp. 6–11.

Yazov, D.T., 1987a. *Na strazhe socializma i mira*. Moscow: Progress.

Yazov, D.T., 1987b. 'Warsaw Treaty Military Doctrine—for Defence of Peace and Socialism', *International Affairs*, no. 10, pp. 1–8.

7 Ideologies of Stabilization— Stabilization of Ideologies: Reading German Social Democrats

Ole Wæver

This is (not) about the political consequences of nuclear disarmament

This chapter is an attempt to analyse the political consequences of nuclear disarmament in Europe by discussing the critical questions relating to stabilization and change, ideologies and political order. The basic idea is that the present changes—of which a certain denuclearization is an important part—have a general effect in the direction of a 'politicization' of European security. The whole situation becomes more mobile: hopes and fears might increase in the non-military sphere. As this happens in a general atmosphere of *détente*, the threats will generally not be labelled as 'security problems' although these problems might in some objective sense be increasing. In a political crisis we might suddenly discover that insecurity has increased. The game of the *political order* in Europe has become *open* to an unprecedented degree. The chances and risks inherent in this should be anticipated.

This chapter presents an investigation of the rules of the game and outlines the main suggestions for what constitutes the inner logic of the situation. The first half presents some elements of a political analysis of European security.[1] In order to get closer to the core of the question, an indirect approach is used in the second half.[2] What is initially postulated as the crucial question is investigated through a reading of some Social Democratic texts dealing especially with *Ostpolitik* and the 'second *détente*'. The views of the four writers concerned are generally very much along the same lines as regards the proposed policy. However, it will be shown that the logic of their arguments in favour of this policy are markedly divergent, if not contradictory.

The most important effect of physical and mental denuclearization will be seen as a change at the symbolic level, entailing a self-fulfilling expectation of political change and manoeuvre in a Europe less exhaustively defined by the bloc structure. In this sense the essential questions should be the goals and means of mutual influence in this less frozen Europe. In this chapter we shall not deal with the question of whether new 'military options' (options for political intimidation) could arise in this process (cf. the chapters in this volume by H.G. Brauch, S. Duke and P. Sivonen). The issue will instead be the non-military dimensions of the security problems and the security solutions in a 'new Europe'.

The setting

After INF: disarmament, politics and Europeanization

Nuclear arms are fundamentally not military but symbolic entities. They cannot be fitted into a military strategy. Therefore it is also impossible to ascribe a definite meaning to them on military grounds.[3] When the Pershing and cruise missiles were deployed in West Germany, for instance, the final decisive argument was that if West Germany did not support deployment, then others, both in East and West, would say that West Germany was floating freely in the centre of Europe, open to Soviet influence, even if the same people in West Germany argued that in military terms the importance of the new nuclear weapons was obscure and ambiguous![4] And now the missiles are being dismantled. There is a broad consensus of opinion that this means an opening in Europe. Some sort of Europeanization is taken for granted. Then this is what the INF agreement means: however much (or little) progress the superpowers make in their negotiations we shall in Europe have *détente* dynamics, European-ization, for some time to come.

Now there is a tendency pointing towards *détente*. What, then, could go wrong? Not only could other projects mobilize their power resources. Rather more important are the problems that the *détente* project may run into itself, because *détente* has always been marked by a reciprocal interaction ('dialectics') between the rapprochement that leads to demarcation and the demarcation that leads to rapprochement.[5]

A *détente* process bringing East and West closer to each other involves more interchange (personal, economic, etc.) which invariably will mean mutual influence, i.e. have political consequences. Where political effects may be seen as threatening—and I presume it is in the first instance in Eastern Europe that this understanding will make itself felt—there will be a tendency to control and regulate East–West contacts and their effects. This will be seen by the other side as illegitimate, as an abuse of the label 'security considerations'. And conflicts of this sort may (if clearer rules are not developed) easily lead to a backlash for *détente*.

What is at stake in the long run is, of course, the political order in Europe.

Political orders: making history

To begin with we ought to focus on the difficult questions arising around Eastern Europe. These are basically of a domestic nature, but because the domestic order is unstable, interaction with Eastern Europe may easily cause security problems. The West must therefore have a discussion of policies and politics for East and West. It must come to grips with internal questions in East and West, for internal problems are central to European security. Similarly, from the Eastern point of view, threats are not only defined by intentions and actions but also by the receiver's (i.e. the East's) vulnerabilities.[6] Growth has been seen as aggression many times in history, and the EEC of 1992 can hardly avoid effects in Eastern Europe. Therefore, the form of Western European economic and security integration must be discussed in relation to its effects on and in Eastern Europe. Furthermore, in a relaxed atmosphere there will most likely be increased integration of Eastern Europe into structures based in Western Europe. At the same time there will be a growing 'pan-Europeanization', possibly implying some Soviet influence in Western Europe. The main form of security problems in this context will be an integration race.

There is no distinct dividing line between 'politics' and 'security politics': European security politics is politics in Europe. Therefore, Europeanization is a question of competition between different security-political orders, which are also different political orders.

There are many political interests at stake. This is why optimal security is presented differently in various quarters. And with the rediscovery of the 'European identity', each region finds its own identity—e.g. central European or Scandinavian—now all of a sudden labelling it 'European'.

After 40 abnormal years we are heading back from one predominant conflict towards the hilly landscape of the classical questions: power and the social order, political-economic interests and ideology—the pattern of the European states system.

In the establishment circles, where 'Europe' and 'European security' were previously seen as a very narrow problem of integration in Western Europe and of strengthening the alliance, there is now a growing awareness of new questions, new challenges and new chances. With more or less enthusiasm it is widely perceived that we are moving out of a period where the structures of the Cold War were narrowing the relevant debates to a very small and easily recognizable repertoire. The possibility that a vast number of fields may be interesting is now opening up. Security politics is suddenly once again seen as part of European history.

We act politically, we participate in the creation of patterns; we may err and things may go completely wrong, or we may end up in new exciting places. Earlier we did not pursue our security policies in such an atmosphere: security policy did not lead anywhere. It was a static guarantee of what we have and what we are. The best outcome would be that it did not go wrong. There might be various initiatives (the Helsinki process, etc.) aimed at the creation of careful development. But that our 'security politics proper' is flowing into our politics which on its side turns into historic action—that is new.

Security can therefore not be debated as an unpolitical, 'technical' problem. Even as 'high politics' it is a discussion that must be taken seriously by activists, politicians and researchers, whether they like it or not. What this 'high-political' discussion is most congenial to is, I suppose, the way in which we now view the European history of the previous centuries: the rise and fall of dominant powers; changes of systems; the struggle over the political order, domestically and internationally.

In a militarily stabilized and more European Europe the internal politics will not disappear. On the contrary. And fundamental political changes may have effects on the foreign policy of a country—and consequently on European security. Quite a few in East and West contemplated this, for example in connection with the Polish situation in the early 1980s. In a Europe less in the grip of the bloc logic there will still be social changes and developments, probably more than during the last 40 years, during which time certain basic patterns or main orientations were settled more steadily than in any other period over the last couple of centuries in European history. And at the same time we think that the 'development' is moving faster than ever. Obviously, the specific international (bipolar) structure has been a socially limiting factor. In a less one-dimensional Europe social development (economics, politics and ideology) will be more important to security than hitherto.

Since the mid-1980s there has been a certain shift towards an interest in the 'non-military aspects of security'. In many different senses there is a general assumption about the decreasing role of military compared to non-military factors. It is less clear what should be meant by non-military aspects. Sometimes this is synonymous with 'co-operation', as is often the case in writings on 'common security' (Wæver, 1989a). In other places it means policies for disarmament (!). The latter seems to be the case when Gorbachev repeatedly states that security is basically a political phenomenon. This talk of 'non-military security' runs the risk of obscuring the picture of European security and excludes precisely the non-military aspects of security. There is a danger of European security consisting of only mute, *military* factors and purely constructive *non-military* factors. What gets lost then is *politics*.

'Non-military aspects' are not the 'good' to take over from all the 'evil' military aspects. There are not only non-military security policies but also non-military insecurity policies. There are not only non-military solutions, but non-military problems as well. The coming years can show that some of the problems may well become bigger or occur in new forms, demanding new answers which we would be well advised to prepare for. This presupposes that we face the non-military (security) problems now.

The central non-military security problem is that *détente* is danger-ous to *some* and consequently unstable for *all*. If East and West are to have more to do with one another, in reality that will mean influence. Influence is politics. And, except in Germany, we have not come very far in discussing how to relate to changes and how to accept certain given limitations to change.

Future security-political developments depend on solutions to problems such as the question of Germany's place in Europe; of France's rank in world politics; of conditions for Social Democratic/left-wing alliances in Western Europe; of socio-political development in Eastern Europe; and of the relationship between Eastern Europe and the Soviet Union. Why is it relevant to point out these issues as problems? Why not just settle for favourable futures and start pressing in that direction?

Because of a specific dilemma related to ideals and utopias—which is even more acute in security and peace politics than in politics in general. Ideals and utopias are at one and the same time often necessary to uphold the enthusiasm that sustains larger social move-ments which are often necessary in turning points. But at the same time they block organic change. There is a general law of action and reaction that also covers the political area. But more than that: in security politics radical visions will usually mean radical losses (of power, identity or life) for some power-holders.

There are simply too many veto-holders. Take the case of Germany: no solution or major development can be imagined over the heads of the Germans, nor can the Germans decide without the consent of the four powers. As Pierre Hassner (1968b, p. 9) noted,

the great powers cannot find or impose a solution, but they can prevent one that does not meet their favour. The dislikes and objections of the various powers, some of them shared, some contradictory, some held by all or some of the Germans, and some directed against the Germans, tend towards the production of a cumulative pressure in favour of the *status quo*.

This likely option of radical pressures and fear-blocked status quo will then be a cover underneath which processes for change will slowly accumulate—surely a recipe for disaster, because then no mechanisms for handling *change* in the system will have been developed (cf. Grela, 1989). This is simply the ancient problem of 'peaceful change'. This can not happen without some 'minimum consensus' on a dynamic status quo (or a 'stable evolution').

The specific character of the security area should be no surprise to us. First, 'security' is historically a tool for attempted conservatism. 'Security' is basically a speech act, or more precisely an 'illocutionary act' (cf. Austin, 1980). Security is the sound coming forth when power-holders claim the need to use their special right to block certain developments by reference to the 'security' of the state (or political order); a special right to use extraordinary means going beyond their register in 'everyday politics'; a special right grounded in the basic image of the modern state having the supply of security and stability as its primary task (cf. Hobbes's *Leviathan*). Usually the threat is then described as coming from the outside, even though it will most often be a combination of internal and external (cf. Wæver, 1989b).

Second, specifically in our nuclear times, it is in Europe impossible to force one's will upon others. The military instrument is hardly useful and the other instruments can almost always be met at some cost through isolation, whereby crucial questions for the fate of the political order are transferred totally to the domestic scene. There is the 'special right' for power-holders (the official representatives of a state) to block threatening developments by referring to 'security'. This has now become—by definition—almost a guarantee for the availability of the *status quo*.

Stabilization and Change

A dynamic process is only possible when the actors concerned engage in a certain amount of mutual stabilization and reassurance. Here one can compare Brandt's *Ostpolitik*, which aimed at overcoming the political and social status quo by stabilizing the territorial status quo, with the fruitless attempt towards reunification entailed by Adenauer's policy of strength and maximum demands.

Political change is only possible in an atmosphere of *détente*. And *détente* is only possible when the fundamental structure is stable. As long as there was hope in East or West for major gains (changing of sides in the conflict, etc.) in the ideological and political-military competition between the two, there was no foundation for *détente*. 'Though, in reality on both sides little happened with the aim of undermining the other and to bring him to fall; the fear of this was great' (Bender, 1986, p. 343). That is why the events in Paris and Prague in 1968 in a way were catalysts for the acceleration of *détente* from 1969. The events of 1968 showed that the alliances and the socio-political orientations were not to be changed. All kinds of selective or divisive *détente* could just as well be dropped; there was no alternative to the slow and less promising process of status quo-based *détente* (Hassner, 1976, pp. 20ff).

This is why one should be very careful not to tamper with the alliances—and why especially individual countries unilaterally leaving an alliance would be highly negative for *détente*.[7] It would reopen the more optimistic and more pessimistic game of greater relative gains and losses by neutralizing allies of the opponent, winning new allies or shifting the 'type' of neutrality by existing neutrals. That would mean a more propagandistic, more manipulative policy oriented less towards stability and *détente*.

However, there is also no hope related to a total status quo policy in the midst of social and technological change. Especially regarding political changes on the other side, stabilization/destabilization is a difficult problem. Certain societies might be so unstable (due to lack of legitimacy for the governing) that some amount of domestic change is necessary before that society could be seen as a stable component of European security. Here a *status quo* policy (stabilization) is not wise security policy. On the other hand direct support for the oppositional forces (destabilization) is obviously also detrimental to *détente* and thereby to European security.

This looks like a dilemma between stabilization and destabilization where the natural reaction, at least for political parties, would be to avoid it by choosing neither. This is the explicit position taken by

Horst Ehmke (1985) of the West German SPD in one of the most careful investigations of these problems, and the implicit position taken by the present government in Bonn (Wæver, 1989a). And this position is wrong.

What is needed is an upgrading of both stabilization and destabilization. Many political forces in the East and the West need to be more conservative on some dimensions (those relating to existential fears on the other side) and more radical/progressive on other dimensions (where organic change should be possible on the other side without causing ruptures).

Horst Ehmke (1985, p. 1009) says that 'the domestic dimension of *détente* policy can be neither "destabilization" nor "stabilization". It is reform.' But this leads him to a one-dimensional orientation towards the official representatives on the other side and what they posit as security interests and domestic possibilities. Neither on the Western nor on the Eastern side can consensus be achieved by only pursuing the East–West policy that is sanctioned by the current power-holders on the other side. It must be possible to relate positively to critical social forces on the other side that work for goals that one is agreeing with as long as it is done inside *certain* limitations relating to *political stability* (domestic and international).

This is only possible by specifying the existential or non-existential character of different spheres and by clarifying within each of these rules of the game (Hassner, 1968a, p. 9; 1968b, p. 6). The second part of the present study will try to contribute to this.

In effect this is all about what Kissinger (1957, pp.1–6) in his study of Metternich and Castleraigh labelled 'a legitimate order': a situation where there is agreement among the major powers about what is legitimate. In a struggle over the rules of the game ('a revolutionary order') there is no common basis, no common yardstick. Therefore in the struggle all moves become tactical, oriented towards unilateral gains. A struggle inside a legitimate order can be handled using diplomacy, compromises, etc. The most difficult element, in this kind of agreement on the rules of the game is the rules of change and the status quo:

A legitimate order confronts the problem of creating a structure which does not make change impossible; a revolutionary order faces the dilemma that change may become an end in itself and thus make the establishment of any structure impossible (Kissinger, 1957, p. 172).

'The search for an immutable *status quo* is as sterile as the search for perfect security, and for the same reasons' (Hassner, 1968a, p. 10). But total or rather uncontrolled change is also impossible. Whatever new and European security structure can be devised in the coming years will therefore have to be seen fundamentally as a stabilization and evolution of the alliance system—as an alliance of two alliances. What one should hope for, then, is not that some day we will reach the point where the alliances are dismantled. Rather a day may come when we forget that we have these alliances; when we forget them because they are no longer felt as structuring the ongoing processes.

The European figuration[8]

A method of analysis must be developed which is capable of handling these issues. This is not done by starting from any general theory of international security giving European security some 'essence'. 'Security' is basically national security. The analysis of European security must therefore be based on an interlinking of national vulnerabilities and policies (Buzan, 1983; Jahn et al., 1987; Kissinger, 1957; Lodgaard and Birnbaum, 1987). This could be called the regional 'security complex' (Buzan, 1983, pp. 105–15).

By investigating empirically this network of vulnerabilities and threats (structural and intentional) one can at any specific time localize certain patterns identifying the core problems. At present there is a simple overall pattern relating to the East–West figuration (cf. Wæver. 1989b, Fig, 17.2) and some additional problems especially relating to Germany, ethnic problems in the Balkans, and a South–North link operating via the Northern flank and maritime strategies (Lodgaard and Birnbaum, 1987).

The main pattern is a fear in the East of 'low politics', i.e. threats towards economic security and ideological defence or fears relating to the effects of increased interaction at the societal level in trade, tourism and talk. In the West the focus of security is on the military-political and diplomatic 'high politics', i.e. a fear of disarmament policies leading to military semi-options for the East that could be exploited for intimidation. And there is a fear of Gorbachev being an all too able player on the diplomatic arena and on the transnational media screen. There is in Western establishment circles a fear of being outmanoeuvred on the level of *states-policy*, in contrast to the interaction of *societies* causing fears in the East.

On the basis of this specific precondition for stable change is a stabilization of West–West relations at the state level and a securing of some basic elements of the political/social system in the East. All this within the overall framework of temperate change.

Since its structure is generated from below, this figuration is necessarily complex and impossible to capture in a formula. One component of the figuration is the 'pure' East–West conflict in its neat one-dimensional form. In the future there must be a continued role for the Cold War in the figuration. In some quarters there is a thinking in coalition logic (Iklé *et al.*, 1988, pp. 2, 10, 14ff, 23f, etc.). All European states are seen as open to pressure and attempts at influencing the degree of their alignment to the two superpowers. This struggle for allies and semi-allies, for cohesion and divisions, operates in war, crisis and peace. One of the logics securing the position of Gorbachev and *perestroika* is the hope of competing better. Eastern European elites also operate consciously with transnational links making Western actors relevant to domestic developments (cf. Lemaître, 1989a; 1989b). A process of *détente* will be blocked if it is seen as a security problem by these groups, these self-appointed guardians of the 'national interest'.

Why accept this? Because there are security elites in all countries— there have to be.[9] All nations have hawks. All countries have a security establishment; some people are professionally predisposed towards pessimism.

As argued above there are a lot of veto-holders. The veto-option is especially easy in relation to *détente* because this possibility is a *constructive* endeavour: the common interest is not given—it is that which is not there (Wæver, 1989b). The *détente* project must enlist a certain amount of participation. It must necessarily pass through some form of agreements and co-operative projects. It is only possible if the overall development is seen with confidence by all major actors. It must not lead to existential threats.[10]

Changes do not necessitate *agreement* among all actors on a full programme. This is obviously absurd. What is necessary is a 'package deal' where A can accept what B starts to do as long as A is at the same time allowed to pursue its policy *a*. The process *b* can be tolerated as long as it is offset to a certain extent by process *a*. Then the process *a* and *b* should not just cancel each other out but in combination lead to some degree of transformation of the system. This would amount to a process containing a 'balance of imbalances'. Thus the interlinking of the different levels in a concrete manner is decisive (cf. Hassner, 1968b, p. 19). The overall process has to be unpredictable in the long run—otherwise someone would block it—and at the same time in the medium term stable enough for all to go along.

In this complex figuration some questions are more pressing than others. Now the crucial two are: Western Europeanization and Eastern European domestic developments; that is, state-to-state developments in Western Europe and societal developments in the East. This gives an extraordinary importance to the intersection of the two: Western European policy for Eastern Europe. Or in broader terms: the effects of the forms taken by Western Europeanization on Eastern Europe.

The future of European security is decided by the many factors involved in the question of the possibility of giving a new dynamism to the complex configuration. However, if there is one point that at the present looks as if it is condensing questions into it, then it is the relation between West German and French views on *Eastern policy*. At this point, of course, the controversies contained in the question of Eastern policy as such (including views from the East) enter the picture.

In this process the superpower interests, the strict East–West conflict, has to be *internalized* by the European actors in order that we can free ourselves from it. Stability is achieved only by fundamental concerns becoming self-evident (cf. Kissinger, 1957, p. 192). Self-restraint and spontaneous obligations towards stability are necessary for the opening towards social and security political change. A real chance for steps towards a socially and politically more plural Europe exists now after the INF agreement.

The German political landscape

The general traits of SPD policy can be discerned through a structural analysis of the West German debate. An investigation of the operations of the parties in relation to each other can define the position of the SPD in the post-1982 landscape.[11] The common demands on all the main characters in SPD are urgency, a new and different policy and a continuation of the social-liberal *détente* policy. This continuity and change typically takes forms like the 'second phase of *Ostpolitik*', 'second *détente*'.

They must keep a distance to the *right* (a European peace order does not follow from the victory of one over the other) and to the *left* (there should be no radical change in the relationship to the West). This, of course, relates to the attitudes towards the recent past of the party: there should be continuity as well as discontinuity in relation to the SPD of Schmidt.

Now it is time to turn to the actor *in medias res*. The SPD played a key role in the instigation of the 'first *détente*' with its 'new *Ostpolitik*' from 1969. Again today a lot of very different observers believe the SPD is the key actor for a possible 'second *détente*'. Whether with hope or fear, one views the SPD as a party pushing for *change* and doing it in a way that at least *seems* realistic enough to make it operate inside the 'serious' part of the political spectrum (cf. the sceptical analysis of Asmus, 1987).

The Social Democratic text(s)

There is a Social Democratic text. It is possible for an SPD leader such as Vogel to use elements from all the different 'thinkers' and to make an effective speech out of it.

Looking more closely at the security thinking of the SPD, one will find not one coherent text but several logics pulling in different directions. This holds generally for all texts. A text is layered, not unitary (cf. Freud). In us we all have different levels 'discussing' with each other.[12] Similarly a *text* will never be able to stabilize itself with a fixed meaning. There will still be the noise from a different logic present in the text; this could be unfolded but never laid to rest with itself; etc. The different layers in the text write against each other (cf. Derrida, 1978). Furthermore, there is *performative inconsistency* between what the text *says* and what it *does*. This goes for the Social Democratic text, too.

Searching for the characteristic logic of the individual politicians is not done in order to reconstruct any 'real' political compromise in the SPD.[13] Nor is the aim to cut canals in the party. The purpose is to cultivate specific logics of the situation. The SPD and some other actors propose a new policy for Europe. This links together a lot of elements and it can be very difficult to get a hold on it—and thereby difficult to get a constructive debate. It might be possible to decompose these very broad ideas of *détente* and change, discover their constituent components by highlighting variances in emphasis among the different writers. Then the focus will be on the specific (often latent) logic of each and this logic will thus be fully developed in a way which would most likely not be accepted by the author. Our focus is not mainly on what the texts *say* but what they *do* (Derrida, 1974); how the totality of logic, style and rhetoric constitutes some patterns where only certain things can be said. The purpose of these readings is threefold. We learn something about the thinking of the SPD. We learn about European security as such, about dimensions of the change/stabilization problematic. We might even learn something about the difficulties and preconditions for conceptualizing and us changing this area. The latter would amount to some theoretical and methodological guidelines for the study and practice of European security.

Egon Bahr: common stability

I am not going to deliver here what might by now be seen as the 'usual' critique of 'common security' (Jahn *et al.*, 1987, pp. 49–55; Wæver, 1989a). The present analysis will go for the specific logic of one text—Egon Bahr's book *Zum europäischen Frieden* (1988). However, a lot of interesting questions relating to this book will not be touched upon: the proposals for *Deutschlandpolitik*, the claim to be more or less the father of Gorbachev's 'new thinking', the more specific arms control ideas, a surprising revitalization of Bahr's own concept of *Wandel durch Annäherung*, etc.

One thing is immediately striking in this book: it presents our times as carrying possibilities for dramatic changes. Nothing less than 'peace in Europe' is possible—a peace which is more than the 'negative peace' we have had for over 40 years. Bahr definitely lives up to the demand of presenting options for *change*. Things could be *so* different. The title is no coincidence. Nor the sub-titles: a change to a world 'beyond war' is possible *now*.

This raises two primary questions to discuss. First, is it so close? Or rather how does Bahr construct a logic that makes it so close? Second, how can such an important development be located as a purely 'security' question—without *political* effects? Who will guide this process, where will it lead, who will be threatened by it, etc? The second question is not addressed in the book. And as we will see, the explanation follows from the answer to the first one.

It is possible to create a structure where war is impossible. This conclusion is reached via the concept of *stability*, defined as a situation where none of the parties is capable of carrying out a successful attack. This should be a situation which none of the parties could change unilaterally (Bahr, 1988, p. 61).

In this way Bahr succeeds in cutting out some factors that can be connected into a logically strong argument.[14] The impossibility of war leads to a possibility of stabilizing definitively the military situation. This is presented as a guarantee of security. Then the rest follows—'security is the key to everything' (Bahr, 1988, p. 35).

Military threats and the related fears have constituted the security problem and the grounds for the division of Europe. Stability in the form of non-offensive defence ('structural incapability of attack') will therefore make war impossible and as the implementation of this defence will be more than ephemeral, Europe will as a historical event be moved beyond war. This is peace. As a definition of peace this is probably a very good choice (cf. Jahn *et al.*, 1987, pp. 39–46). The problem relates to the very narrow conception of what could cause war or existential fear leading to the revisions of policy.

As soon as there is conventional stability, Bahr says, we can dispose of the alliances and create a system of collective security. With this in place the superpowers can disengage themselves from Europe and we have 'European peace'. By solving the security problem, one can set free energy in all other spheres. This is a well-known argument which I find very convincing (cf. Jahn *et al.*, 1987, p. 46). However, it presupposes that existential threats be removed in their totality. And Bahr does not discuss the question of whether these change-blocking fears also exist in the non-military spheres, whether they might even be aggravated by a stabilization of the military dimension.

A premise for Bahr's argument is that security is a purely military question. Whether systems are or could be threatened by other factors is not part of the basic argument. All non-military elements are redefined as 'co-operation'. And all kinds of 'negative' acts are banned by reference to the logic already established by the analysis in the military sphere (since unilateral security gains are impossible). This analysis would not hold if the non-military dimensions were part of the security analysis from the beginning (then unilateral security gains would be possible).

Through the many connotations of 'peace' it is possible to set up a picture where non-military worries will seem dated. Who is afraid of these developments when we have *peace*?

The logic is built upon sharp divisions (Bahr, 1988, p. 36) between power, economic-technological competition, and argumentation or dialogue (in some ideal sense). And power is defined as *military*. There can thus be no threat or intimidation in the non-military sphere. This is expressed in the well-known phrase: 'Ideological conflicts should not be allowed to enter the level of states' (Bahr, 1988, p. 31).

On the penultimate page (Bahr, 1988, p. 99) there is an argument about the possibilities for closer co-operation within Western Europe and within Eastern Europe. It becomes clear that the European peace as stabilization could take the form of Western Europeanization and Eastern Europeanization. There is throughout the book very little stress on human-dimension issues. The project is not to sew Europe together, therefore the non-military questions are not in the forefront. The core of the strategy is dissociative. The aim is independence and power for Europe—not more pan-European culture and 'domestic-European politics'. After removing the danger of war from Europe, the superpower presence can no more be legitimized. And European energy can be used for new purposes.

There is nothing to prevent stabilization of East as East and West as West. European peace would still be achieved. This is not to claim that Bahr's motives are these. Quite the contrary, he is most likely to be interested in some East–West dynamics—especially in Germany! But it is remarkable how the logic of the argument has to exclude this.[15] A general, societal rapprochement between East and West would inevitably raise political issues—maybe even *security* problems. Thus this kind of *Wandel durch Annäherung* must be excluded from the analysis of European security proper. Symptomatically, the term *Wandel durch Annäherung* is in the book reappropriated for a new meaning. It stands for a general change of the European security system through security co-ordination. As if the phenomenon of domestic change as an effect of *détente* could be muted by taking back from it the name originally given by Egon Bahr in 1963.

In order to cope with this, Bahr has to make *military stability* equivalent to peace and security. Not partly, but fully. Thus security problems cannot be non-military. Otherwise non-military fears might motivate some actor to move away from the 'rational' policy of common stabilization.

Erhard Eppler: stable competition of ideologies

Eppler is aware of the necessity of setting limits *inside* the non-military sphere as well. This is in direct opposition to Bahr. Eppler (1988, p. 19) explicitly refutes the argument about not transferring ideological conflicts to the state level. The limits should set free a dynamic for a peaceful unfolding of competition (*Wettbewerb*) and struggle (*Streit*). The systems are then supposed to compete in their performance. This new competition in fulfilling human needs should be based on the declared goals shared by the systems: democracy, human rights, welfare, humanism, etc. There is a core logic to Eppler's endeavours, his writings and the negotiations with the East Germans leading to the 'common paper' agreed upon between the East German SED and the SPD.[16] The competition of the systems will have to continue without war—war is no longer a political means in Europe. Thus the systems have to work from the premise not of any kind of victory, but the premise has to be open-minded coexistence. Development will depend on the ability of both systems to reform themselves.

Getting the best out of this situation is at present hindered by certain ideological evaluations by each system of the other, e.g. saying the other system is inherently leading to war. Peace politics is therefore necessarily directed against the other side. A core sentence of the common paper is therefore that both systems have to see the other as *friedensfähig* (capable of peace). This caused trouble in the GDR! 'Living together' cannot be limited in time, but must be open-ended. One system might 'win' some day—'but then it would no longer be the system from that day' (Eppler, 1986, p. 11).

Eppler's (1986; 1988) work is a sophisticated analysis trying hard to find possibilities for adjusting ideological dogmas in ways that do not undermine the basic identity of the system in question. Finding such ways makes it possible for the two sides to enter a more constructive interaction. At points it might even seem like an overly idealistic interest in the logic of ideological statements. In the present analysis this is viewed as extremely important—and Eppler (1988) could be of immense value as a 'debate book' for a broader public. For instance, the importance of the twists and turns in the Soviet concept of 'peaceful coexistence' are here set into a highly meaningful framework.

One of the outlets of this approach is the attempt to develop together with the East some 'rules of the game', a *conflict culture*. (For more detailed elaborations of this aspect, see Eppler, 1988, pp. 73ff, 109ff; Kaiser, 1986; 1987; 1988; Meyer, 1987). This includes some improvement in the direction of agreement on the core issue: the West accepting certain limitations on non-military intervention, and the East accepting that Western criticism must be otherwise tolerated. That is, one must take up the debate—not use the labels 'interference in domestic affairs' or 'a threat to national security'. This necessarily leads to an acceptance of debate in society that is not allowed in East Germany today even when no external forces are present. It is therefore pointed out how implementation of the paper will necessitate a more open domestic debate (cf. Voigt, 1988a; *Spiegel*, 1987).

The 'common paper' has been vehemently criticized, not least because it states explicitly that certain things are to be conserved, things that are nevertheless never seriously challenged by any serious political forces in the FRG. Thus, there are certain things you can do but not say. And, to the extent that what is said becomes of importance for what can be done, there is a problem. It is a structural problem of the European security area that the necessary ideological debate is a losing issue for politicians (Wæver, 1988). Reproaches for treachery easily spill over into the more important domestic arena. Against the background of the first half of this chapter it should be clear that this is not a minor problem. In a dynamic process of mutual stabilization it is necessary to learn to speak about that which one has already *de facto* accepted on the other side.

In some instances the 'common paper' and Eppler (1988) make things worse for themselves (this is of course not accidental, it is necessitated by the logic of other arguments). There is a certain tendency to use euphemistic phrases regarding who or what is to be stabilized: there is quite a lot of talk about 'sides' ('not deny[ing] the other side the right to exist', etc.).[17] It could be useful to make a simple distinction between power-holders, states and systems. There are already rules for the intercourse of *states*—after all the states in East and West do recognize each other. Even the two German states do so, *de facto*. The counterreaction to destabilizing effects of *détente* does not come from 'system' or 'sides' but from concrete social actors.

One could state explicitly that this is about the *Realpolitik* of change which necessarily entails the avoidance of 'mortal' threats against power-holders. This will often imply at least a *de jure* preservation of key elements of ideologies ('the leading role of the Communist Party'). But by being more explicit about the object of stabilization, one could avoid reifying in many cases the 'systems' and 'ideologies'. (This often happens indirectly through the metaphor of 'sides'.) Eppler's formulations have the paradoxical effect of making it sound as if the aim was to stabilize ideologies.

There is, however, one problem that is more striking. The final criticism of the Eastern concepts of peaceful coexistence and of the Western theory of totalitarianism (Eppler, 1988, chs 4 and 5) relates to the effects of the theories on the perceptions and thus the policies of the other side. The opponent might be overly frightened by the rhetorics. Thus, the logic of the conflict is power and perceptions—geopolitics and enemy images. Not 'ideology' in the sense of systems of thinking, goals and interpretation, but the ideology concerning the opponent's ideology!

The effect of this logico-rhetorical operation is to exclude the 'real abstraction' of East–West relations as a conflict as such. Eppler is right in pointing out how it is necessary to see the conflict as open and more complex in order to inject an evolutionary perspective into it.[18] However, the reductionist view of strict bipolar logic is real, too. And to a certain extent the East–West conflict must also be viewed as relative; a conflict over relative gains in competition between the two dominant systems.

If one starts from the empirical (not from an abstract structure) it is, as Eppler shows, possible to admit the role of values and aspirations (the continuing competition of ideas). However, these will in this logic be seen as positive, as defined by and in themselves—thus possibly competing in a positive-sum game. To a certain extent, however, the East–West conflict has been a conflict built on the 'abstraction' of a duel over world history. This image cannot simply be refuted as an empirically incorrect reflection of reality. That would be as if the criticism of capitalism by Marx had taken the form of criticizing individuals for acting according to the abstract exchange-value concept instead of the 'real' use-value one. These abstractions are socially real and thus self-fulfilling. What must be analysed and possibly criticized is the effects of a social system built on these abstractions.

This is exactly the perspective excluded by Eppler: statesmen are not motivated by a perception of the East–West conflict as a real life-and-death struggle of two social systems.[19] They use this as window-dressing and they might react to the others' use of this language. Basically they think in terms of power and geopolitics. And they are caught in enemy images leading them to overinsurance.

Eppler's book at first seems to be an attempt to stress the importance of ideologies. In the first chapters he repeats over and over again the statement that peace politics can no longer skirt around the issue of ideologies; the ideology problems must be addressed, too. In accordance with his own moral, value-based (religious) approach, it is natural to see the conflict as a struggle for something. The book scores over many left-wing analyses and analyses in peace movement circles in presenting the East–West conflict as a conflict about something. However, Eppler's analysis has the effect of redirecting this argument into the form of the 'enemy image' problematic. This can be seen as related to his personal political experience of anti-communism (Eppler, 1988, pp.8ff), typical for this new generation of SPD leaders (cf. Voigt, 1988a, p. 603).

Eppler's project is to take Reagan statement that armaments are not the cause of mistrust literally; it is the lack of confidence that causes armament (Eppler, 1988, p. 18). If the source lies in the opposition of systems and ideologies, Eppler thinks we should search for new ways to compete. The task is to make relatively minor but principled adjustments to the ideologies so that the systems can compete without turning each other into enemies. But Eppler's analysis is paradoxical, since the central most analytical part (Eppler, 1988, chs 2–6, based on Eppler, 1986) carefully establishes a logic where the foreign policy of states follows not from ideologies but from interests—and misperceptions. States do not really act because of systems and ideologies. The one dimension distinctively absent from Eppler's figuration is the political manoeuvre war between East and West for relative gains. In order to avoid this as a totalizing interpretation, he makes a move to the effect of excluding it as a component. His model becomes thus unable to handle this problem—his original worry.

Horst Ehmke: Western Europeanization and détente *from above*

In two areas of SPD policy the main source—usually referred to by researchers and the party alike—are the writings of Horst Ehmke. Regarding the attitude of the SPD to West–West relations and future security co-operation in Western Europe, the main source is Ehmke (1984). As to the issue of responsibility towards critical groups in Eastern Europe, together with the broader question of the role of independent groups (East and West) in the process of détente ('détente from above' versus 'détente from below'), the most balanced and authoritative source is Ehmke (1985).

Ehmke (1984) attempts to localize and talk openly about West–West problems. This in contrast to the conservatives, who do not want to talk about it; and in contrast to the Greens, who would not like to see this as a pragmatic problem to be handled. It should be a natural task for the SPD to ease the situation and to try to formulate this problem pragmatically.

Ehmke (1984, p. 197) suggests, first, that both sides of the Atlantic must agree on the future of the alliance; and second, that the Europeans should agree on their own policy inside the alliance.

As regards the Americans and what was expected from the SPD at the time of the writing, Ehmke is quite obliging (Ehmke, 1984, p. 201) on several issues. He in fact only puts things bluntly when refuting 'horizontal escalation': Europe is not to be integrated into the global strategy of the United States. This is the essence of his paper. If this can be secured he is quite pragmatic on the rest. And the paper labours mostly on quite well-known concepts and issues: the two-pillar concept, concrete institutions in Western Europe, and all that.

His conclusion: for Europeanization, the code word is 'stability'— 'stabilizing the military and *political* balance' (Ehmke, 1984, p. 204, emphasis added). This naturally leads to the other issue.

As a reaction to some arguments over the peace movement strategy of 'détente from below', Ehmke (1985) formulated some principled considerations regarding 'Peace and Freedom as Goals for *Détente* Policy'. It is argued that détente from below can hinder real détente because it creates counterreactions with the governments in the East. This was not the effect of the original Social Democratic policy of détente, Ehmke claims. It has all the way been a question for the design of détente whether it would have 'ideological effects that would make the Eastern bloc turn its back upon it' (Ehmke, 1985, p. 1004). The regimes in the East have domestically 'endured' détente surprisingly well, Ehmke notes. He obviously views this as promising; whereas 'a policy wanting to destabilize the Eastern regimes—be that from "outside" or "below"—would serve neither détente nor peace' (Ehmke, 1985, p. 1005). The 'dissidents' in the East are presented as nice and good but not very realistic—they want 'all or nothing', and now. Thus, we should neither condemn nor actively support these groups, Ehmke writes. 'The domestic dimension of détente can mean neither "destabilization" nor "stabilization". It means reform' (Ehmke, 1985, p. 1009). So Ehmke's article ends up reflecting on the possibility for reform in the Eastern regimes and on the options for the Soviet Union for fulfilling its security needs in Europe better with reform than with armour.

The article triggered an interesting reply by a leading Solidarność spokesman (Anon, 1986). This cannot be presented in detail, but among other things it pointed out how Ehmke's view of Eastern Europe is lopsided. The destabilizations have come neither from below nor from the outside—but from inside; they are generated by the system. And the opposition is not 'dissidents', courageous, extreme and irrelevant individuals. They are strong social forces rooted in the processes of these societies; forces of 'continuing potential relevance on the political scene' (Anon, 1986, p. 550). The image of reform in the East is therefore completely different. Reform is not just enacted from the top. It is the outcome of a political process involving various forces. Thus several political actors are relevant to the combined European development that will in the last instance be equivalent to the process of *détente*. Relating to only one part is not 'neutral', but reinforces certain dimensions of reality, in this instance the monopoly claims of the regime.

As pointed out in the first part of this chapter, the conclusion should therefore not be to forget the terms 'stabilization' and 'destabilization', but to understand them. The alliances, representative democracy in the West, and a formal 'leading role' for the communist parties in the East, should all be stabilized in order to secure continuity. On the other hand, an *Ostpolitik* should destabilize the arms race, the form of public debate in the West, the monopoly position of the regimes in the Eastern societies, etc.

The Solidarność spokesman points out how in the other direction the East *is* making the links Ehmke warns against. Eastern elites do not shy away from relations with peace movements in the West. But Ehmke warns Western governments, parliaments and parties against having relations with Charter 77 and Solidarność. So, the Solidarność spokesman concludes, Ehmke's policy is in reality '*détente* from above' even though he claims it is a 'both-and' policy. It could be added: also in the West, Ehmke's policy is purely 'from above'. The role he ascribes to the peace movement is only one of supporting the Social Democratic policy. He does not talk at all about *direct* East–West policies being conducted by Western 'unofficial' groups.

In Ehmke (1988) the issue of the role of social movements is handled by referring to the distinction between the first *détente* (or *Ostpolitik*) and the coming second phase. In the first phase the SPD was very one-sided in its work at the official level, but precisely through this an option has now been created for broader participation in the second phase (Ehmke, 1988, pp. 103. 268). A heavy burden is laid on the distinction between the first and second phases of *détente*—a distinction that has to my knowledge never been carefully specified. Especially not by Ehmke.

Is there anything common to the two arms of Ehmke policy? Yes, they both take the form of immediate *Realpolitik*. They both find their ground in a kind of Social Democratic *raison d'état*. They are answers to the questions a new foreign minister would immediately have to face.[20] His version of SPD policy is marginally adjusting the status quo in East and West. One could speculate about the ability of precisely this version to function as 'place-holder' in the political landscape described in the first part of this study (cf. Wæver, 1989a).

Karsten D. Voigt: *Radical Neo-Atlanticist* Ostpolitik

The plot of Karsten Voigt's (1983) intervention in the deployment debate in the Bundestag was to show that NATO membership can lead to different policies. This was quite a clever strategy of pointing out how the government, by positing an unquestionable link between NATO membership and missiles, made opponents of the missiles opponents of NATO (cf. the Greens).

This is the general form that Voigt's speeches take: to turn arguments against their proponents; the logic of we do better what you claim to be doing. It is necessarily the *same* that should be delivered then—not something different, no 'alternative' ends, only alternative means.

Yet another case of turning arguments around is Voigt's (1983, p. 2448) accusing CDU/CSU hardliners of political and psychological weakness:

this policy of military strength is the expression of political weakness, and by many an expression of psychological weakness, too. I cannot see the fixation of Franz Josef Strauss and Alfred Dregger on the Pershing 2 any different. I understand it as a compensation for their Spenglerian visions of internal decline, external vulnerability towards blackmail and for a threatening

Untergang des Abendlandes. The aggressivity is an expression of *Angst*, *Angst* for the Soviet Union, *Angst* for communism and *Angst* for the domestic opponent. *Angst* is a bad adviser. When you reproach the peace movement with *Angst* then I tell you: Your policy is marked by *Angst*, born out of *Angst*.

On several occasions Voigt has given speeches that have brought the debate on *détente* into conservative human rights territory. Social Democratic *Ostpolitik* delivers what the West allegedly stands for: dynamics in the East and security of the West (Voigt, 1987).

Implied in this politically offensive strategy is that there is only talk of political change on their side (cf. especially Voigt, 1987; 1988c). In a way Voigt is on these occasions the one who comes closest to the original *Wandel durch Annäherung* approach.

This fits well with the fact that he is the one who works actively in the NATO community. He is the author of several reports for commissions under the North Atlantic Assembly. A correlate to this was an active polemic with the Greens in the deployment debate in order to show that one is taking part in NATO politics—not just grudgingly accepting the unavoidable nature of membership.[21] On these occasions, there is a complete block on what might in a way be his own motive: changes in the West.

What about some other papers by Karsten Voigt (cf. 1985, 1988a; and 1988b, pp. vii, and 181ff.)? He stresses that Social Democrats are basically and historically in favour of reform, domestically as well as internationally. They are *reformists*. This descriptive (or even pejorative) term is turned into a programmatic label. Abrupt societal change is impossible in East as well as West. Responsibility therefore spells 'reform'. Reform in international relations (*détente*) is the best framework for these changes. By stressing emphatically the specific links among these processes of change, Karsten Voigt develops a conception of *Ostpolitik* where *détente* is closely linked to change on our side as well.

Generally Voigt is in many ways close to the perspective presented in the first part of this chapter. He stresses the continued role of the alliances, and delivers generally one of the most convincing versions of a European security policy, one recognizing that security policy is political, that there is a struggle over what peace it should be, etc. (Voigt, 1985; 1986). He stresses sometimes very clearly how the peace problematic is intimately linked to the issues of future developments of the societies (e.g. Voigt, 1988b, p. 258).

The two parts of his writings fall apart openly contradicting each other at a point defined by themselves as crucial: reform in the West. Maybe this is not just bad luck or coincidence; it might be irony of 'unhappy consciousness'. With this awareness of the political nature of the matter and with a strategy of showing all groups how the same can be achieved better in another way, one will inevitably have to take on extremely explicit contradictions—if it should not be so that all interests are basically in harmony. The present reading might be an indication of the lack of this harmony! If the aims and aspirations of all groups should unfold this must entail conflict; it might be possible that they can be manipulated into agreement on one policy but then conflict will be displaced to other areas where the premises will contradict.

There is an attempt to mediate between the two groups of writings. 'Learning process' is then the (typically German) key term (Voigt, 1983, p. 2449; and 1988, p. 156f). Even in the NATO report, Voigt (1988c, p. 33) writes:

In [my] opinion . . . arms control constitutes a civilizing process of peace politics through which both sides gradually learn to resolve conflicts without recourse to the use of force. The discussions about to begin between East and West on conventional stability are very much part of this learning process. The very debate itself alters attitudes and perceptions, in turn civilizing the participants.

It is hardly coincidence that leads Karsten Voigt to the particular ambiguity of 'learning' and 'civilizing'—terms indicating reform and non-reform. In the West it will not be the same or different, just 'better'.

Stabilization, change and ideology

We have already seen in the preceding sections how *each* of the Social Democratic texts tended to point towards its own blind spot. Bahr wants to achieve a change in East—West relations. But in order to do this he has to shut off East and West from each other. Eppler wants to emphasize the importance of ideology and therefore conscious change in our and our opponent's ideology (including a mutual stabilization of the ideologies). In order to achieve this he sets up an analysis where the foreign policy of a state is not an effect of its ideology. Ideologies only have effect on the opponent's policy, not directly upon their holders. Thus foreign policy is based on raw interests and the ideology about the opponent's ideology. Rather paradoxical. Ehmke in a way fails to meet the structural demand for a neo-SPD policy, of urgency and novelty but he, in fact, argues like a minister of foreign affairs. His logic is basically built on the responsibility of the state; his direct claims are for a formulation of the 'new' SPD policy. Occasionally this—non-present—novelty is necessary to uphold the argument, as in the case of the two *different* phases of *détente* getting him past a problem relating to broader participation in the process of *détente*. Voigt came out as a double structure almost presenting itself as based on a mirror-effect.

However, it is probably more important to notice how the texts in their more basic narratives mutually debase each other. Voigt stresses the inescapable link between peace politics and societal developments. This is deeply problematic for the other three as they want to present a 'necessary' peace and security policy above 'political' interests. Ehmke's text is basically framed as pragmatic foreign policy whereas the other three have emergency as their basic premise (cf. the title of an article by Bahr from 1982: 'Peace: A State of Emergency'). [22] But the most interesting is the contrast between Bahr and Eppler. Bahr wants to stabilize the military sphere and it is decisive for his project to make a clear demarcation between 'military' and 'non-military'. Eppler wants to stabilize a broader field. His main idea is built around the broad societal competition. This is absent from Bahr's picture—and has to be because his basic, tight argument about 'peace at hand' would be questioned by the possibility of threats to social systems (and power-holders) other than the military ones. Eppler needs the arguments of a continuing danger of East–West war. It gives impulses to limitation on competition in other spheres, thus civilizing the conflict behaviour. By contrast, Bahr starts from the premise that war is now ruled out as a relevant option. And his approach definitively excludes this possibility—thereby freeing new dynamics. According to Eppler (1988, p. 37) the security problems are shifted from the military to the non-military spheres. In Bahr (1988) non-military security problems are a contradiction in terms.

What is to be learnt from this deconstruction? It is impossible to enclose a specific area of 'security' and make unpolitical arguments from this basis. Security will always be drowned out by politics.

One might be misled by the conservative connotations of security or the seemingly unproblematic nature of stabilization. However, any such project reinforces or destabilizes certain elements of present reality, thereby invoking political effects and political reactions:

A formalization of the *status quo* is one type of political settlement, and, as with all political settlements, it means reinforcing certain elements of the *status quo* (e.g., the division of Germany into two states) while weakening certain others (e.g., the ties between Germany and her Western allies, the psychological grounds for the American presence in Europe). There is therefore a case for handling political problems politically and attempting to use military stability as a means of solving the open questions of political settlement instead of pre-empting them under the guise of normalization (Hassner, 1968a, p. 6).

The alternative to this must be much more clearly to launch the debate on European security as a debate on European politics. About the future of Europe; not in the sense of some 'Europe' having a natural, historical essence to be preserved or regained but as an area of peoples, states and possibilities—of conflicts and controversies that are inter-related across a continent. Of politics.

The political approach—in politics as well as in research—could be to point out these interrelated effects and show how they are choices and options, the object of action. This interrelated figuration contains elements that relate to 'security' proper as well as to issues of an economic, social or political nature. Debating this constellation of conflicts as such would most likely raise the level of controversy. It hinges critically on the 'will to power': on the willingness to stand up for projects and take responsibility as *creator*, not just *conservator* (Wæver, 1989b).[23]

Notes

1. The first part of the present study is an abridged version of a paper originally presented at the TAPRI workshop on Political Consequences of Nuclear Disarmament in Europe (Wæver, 1988).
2. In many cases a text on a text says more than a text. The specific patterns and problems created in the textual work might be doubly revealing—and easier to read than 'reality'. Or more correctly: we never work directly on 'reality'; we are always commenting on something already said. It can then be revealing to focus directly on the textuality of what has already been said. Not least the 'blind spots' of texts might be very telling: 'The insight exists only for the reader in the privileged position of being able to observe the blindness as a phenomenon in its own right—the question of his own blindness being one which he is by definition incompetent to ask—and so being able to distinguish between statement and meaning. He has to undo the light only because being already blind, he does not have to fear the power of this light. But the vision is unable to report correctly what it has perceived in the course of its journey. To write critically about critics thus becomes a way to reflect on the paradoxical effectiveness of a blinded vision that has to be rectified by means of insights that it unwittingly provides' (de Man 1983, p. 106). The obvious price of this approach is that one remains dependent on the text one uses. The chosen text is at the same time contamination and cure (Derrida, 1981, pp. 61–171).

3. The reason for this is basically the disappearance of the only meaningful yardstick—the battle. Cf. Clausewitz, who writes that 'the decision by arms is, for all operations in War, great and small, what cash payment is in bill transactions' (*On War*, Book I, Chapter 2).

4. See especially the speech by Foreign Minister Dietrich Genscher of the FDP in the deployment debate of the West German Bundestag, *Plenarprotokoll*, 10/35, pp. 2356–64.

5. *Annäherung* and *Abgrenzung* in German.

6. Thus it is possible to be even an 'unwitting revisionist' (Hassner, 1968a, p. 10).

7. Here one could note that even the intellectual leaders of END (the part of the European peace movement most interested in overcoming Europe's division and superpower dominance) are aware that the more independent ('beyond the blocs') policies of European states are most likely to come about as policies of still-allied states. However, that being so, the chosen key term 'dealignment' seems a very unfortunate choice. The essence of the thinking in these quarters is a decrease in bloc logic without a break-up of the alliances. In that case the term 'dealignment' should be avoided—even if 'deblocification' is an impossible term!

8. This section is mainly based on Wæver (1989b).

9. An attempt to circumvent these groups most likely leads to some kind of non-military civil war—and a divided state, as the case of Sweden tends to indicate (Tunander, 1989, ch. 9).

10. Or more precisely: the process must lead to less existential fears than non-action would do. Some states might be in a weak position—a kind of double-bind: cf. the Eastern European problem of 'economic security' where the choice seems to be between plague and cholera: political instability due to economic crisis or political instability due to impulses from the West relating to increased trade and co-operation.

11. This section is based on Wæver (1989a).

12. This is why Jacques Lacan says that 'the unconscious is structured like a language'—if it were not it could not interact (debate) with our conscious part. This psychological insight is often obscured by talk about the 'subconscious', creating an image of an unstructured, floating, boiling underworld in us. 'For Lacan, as for many writers, Freud's essential insight was not—clearly not—that the unconscious exists, but that is has structure, that this structure affects in innumerable ways what humans say and do, and that in thus betraying itself it becomes accessible to analysis' (Bowie, 1987, p. 102). See especially Freud (1960).

13. Accordingly there will be no integrating of information regarding the particular positions and posts held in the party. Suffice it to note that the four are the leading thinkers and spokesmen of the party on foreign and security policy.

14. 'Bahr has a total conception (*Gesamtkonzept*) of rare compactness (*Geschlossenheit*) and breathtaking boldness' (Baring, 1988, p. 8).

15. One could even say: *if* the project achieved what it wanted it would remove the grounds for itself. This extends the often demonstrating problem for

'common security' that it wants to overcome deterrence—and at the same time has a deterrence relationship as a basic premise.

16. Common paper agreed upon between the Academy of Social Sciences under the Central Committee of the Socialist Unity Party of Germany (GDR) and the Basic Values Commission of the SPD (FRG): 'Der Streit der Ideologien und die gemeinsame Sicherheit', printed numerous places, e.g. *Neues Deutschland*, 28 August 1987, p. 3; *Frankfurter Rundschau*, 28 August 1987; *Blätter für deutsche und internationale Politik*, 1987, no. 10, pp. 1365ff.

17. Also a statement like 'We should not force our standards on the other side' (e.g. Voigt, 1988a, p. 602) becomes ambiguous in the instances when the majority 'on the other side' would love to have 'our' standards forced upon them, instead of the standards decided 'on their own side'—by a minority.

18. From 1985 to 1988 this has been the essential argument of most of what I published myself, mainly in Danish. For a very clear analysis stating many of the basic ideas that structure the writings in and around 'the common paper', see Jahn (1981).

19. Eppler (1988, p. 36) is aware that the two global powers will necessarily be focused on each other (p. 36). This is, however, presented as a pure logic of power—explicitly geopolitical and with some touch of pure conflict logic. It does not follow from the systems conflict.

20. After discovering this pattern it is almost embarrassing to read Ehmke (1988, pp. 267–9).

21. Cf. Margrethe Auken and Ole Wæver, 'Fra fodnoter til virkelige skridt', *Information*, no. 23, May.

22. In *Vorwärts*, 1982, no. 22; English translation in R. Steinke and M. Vale (eds), *Germany Debates Defence*. New York: Sharpe, 1983.

23. A note for SPD (and its fans): In this situation the SPD text—with all its tensions and intentions—is likely to be seen as one of the most attractive by wide segments of European societies. The policies and a lot of the arguments fit well with the aspirations of many a political force and social group. However, this is not achieved by presenting the text as the necessary security policy following from an indisputable security analysis above politics. This depolitization is most likely to be counterproductive.

Bibliography

Anon, 1986. 'Entspannungspolitik—in einer anderen Sicht. Eine Antwort', *Die Neue Gesellschaft*, vol. 33, no. 6.

Asmus, Ronald D., 1987. 'The SPD's Second Ostpolitik With Perspectives from the USA', *Aussenpolitik* (English language edition), vol. 38, no. 1.

Austin, J.L., 1980. *How To Do Things with Words*. Oxford: Oxford University Press (first published 1962).

Bahr, Egon, 1988. *Zum europäischen Frieden: Ein Antwort auf Gorbatschow*. Berlin: Corso bei Siedler.

Baring, Arnulf, 1988. 'Der realistische Traumwandler: Egon Bahrs europä- ischer Friedensentwurf', *Frankfurter Allgemeine Zeitung*, 28 March.

Bender, Peter, 1986. 'Sicherheitspartnerschaft und friedliche Koexistenz: Zum Dialog zwischen SPD und SED', *Die Neue Gessellschaft/Frankfurter Hefte*, vol. 33, no. 4, April.

Bender, Peter, 1987. 'The Superpower Squeeze', *Foreign Policy*, no. 65, Winter.

Boutwell, Jeffrey, 1988. 'The Politics and Ideology of SPD Security Policies', in Barry M. Blechman and Cathleen S. Fischer (eds), *The Silent Partner: West Germany and Arms Control*. Cambridge, MA: Ballinger.

Bowie, Malcolm, 1987. *Freud, Proust and Lacan: Theory as Fiction*. Cambridge: Cambridge University Press.

Buzan, Barry, 1983. *People, States and Fear*. Brighton: Wheatsheaf Books.

Buzan, Barry, 1989. 'The Future of Western European Security' in O. Wæver, P. Lemaître and E. Tromer (eds), *European Polyphony*. London: Macmillan.

De Man, Paul, 1983. *Blindness and Insight*, 2nd edition with five additional essays. Minneapolis: University of Minnesota Press (first published 1971).

Derrida, Jacques, 1974. *Of Grammatology*, translated by Gayatri Chakravorty Spivak. Baltimore, MD: Johns Hopkins University Press (first published 1967).

Derrida, Jacques, 1978. *Writing and Difference*, translated by Alan Bass. Chicago: The University of Chicago Press (first published 1967).

Derrida, Jacques, 1981. *Dissemination*, translated by Barbara Johnson. Chicago: The University of Chicago Press (first published 1972).

Ehmke, Horst, 1984. 'Eine Politik zur Selbstbehauptung Europas', *Europa-Archiv*, no. 7.

Ehmke, Horst, 1985. 'Frieden und Freiheit als Ziele der Entspannungspolitik', *Die Neue Gesellschaft/Frankfurter Hefte*, vol. 32, no. 11.

Ehmke, Horst, 1987. 'Feinbilder und politische Stabilität', *Die Neue Gesell-schaft/Frankfurter Hefte*, vol. 34, no. 12.

Ehmke, Horst, 1988. 'Einfuhrung in das Seminar'; 'Bei den Schulden zu helfen, ist schon eine ganze Menge'; 'Regierungen mussen Kompromisse machen'; and 'Ich will keine Zusammenfassung versuchen . . .' in Greune (1988).

Ehmke, Horst, 1989. 'Der Binnenmarkt—unsere wirtschaftliche "Peres-troika" ', speech in the Bundestag on 19 January, printed in *Das Parlament*, vol. 39, no. 5, 29 January.

Eppler, Erhard, 1986. 'Friedenspolitik und Ideologie', *Mediatus*, vol. 6, no. 4.

Eppler, Erhard, 1988. *Wie Feuer und Wasser: Sind Ost und West friedensfähig?* Hamburg: Rowohlt.

Freud, Sigmund, 1960. 'Das Unbewusste', *Gesammelte Werke*, Vol. X. Frank- furt am Main: Fischer (first published 1915).

Grela, Marek, (1989). 'The Debate on European Security in Poland' in O. Wæver, P. Lemaître and E. Tromer (eds), *European Polyphony*. London: Macmillan.

Greune, Gerd (ed.), 1988. 'Die Dialektik von Entspannung und individuellen wie kollektiven Menschenrechten in der zweiten Phase der Entspannungs- politik' in *Dokumentation des internationalen Seminars der Friedrich-Ebert-Stiftung*. Bonn: Friedrich-Ebert-Stiftung.

Hassner, Pierre, 1968a. 'Change and Security in Europe. Part I: The Background', *Adelphi Papers*, no. 45, February.

Hassner, Pierre, 1968b. 'Change and Security in Europe. Part II: In Search of a System', *Adelphi Papers*, no. 49, July.

Hassner, Pierre, 1976. 'The Politics of Western Europe and East–West Relations' in Nils Andren and Karl E. Birnbaum (eds), *Beyond Detente: Prospects for East–West Cooperation and Security in Europe*. Leiden: A.W. Sijthoff.

Iklé, Fred *et al.*, 1988. *Discriminate Deterrence—A Report of The Commission on Integrated Long-Term Strategy*. Washington, DC: US Government Printing Office.

Jahn, Egbert, 1981. 'The Tactical and Peace-Political Concept of Detente', *Bulletin of Peace Proposals*, vol. 12, no. 1.

Jahn, Egbert, Lemaître, Pierre, and Wæver, Ole, 1987. 'Eruopean Security: Problems of Research on Non-Military Aspects' in *Copenhagen Papers 1*. Copenhagen: Centre of Peace and Conflict Research.

Kaiser, Carl-Christian, 1986. 'Wandel durch Wettbewerb?' *Die Zeit*, 7 March.

Kaiser, Carl-Christian, 1987. 'Kultur des politischen Streits', *Die Zeit*, 28 August.

Kaiser, Carl-Christian, 1988. 'Wenn's im Dialog kritisch wird', *Die Zeit*, 6 May.

Kissinger, Henry, 1957. *A World Restored*. Boston: Houghton Mifflin.

Leciejewski, Klaus, 1988. 'Freiheit durch gemeinsame Reformen?', *Deutschland Archiv*, vol. 21, no. 10.

Lemaître, Pierre, 1989a. 'Osteuropa im europaischen Sicherheitssystem' in C. Wellmann (ed.), *Frieden in und mit Osteuropa*. Frankfurt: Suhrkamp.

Lemaître, Pierre, 1989b. 'Hungarian Concepts of Security Policy and the Security Policies of Hungary' in O. Wæver, P. Lemaître and E. Tromer (eds), *European Polyphony*. London: Macmillan.

Lodgaard, Sverre and Birnbaum, Karl, 1987. *Overcoming Threats to Europe: A New Deal for Confidence and Security*. Oxford: SIPRI/Oxford University Press.

Meyer, Thomas, 1987. 'Ein neuer Rahmen für den Ost-West-Dialog', *Die neue Gesellschaft*, vol. 34, no. 10.

Reinhold, Otto, 1987. Interview 'Ideological Disputes and Mutual Security', *New Times* (Moscow), no. 45, November 1987.

Spiegel, 1987. 'Ein System kann das andrere nicht abschaffen', interview with Erhard Eppler and Otto Reinhold, 31 August.

Tunander, Ola, 1989. *Cold Water Politics: The Maritime Strategy and Geopolitics of the Northern Front*. London: Sage.

Voigt, Karsten D., 1983. Speech in the Bundestag, 21 November, in the debate on deployment of cruise and Pershing. Published in Deutscher Bundestag, *Plenarprotokoll*, 10/35.

Voigt, Karsten D., 1985. 'Die Funktionen von NATO und Warschauer Pakt auf dem Wege zur Sicherheitspartnerschaft', *Die neue Gesellschaft*, no. 2.

Voigt, Karsten D., 1986. 'Strategic Policy Options and the Implications for Arms Control, Stability and East–West Relations', *Adelphi Paper*, no. 206.

Voigt, Karsten D., 1987. 'Perspektiver for Vesten: en ny Ostpolitik', speech (in Danish) at a seminar on the relationship between the Soviet Union and Eastern Europe held by the Danish Commission on Security and Disarmament, 25 November.

Voigt, Karsten D., 1988a. 'Gesellschaftliche Reformen: Gemeinsame Freiheit?' and 'Von der lagermentalitat zur systemoffnenden Zusammenarbeit', *Deutschland Archiv*, vol. 21, no. 6 and vol. 21, no. 10.

Voigt, Karsten D., 1988b. 'Sozialdemokratische Menschenrechtspolitik'; 'Sicherheitspolitik als Lernprozess zwischen Ost und West'; 'Gesellschaftliche Reformen—gemeinsam Freiheiten?; and 'Es Geht um Entmilitarisierung des Konflikts', in Greune (1988).

Voigt, Karsten D., 1988c. *Draft General Report on Alliance Security: Towards Conventional Stability in Europe; The US Maritime Strategy and Crisis Stability at Sea*, draft by the Gerneal Rapporteur for North Atlantic Assembly's Military Committee, November.

Wæver, Ole, 1986–7. 'Afspænding hvorfra?, *Krig of Fred*, vol. 2, no. 2.

Wæver, Ole, 1988. 'New Non-military East–West Controversies in a Denuclearizing Europe', paper presented at the TAPRI Workshop on the Political Consequences of Nuclear Disarmament in Europe, 8–10 June, Tampere, Finland.

Wæver, Ole, 1989a. 'Conceptions of Detente and Change: Some Non-military Aspects of Security Thinking in the FRG' in O. Wæver, P. Lemaître and E. Tromer, (eds), *European Polyphony*. London: Macmillan.

Wæver, Ole, 1989b. 'Conflicts of Vision—Visions of Conflict' in O. Wæver, P. Lemaître and E. Tromer, (eds), *European Polyphony*. London: Macmillan.

8 European Nuclear Weapons: The Case of the United Kingdom and France

Peter Jones and Janet Bryant

Introduction

The main aim of this chapter is to discuss the reasons why the United Kingdom and France have nuclear weapons, their view on when and if these weapons should be the subject of disarmament proposals and the difficulties that face those who hope to see such negotiations reach a successful conclusion.

The chapter will concentrate far more on the French position because readers may be less familiar with the French case. The British case has been much examined in all its aspects in earlier works (see, for example, Alternative Defence Commission, 1983; Dillon, 1983; Freedman, 1980; Malone, 1984; Simpson, 1986). Literature on the French case is far less common in English. Where appropriate, the chapter will look in detail at the French position whilst drawing comparative conclusions from the experience of both the British and the French.

Why did the British and French acquire nuclear weapons?

Unlike that of the United Kingdom, French security policy has always been, and in many respects remains, a subject of ambiguous controversy. One example of this is the speculation surrounding the French position which has dogged NATO strategists since 1966. This has given rise to several questions. What is France's true relationship with, and commitment to, the Western alliance? In the light of these assessments, what form should proposed battle plans take? Does France really intend to abide by her declared option of non-belligerence? Would she indeed participate in the forward battle? These are the sorts of question which are perhaps more open to discussion in the case of France than in the case of the United Kingdom, whose deterrent posture within Western defences is necessarily more succinct. There is, in addition, one other point of fundamental contrast between the French and British perspectives on the issue of nuclear defence: the question of consensus. French nuclear forces have been developed and cultivated by successive governments over the years, and this political consensus surrounding the utility, rationale and operational viability of French nuclear weapons has been continued by the parties of the Left, following their nuclear conversion in the late 1970s. This is to some extent a mirror image of the British experience where nuclear weapons have become the subject of much controversy in recent times. However, there are some signs of a return to the previous consensus on the need for the United Kingdom to retain its nuclear weapons for some time to come.

Nation-states proffer numerous vindications for the acquisition of an atomic capability—the validity of these pretexts may, of course, be open to some debate. But it becomes clear from an analysis of factors which influenced the French and the British decisions to develop nuclear weapons that common elements and appraisals exist—or existed—in both countries' perspectives. Other reasons, though, are more easily attributable to fundamental nationalist concerns of the individual state.

In the case of France, like the United Kingdom, one can trace the embryonic beginnings of *la monarchie nucléaire* back to the war years. Although France, like the United Kingdom, had participated in the wartime Manhattan project, it was no longer privy to American nuclear secrets in the immediate post-war years, protected as they were by the strict application of the McMahon Act. Despite this the British did have some unofficial assistance from the United States and in 1958 the Act was amended in its favour but not in favour of the French (Baylis, 1984).

The United Kingdom thus led the way down the road towards an independent nuclear deterrent, impelled as it was by the pre-war and wartime experience and its perception of itself as possessing great power status. France also believed itself to be a great power but since one of France's leading nuclear scientists had served in a communist-led Resistance group, the French found their way doubly barred—and they like the British decided to 'go it alone'.

What then followed constituted a series of foreign policy dilemmas which served to reinforce in French minds either the perceived unpredictable and ephemeral quality of Anglo-American guarantee to allies, or a growing belief that a remedy to the impotent frustration and *immobilisme* of the 1950s lay in the nuclear path. These foreign policy setbacks relate largely to the anachronistic approach the French adopted in the face of the world-wide movement for national self-determination in the post-war era. As a result, the French experienced a much more painful decolonization process than did the British in the shape of the 'loss' of Indo-China, Algeria (and the related fiasco of Suez), and to a lesser extent two other humiliations in Tunisia and Morocco. In many respects, it was hoped in 1958 that the acquisition and development of a nuclear capacity would actually aid in reconciling the French military establishment—which had become dangerously alienated from Paris, as events in Algiers in 1958 testified—to the end of the Empire.

The change in NATO and US strategic policy from massive retaliation to flexible response in the 1960s again raised the spectre of an abandoned and dispensable Europe and this Euro-interpretation was matched by the French refusal to water down, as it saw it, its own strategic precept. In the most material sense, it was in any case impossible for France to elaborate a posture of controlled and graduated response at this date—it simply did not have the necessary delivery systems. The seemingly crucial shift in American thinking was therefore unacceptable to the French on both counts.

During the infant stages of France's nuclear programme, a *de facto* alliance between the civilian and military bureaucracies (which wanted to strengthen the autonomy and political effectiveness of the state) had been established. By 1958, all the avenues of French national assertion had been turned into dead-ends. France had witnessed or was experiencing, for example, the collapse of the empire. Her continuing inferior status within the alliance, particularly in comparison to the British role in NATO and in nuclear strategic questions, persisted despite de Gaulle's failed attempt to create a triumvirate of nuclear powers at its heart as well as the earlier failure of the EDC. These stark facts were compounded by the gap between continuing aspirations, on the one hand, and the increasing operational limits on French action, on the other. Only the nuclear programme, begun by a Fourth Republic ministry, remained and, aided by its vocal lobby of supporters mentioned above, it became increasingly—and still is largely—synonymous with a political, economic, technological and military panacea for French ills. An interesting irony is that in both the United Kingdom and France it was essentially left-of-centre administrations which began the nuclear programmes but right-of-centre administrations which were able to exploit their development.

The continuation of the nuclear programme under de Gaulle and his withdrawal of France from NATO can be understood as a rejection of subjugation to foreign decisions which could have been contrary to France's vital interests, and a limitation on its freedom of action. This has been felt most keenly subsequently as has the belief that only

France's own strategic nuclear forces can offer it the means of total self-reliance and the option of non-belligerency in conflicts foreign to its national interest. At the most fundamental level, therefore, it is evident that the considerations of rank and independence have been enduring preoccupations of French statecraft, and both these preoccupations are deemed to be largely satisfied by a nuclear capacity. As is often the case in international politics, it is at this point that one enters the world of the perceived advantages of belonging to the atomic club and the supposed additional respect and prestige that membership bestows upon a state as a result. It is perhaps no accident that all five permanent members of the United Nations Security Council are nuclear powers. Similarly, neither British nor French public opinion would seem to be enthusiastic about its government giving up nuclear weapons until all other nuclear powers have reduced their arsenals substantially and, in any case, only simultaneously with the other European nuclear state.

Finally, there are the two-centres-of-decision-making and 'wild card' type arguments which have also figured in the official reasons given for British and French nuclear acquisition. Both claim that their deterrent posture aids the recognition of purely European interests in the superpower relationship and that in addition their forces necessarily complicate Soviet attempts at planning and/or control of a future conflict. Lastly, one must never overlook the importance of economic considerations. At the start of their nuclear programmes, nuclear weapons represented the 'cheap fix' in defence matters, giving both countries 'more bang for the buck' when compared with conventional capabilities. The utility of atomic energy by-products from a nuclear defence programme was also considered important at a time when both states were seeking cheap energy sources to continue their post-war redevelopment.

What security and other functions do British and French nuclear weapons have?

Since the famous 1952 'Global Strategy Paper' by the Chiefs of Staff, the British have seen nuclear weapons mainly in terms of their deterrent value, with usage only being envisaged in terms of massive retaliation and in line with NATO policy. The British have, thus, developed a clear view of the role that their conventional tactical and strategic nuclear forces would play within the context of a war occurring in Europe (Lider, 1985). In addition, the British have reserved the right to use their nuclear weapons *independently* of

NATO should there be a threat to British national interests which fell outside the terms of the Atlantic alliance.

Similarly, the official military rationale for French possession of nuclear weapons is equally simple: they constitute the physical guarantee that the national 'sanctuary' will not be violated by a hostile force. Of crucial importance in the understanding of the security functions of the *force de dissuasion* is the French belief that strategic nuclear forces can only purport to protect national sanctuaries—hence the traditional French scepticism of American guarantees to European allies. The security of France cannot and will not be delegated. At the same time, there has been a tendency until recently to obscure the role that French forces (nuclear and conventional) might play in a European conflict. This has always been portrayed by the French as a security asset, since they hold that the inherent vagueness of their position helps to promote more effective deterrence. Although the old version *sanctuarisation* and the 'two battles' concept of Noiret, Messmer and others has been converted into *sanctuarisation élargie* by the 1980s moves to extend security guarantees officially to West Germany, the precise nature of French engagement remains under wraps for essentially the same reasons.

Yet given the geographical dimensions of the European theatre and the effects—both military and political—that any nuclear confrontation within it would have for France, the practical utility of her no-automaticity-of-commitment and non-belligerency options seems to have more rhetorical value than anything else. Nevertheless, the French have never abandoned the declared option of non-belligerency adopted in 1966 since this is what guarantees France's total liberty of decision, frees her from a permanent commitment to NATO policies which could leave France tied to a strategy which is not of her own making, and guards against the danger of being dragged inadvertently into out-of-area conflicts.

The security function of French tactical nuclear weapons deserves some mention since it contrasts with the position taken by the United Kingdom. The French view their tactical nuclear weapons as fulfilling essentially 'warning shot' functions, as one small rung on a rapid ladder of escalation to strategic-level exchange. In officially labelling them *les armes préstratégiques* rather than *les armes tactiques*, French tactical weapons represent the final warning—*l'ultime avertissement*— and accordingly have a largely political role (Smouts, 1984/85). French doctrine does *not* envisage a long tactical battle since the 'war-fighting' concept for tactical weapons is rejected, and is replaced by a determination to use such hardware promptly and far forward. So the way in which the United Kingdom and the NATO allies envisage a relatively prolonged tactical battle before escalation to strategic level is contrasted with the French policy of threatening the early nuclearization of a war in Europe. This, the French argue, contributes to effective deterrence and thus to the long-term security of the allies. Such arguments have not found an echo in Bonn.

The whole of France's security posture is anchored in the concept of proportional deterrence. However, as medium-sized nuclear states, neither France nor the United Kingdom is under any illusion as to the existence of a gross disparity between their forces and those of the superpowers. Nevertheless, neither state aspires to parity with the superpowers because they believe that their threat of strategic nuclear retaliation against an enemy —however powerful—would deter an aggression. This is because the damage that France or the United Kingdom *alone* could cause the perpetrator by targeting the latter's cities would exceed what the enemy would stand to gain in conquering or destroying French or British territory. The strategy of both the British and the French has always, therefore, remained essentially one of countervalue rather than counterforce strikes for both strategic and technological reasons.

France's years of isolation from NATO may be coming to an end as, once again, the French are developing a very keen interest in European defence measures. The subtle change which is occurring within French defence circles is currently highlighted by the way in which France is increasingly identifying her security with that of the continent as a whole. This is another function for her deterrent—and a role which France believes she can fulfil far better than the Americans, who are too bound up with their own concerns to be able to identify completely with European fears, or the British, who are similarly too bound up with the Americans. Since the beginning of the Mitterrand years, France has devoted much effort to the recasting of European defence co-operation within the framework of the WEU, for example, and through the pursuit of bilateral ties or agreements with West Germany, the United Kingdom, Italy, Greece, Spain, Denmark and the Netherlands, among others. In general, France appears to be working harder than the United Kingdom to foster such links.

Finally there are a number of non-security related functions which the French *force de dissuasion* also currently fulfils. These can be defined as serving political, diplomatic and nationalistic ends, and are of considerable symbolic value to the French. The development of a deterrent force has not been easy for France, but to its credit it has persisted and today can offer an impressive triad of both tactical and strategic forces. This achievement is viewed with substantial pride and has allowed France to move from the original 'trigger' role for its nuclear weapons, to one in which they, *of themselves*, are seen to guarantee national freedom. Finally, as we have already noted, France, like all nuclear states, believes that nuclear weapons are the physical appendages of great power status and that to be recognized internationally as a top state it is essential that they be retained. Therefore, France's nuclear weapons are held to give it a voice at the top table and in the world at large. The British are in a similar but not so advantageous position having since the 1962 Nassau agreement relied on the United States for their delivery systems. Their nuclear weapons may thus be seen as being far less independent that those of the French and they are possibly less convincingly able to argue that their nuclear weapons can guarantee national freedom.

Constraints on present policies—financial and political

The British and French currently face a number of problems with regard to their present policies. These constraints may be broken down into three broad categories: strategic, financial and technological.

Doubts as to the strategic credibility of the *force de dissuasion* have been voiced in many quarters since the doctrine of proportional deterrence was first articulated in the 1960s. The theory's critics stress the disproportion between the damage France could cause an enemy— say, the Soviet Union—and the vestigial Soviet capacity for huge retaliation against France. If one takes this residual Soviet ability to destroy France as a fact, no matter what France might do in retaliation, sceptics wonder if there is any circumstances in which it would make political and military sense for France to implement its enlarged anti-cities threats. This debate has also found a considerable echo in the United Kingdom where some critics of government policy have argued that even the enhanced British force of Trident missiles would be no match for the Soviet Union and could only be used as an irrational retaliation once it was clear that chances of national survival in any acceptable form had disappeared. Clearly there are opponents in both countries who suggest that the implementation of such an option would mean national suicide which they would regard as unacceptable. On the other hand, there is a second group of opponents in both countries who argue that the cost of the nuclear weapons programme is now disproportionate within the defence budget and that the conventional armed forces are being starved of much-needed funds. Finally, in the United Kingdom there is a third group of critics who argue that the Trident system is far too powerful for a country like theirs and that acquisition and full deployment of the system would give it far greater capability than it could ever need.

Several other interrelated dilemma are also of significance in the French case. The first concerns the practical implications of its supposed sanctuarization and non-belligerency ideals. These are political hot potatoes—or have been—in Franco-German relations. Mitterand has done much to clarify the situation, however, and it is now publicly stated by French officials that the defence of France must start at the Elbe. Whereas a direct Soviet strike against France would evidently initiate the latter's immediate entry into a European conflict, even if France were not attacked at the outset, her interests would be so deeply involved in any military confrontation in West Germany that it is unrealistic to assume (especially given Hernu's June 1985 pledge and the deepening of the security relationship between the two) that France could somehow stand aloof. Nevertheless, areas of tension do remain. In particular, the operational doctrine for tactical nuclear weapons has always remained a constant source of concern in Bonn, and the extended range of the Hades system (350 km as opposed to the 120 km of the superseded Pluton missiles) has done little to alleviate German fears. France, however, continues resolutely to reject any possibility of a dual-key arrangement, stating categorically that operational authority must remain solely French. Similarly the British enthusiasm for the modernization of short-range nuclear systems in Europe following the INF treaty has brought the United Kingdom into conflict with the government in Bonn, which has traditionally objected to the singularity of treatment sometimes meted out to West Germany. However, it now appears that the Anglo-American enthusiasm for modernization is not shared by other members of the northern tier of NATO and that it may be that it is the United Kingdom rather than West Germany that is becoming isolated on this issue.

Financial and economic constraints on current policies are clearly giving the French great cause for concern. The crux of the matter for the French and the British alike (although the United Kingdom does not feel it quite as pointedly, perhaps) is that although a deterrent force is relatively easy and cheap for a medium range power to acquire initially, the cost of maintaining and upgrading systems to ensure their continued viability can be extremely high. The French have had to bear the cost by themselves and, coupled with this, their desire to parade not only an impressive nuclear arsenal but also to develop a meaningful conventional posture has meant that the problem of trying to afford both has become virtually insuperable. Jolyon Howorth contends in a May 1986 article in *The World Today* that close scrutiny of the defence record of the Parti Socialiste uncovers a remarkable disparity between declaratory aspirations and projects actually funded. Domestic government opposition forces have not been slow to produce their own statistics to show how the proportion of resources dedicated to defence has been squandered since 1981 (Mesmin, 1986).

A major problem for the French is that a number of its systems and components are becoming—or will become—obsolete at about the same time, ranging from two current aircraft carriers, *Foch* and *Clemenceau*, to the ICBMs of the Plateau d'Albion. Evidently, the ten to fifteen most costly armament programmes cannot all be supplied simultaneously, but, supported by various sections of the armed forces, many projects are either in an advanced planning stage or have been started. These projects include the nuclear-powered aircraft carriers; a new generation of nuclear-powered submarines planned for 1994, several aircraft projects, new satellite and missile systems and new radar and detector equipment. That may all be well and good—a panoply apparently justified by concepts and missions of the moment—but the fundamental difficulty is that the realization of these undertakings will necessitate an effort amounting to at least 4.5 per cent of GNP. This objective seems totally unrealistic at the present time.

Finally, there is the very grave problem of an expanding technology gap. France currently faces a massive technological challenge from the superpowers which threatens to leave it quite literally out of the nuclear running. Superior technological advances obviously have crucial strategic implications for second division nuclear states like the United Kingdom and France. Incapable of keeping up, they are left to contemplate a changing strategic environment and the ramifications that those breakthroughs have for the credibility of their own postures. The current variety of technological possibilities for Soviet military developments threatens the very core of French strategic doctrine—independence, proportional deterrence and countervalue. Independence could be threatened by the growing need to co-operate with the United States and the United Kingdom in developing various aspects of nuclear weapons technology. Proportional deterrence could be undercut by dramatic improvements in Soviet strategic defence capabilities against French systems prior to, and after, launch. The countervalue strategy especially could be undermined by a significant expansion of Soviet BMD capabilities (Heisbourg, 1986). Further development and refinement of Soviet BMD could well make the British and French reliance on ballistic missiles an unfortunate choice.

Furthermore, French IRBM survivability and vulnerability are consequently areas of concern. However, France, like the United Kingdom has invested heavily in the sea-based component of its strategic triad, largely because of its second strike potential and current relative invulnerability. The threat facing the British and French submarine fleets is a possible superpower breakthrough in submarine detection and tracking. Since this ability will be dependent upon satellite surveillance systems, of which the British and French have none of any significance, there is not a lot they can do except wait and hope (Seignous and Yates, 1984).

A second question concerns the survivability of British and French C^3I. This is particularly true of the French, for whom the C^3I support systems are most crucial for the operation and, therefore, the credibility, of their deterrent force. France has been far from sluggish in this domain, having recently hardened the communications systems for the *Forces airennes stratégiques*; invested in more sophisticated radar equipment for the new tactical Mirage 2000Ns and has the airborne transmission system ASTARÉ and the general network RAMES due to become operational anytime. However, the extent of French developments in this sphere pale into virtual insignificance compared to superpower C^3I ventures, as they move into their star wars phase.

The independent flavour of the *force de dissuasion* is further called into question when one analyses the extent to which France is forced in practice to rely on NATO's NADGE and AWACS systems, radar and satellite cover for information and protection. In 1982 the Mitterand government delayed indefinitely the project to develop SAMRO, a military reconnaissance satellite, although some military observation systems will be included in the essentially civil-orientated SPOT satellites. SPOT I was launched in 1985; SPOTs II and III are due in the later 1980s. However, as the superpowers work on the possibilities of extending the arms race into space, the widespread and generally pessimistic conclusion seems to be that France will be lucky to get any military satellites off the ground before its potential enemies are ready to shoot them down.

Independence again has had to be compromised when France has been forced to shop abroad for vital C^3I equipment. In August 1982, for example, the Reagan administration restarted the Carter Agreement it had halted and began sending to France a number of Cray I supercomputers designed to help French scientists solve hydrogen warhead problems. Additional supercomputers have been sent since 1982 to aid France with new land-, sea- and air-launched systems.

British and French attitudes towards nuclear disarmament

The events of the late 1980s have come as something of a shock to both the British and the French in so far as they ushered in a new period of optimism about the future of nuclear disarmament. In the United Kingdom, more than in France, the nuclear issue had become deeply politicized. The INF agreement was welcomed by both sides of the nuclear debate as a triumph for their position. The truth probably lies somewhere in between. One consequence of the INF agreement has been to cause dissension in the ranks of both the peace movement and NATO. On the one hand, as has already been noted, the British and American governments are keen for NATO to modernize short-range nuclear forces, whereas others in NATO wish to see progress on arms control coming before modernization, particularly given the Gorbachev initiatives on conventional forces. On the other hand, those in the peace movement have been deprived of their one unifying and international issue and have, to some extent been forced to return their attention to the less fruitful domestic issues, such as, in the United Kingdom, the Trident debate. This is particularly divisive at a time when international events both in relation to conventional and nuclear arms control seem to be moving in a positive direction and are causing political parties such as the British Labour Party to rethink their stance on the nuclear issue.

Much of the credit for this new optimism must go to the initiatives of President Gorbachev, who has done much to wrest the initiative from the West and has been seen as the driving force, albeit possibly for domestic reasons as much as anything else, behind the new peace offensive. This strategy has already had some success as far as the debate on nuclear modernization is concerned: the Germans, in particular, are seen as being soft on this issue and renewed fears of German neutralism are being expressed within the Bush administration (*The Guardian*, 14 February 1989). Even more clearly, there are doubts as to how to deal with the Gorbachev initiatives. One group argues that it is important to his survival that Gorbachev's initiatives be taken seriously and that he get some return for his actions; another group argues that the initiatives are merely paper concessions; that Gorbachev is unstable and could be replaced and that NATO should keep up the pressure for more real concessions before starting any negotiations. The latter group might be accused of having a desire to see Gorbachev fall because the more 'old-fashioned' Soviet leaders posed a clearer and more definite threat and are not sure what to make of Gorbachev. This may explain the rather lukewarm response by the British government to many of the Gorbachev initiatives, which is in sharp contrast to public perceptions of the Soviet Union and its President. For example, a recent poll found that 27 per cent of those questioned regarded the Soviet Union under Mr Gorbachev as either a 'serious threat or something of a threat to the security of the United Kingdom', whereas

67 per cent answered that it was 'not very much of a threat or no threat at all'. The same poll showed that these figures would alter dramatically if Mr Gorbachev ceased to be leader of the Soviet Union; then 54 per cent thought the Soviet Union would be 'a serious threat or something of a threat to the security of the United Kingdom', but only 32 per cent thought it would be 'not very much of a threat or no threat at all' (*The Guardian*, 20 January 1989).

Moving from the more general questions of nuclear developments in Europe to the question of French and British strategic weapons, it is clear that both states share a number of common ideas. Neither the British nor the French were willing to have their weapons included in the intermediate nuclear weapons talks, arguing that they are strategic and had no place in such negotiations. Since that time, the British Defence Minister, Mr Younger, has argued in an article in *The Guardian* (4 December 1987) that the question of the future of Britain's nuclear weapons was not at issue. This point was subsequently reinforced on two separate occasions. The first time was by Mrs Thatcher a few days later, when she told the press conference after Mr Gorbachev's flying visit on his way to the Washington summit that there would have to be very deep cuts in the strategic forces of both superpowers which went 'a lot further than the 50% reduction, a lot further' before Britain could contemplate having its weapons considered for inclusion in any arms negotiations (*The Guardian*, 8 December 1987). The second time was by British Foreign Secretary Sir Geoffrey Howe, who said before leaving for Moscow in February 1988 that he could not see Britain renouncing nuclear weapons 'for the foreseeable future' (*The World this Weekend*, BBC Radio 4, 14 February 1988). This means that it is Conservative government policy to retain for as long as possible Britain's own nuclear weapons.

Furthermore, the British government has stressed the need for the Soviet Union and its Warsaw Pact allies to reduce substantially their superior conventional forces before there is any reduction in British nuclear forces. A similar position is held by the French government which is equally adamantly opposed to any reduction of French nuclear forces, if ever, until there have been reductions in both superpowers' nuclear capacity and substantial conventional force reductions. This resistance is also related to the arguments of national pride which were of such importance for French acquisition in the first place and which now prevents France from being the first European state to relinquish them. Furthermore there is, in both countries, a strong popular feeling (often shared by politicians) that nuclear weapons should not be given up completely while there are still countries which possess—or might at some future time possess—

nuclear weapons which could be used not only to threaten the national interests of, but also to blackmail, either the United Kingdom or France.

There are, however, two significant points of contrast between the position of the British and the French on the question of nuclear weapons. First, the chances of French retention of a nuclear capability are substantially strengthened by the fact that the French have absolute control over their own nuclear weapons. The British, on the other hand, are vulnerable because of their dependence on the United States for the supply of delivery systems. The Americans could at some future time decide to end the supply or maintenance of the Trident system either of their own volition or under pressure from the Soviet Union, which might well argue that it could make no further cuts in its strategic forces until the United Kingdom and France (and China?) made reductions in their strategic arsenals. This point raises the question of the interdependence of arms reductions among all nuclear states and the extent to which this might lead to a vicious circle in which the Soviet Union refused to reduce further until the United Kingdom, France and China made reductions, while this latter group refused to consider reductions until Soviet and American forces were reduced even further. Pessimists may see this as a logjam which it will be difficult to break.

Second, in sharp contrast to the United Kingdom, where CND and other peace groups have been extremely active in attempting to influence both popular and informed opinion, in France there is very little in the way of popular dissension on the question of nuclear weapons. The absence of a mass peace movement organized on structured lines is an indication that, in many respects, the nuclear issue is *not* an 'issue' in France. Consequently the French government is under even less pressure to relinquish or rethink its atomic capability; and where else can one hear bishops supporting the rationale behind their retention? It seems, therefore, that until there is a substantial modification in the way the French view their nuclear weapons and until literature explaining in detail the consequences of their use becomes widely available (its current availability is woefully inadequate), the prospects for a forced change in official perspectives are minimal.

Conclusions

It is clear that the British and French, while acquiring nuclear weapons at different times, shared similar motivations for their nuclear strategy. It was cheap; it was effective; it brought deterrence into effect; and it brought status and prestige. While the French developed an independent strategic and military posture, along with a fully independent nuclear research, development and production industry, the United Kingdom has become increasingly dependent on the United States for much of its delivery technology. The United Kingdom also tended to regard its nuclear weapons as adding to the strength of NATO and its relationship with the United States, while France saw nuclear weapons as a means of developing both an independent position for itself—outside NATO and no longer reliant on the United States.

In the United Kingdom, the nuclear question may be seen as something which was initially not politically contentious, whereas it has subsequently become so. By contrast, in France the nuclear question has become increasingly less contentious and support for the policy cuts across the whole political spectrum. For this reason, there can be little optimism that a change of government in France, unlike in the United Kingdom, would lead to any substantial change of attitude towards nuclear disarmament. In the United Kingdom, there seems to be more grounds for optimism that a change of government, even possibly a change of leader in the Conservative Party, could lead to a less intransigent attitude towards the possibility of British participation in the serious negotiation of nuclear disarmament. On the whole, however, it would seem likely that for the time being the likelihood of positive British or French attitudes towards their own participation in the process of nuclear disarmament is far from strong.

Bibliography

Alternative Defence Commission, 1983. *Defence without the Bomb*. London: Taylor & Francis.

Baylis, John, 1984. *Anglo–American Defence Relations, 1938–1984*. London: Macmillan.

Dillon, George M., 1983. *Dependence and Deterrence*. London: Gower.

Freedman, Lawrence, 1980. *Britain and Nuclear Weapons*. London: Macmillan.

Heisbourg, François, 1986. 'La France face aux Nouvelles Données Stratégiques', *Défense Nationale*, vol. 42, April.

Howorth, Jolyon, 1986. 'Resources and Strategic Choices: French Defence Policy at the Crossroads', *The World Today*, vol. 42, no. 5.

Lider, Julian, 1985. *British Military Thought since World War II*. London: Gower.

Malone, Peter, 1984. *The British Nuclear Deterrent*. London: Croom Helm.

Mesmin, George, 1986. 'L'Année des choix pour la Défense', *Défense Nationale*, vol. 42, April.

Seignous, George M. and Jonathan Yates, 'Europe's Nuclear Superpowers', *Foreign Policy*, no. 55.

Simpson, John, 1986. *The Independent Nuclear State*. London: Macmillan.

Smouts, Marie-Claude, 1984/85. 'France: Its Defence and International Security', *International Journal* (Toronto), vol. 40, no. 1.

9 Nuclear Weapons in Europe after the INF Agreement

Hans Günter Brauch

Introduction

The treaty between the USA and the USSR on the elimination of their intermediate-range and shorter-range missiles of December 1987 (INF Treaty) is the first time since the beginning of the nuclear age that a nuclear disarmament agreement has been signed which calls for the dismantling of about 5 per cent of the launchers for substrategic nuclear systems globally, or for approximately 20 per cent of the substrategic nuclear systems presently deployed in Europe. The warheads for these systems are not covered by the INF treaty.

While land-based missiles with ranges from 500 to 5500 km are being withdrawn and destroyed, the debate on the modernization of the shorter-range ballistic missiles in NATO European countries continues in 1989, as does the pressure of several NATO governments on the government of the Federal Republic of Germany to agree to the replacement of the Lance short-range nuclear missiles (SNF) during the 1990s. In this mixed background, the present chapter will focus on the following issues and questions. Which political, strategic and arms control considerations of the 1970s contributed to the European missile debate and crisis in the 1980s? How many and which nuclear weapons will remain in Europe after the INF Treaty has been implemented? Which nuclear modernizations have been considered in the framework of the Montebello decision of NATO's Nuclear Planning Group in October 1983? What political lessons may be drawn from the INF case for a continuation of the nuclear disarmament process in Europe? Which political options for a nuclear disarmament in Europe should be pursued by both military alliances in the 1990s? And what impact can nuclear disarmament have on a European political structure based on mutual confidence and stability?

Eleven hypotheses on the history of the INF case

The so-called missile crisis was a consequence of a series of events both in the West and in the East and of serious miscalculations on the part

155

of the political and military elites both in NATO and in the Warsaw Pact states. The following hypotheses try to interpret the events that have contributed in the early 1980s to the missile crisis in Europe (Holm & Petersen, 1983; Joxe *et al.*, 1987; Risse-Kappen, 1988a; 1988b).

The European missile crisis was a direct consequence of serious shortcomings of SALT I

The Interim Agreement of May 1972 (a part of the SALT I Treaty) was instrumental for the future European missile crisis because of:

1. The failure to prohibit multiple independently retargetable vehicles (MIRVs) (Smith, 1980).
2. The political price that had to be paid by the Nixon administration for the ratification of SALT I in the US Congress in terms of new weapons systems such as Trident nuclear submarines, the B-1 bomber and cruise missiles.
3. The political price paid by Leonid Brezhnev and the Soviet leadership that strengthened the position of the military in the Politburo (Payne, 1980; Wolfe, 1979).
4. Three displacement effects of arms control agreements in general (see Rathjens *et al.*, 1974) and of the SALT I agreement in particular:
   (a) to level up (e.g. in the Vladivostok Accord of 1974);
   (b) to introduce bargaining chips for future negotiations (e.g. cruise missiles); and
   (c) to compensate for the freeze in strategic launchers with new weapons systems.
5. The requirements of the Jackson Amendment to SALT I that called for a numerical balance in SALT II and in the Vladivostok Accord in 1974 (Brauch, 1984; Newhouse, 1973).

In the mid-1970s the Soviet reaction to the US request for numerical parity in launchers was to replace a three-stage ICBM (SS-16) with a two-stage IRBM (SS-20) and to add to it a MIRVed warhead.

Soviet specialists tied the background of the SS-20 directly to the Vladivostok Accord in conversations with a West German member of parliament. According to this source the Soviet military leadership is supposed to have called for compensation for the numerical superiority the USSR was granted in strategic launchers in SALT I as a counter to British and French nuclear systems.

The United States and, even more so, Western Europe used this development to legitimize the modernization of the upper level of its TNF in Europe that had been discussed in the NPG since 1975 after the Schlesinger Doctrine had been announced in 1974 (Brauch, 1983; Risse-Kappen, 1988a; Ruehl, 1987; Schwartz, 1983).

While the SS-20 was not the cause for Pershing 2 and GLCM it offered an easy justification for the introduction of new systems that had been planned for different reasons. First, Pershing 2 was considered a follow-on system to the Pershing 1A introduced to US forces and to the Bundeswehr in the early 1970s. Second, the GLCM was part of the political price that the Nixon administration had to pay for the approval of SALT I by its JCS and the Senate.

The NATO dual-track-decision was also a consequence of several political factors

While the SS-20 had first been recognized by US intelligence in 1975 and publicly been admitted in September 1976, it did not become an intra-alliance issue until the autumn of 1977 when the West German Chancellor publicly criticized the US SALT II negotiation position that excluded the substrategic nuclear systems deployed in Eastern Europe and targeted against NATO Europe (Brauch, 1983; Carter, 1982; Schmidt, 1987). Schmidt's criticism was interpreted as a lack of US reassurance of its allies. It was used by the proponents of the INF modernization in the US Department of Defense to call for the procurement and deployment of new missiles in Europe.

Given the tensions between the Carter administration and the West German government, the INF case was conceived by several of President Carter's advisers as a political tool to overcome the neutron bomb débâcle of April 1978 (Hoffman, 1986; Matthée, 1985; Wasserman, 1983) and to demonstrate a renewed leadership within NATO. Contrary to public belief it was not Chancellor Schmidt who had called for new missiles but President Carter who had proposed the deployment of new INF systems at the informal quadripartite summit meeting at Guadeloupe in January 1979 (Brauch, 1983; Brzezinski, 1983; Carter, 1982; Schmidt, 1987; Talbot, 1984).

The NATO INF decision was part of a nuclear modernization process within NATO that had been discussed in NPG meetings since 1974–5.

The strategic context of the theatre nuclear modernization had been laid down prior to and independently of the Soviet SS-20 system. Due to the technical features of the Pershing 2—its short flight time and its high precision (CEP)—this system became the ideal military means to implement counterforce strikes against time-urgent military targets in the Soviet Union from the territory of third countries (Buteux, 1982; Ruehl, 1987; Schwartz, 1983).

The INF decision may be explained, therefore, not as a direct reaction to the SS-20, as indicated in the public legitimation of the INF decision in the West, but as a complex combination of four factors: the shortcomings of SALT I; technological follow-on imperatives; a strategic reassessment; and a political mismanagement of alliance politics especially between the United States and West Germany.

Nevertheless, the emergence of the SS-20 (with its increased precision and its three MIRVed warheads) offered an opportunity to increase the range of the planned Pershing 2 missile to 1,800 km, beyond the 720 km for the Pershing 1A. In 1978, the proponents of a LRTNF modernization in the Pentagon called for as many as 1,500–2,000 LRTNF warheads for Pershing 2 and GLCMs (Ruehl, 1980, p. 106), a proposal that was never accepted either by the Carter administration or by NATO.

The INF decision and its consequences could still have been avoided in 1979 by two options: a Soviet offer of a verifiable SS-20 production and deployment moratorium; and a postponement of the INF decision in December 1979.

In November 1979, INF proponents in Bonn feared that the Soviet Union would table such a proposal to undercut the NATO decision-making process. However, the Soviet leadership under Leonid Brezhnev was too inflexible to introduce the moratorium concept prior to adoption of the NATO decision on 12 December 1979 (for such a proposal, see Brauch, 1983). A postponement of the NATO decision without a serious Soviet offer would have been seen as a lack of alliance cohesion and as a direct success of the Soviet political use of the new missiles.

The political fallout of the INF decision along with the consequences of the Soviet intervention in Afghanistan might still have been reduced in 1981 by a change of the INF decision from land- to sea-based systems and by a shift to a more comprehensive zero option covering sea-based INF systems as well.

However, the sea-based option that seemed to have been preferable to Chancellor Helmut Schmidt was opposed by several NATO countries; Norway, for instance, feared a change of its non-nuclear posture in peacetime (see, for example, Holst, 1983). When a new debate on a sea-based option emerged in West Germany in 1981 (see Brauch, 1981; Scheer, 1981; Weizsäcker, 1981) this proposal obviously had no chance of being accepted by the other NATO countries, primarily for political reasons.

Once the INF decision had been agreed upon it became a symbol of alliance cohesion within NATO

Not surprisingly, its critics were accused of undercutting alliance solidarity. As a consequence, the NATO elites became victims of their proclaimed policies with the goal to strengthen NATO solidarity. However, the political elites had miscalculated the domestic reaction to that very decision. What was meant to strengthen NATO's cohesion became the most controversial alliance decision.

The INF decision contributed to both an independent peace movement in Western Europe and to the freeze movement in the United States

In Europe, the independent European Nuclear Disarmament (END) movement, with its opposition to both SS-20 and Pershing 2 and with its call for a nuclear weapon-free zone from Portugal to Poland, developed a new political vision for the European peoples that combined disarmament with the call for freedom and human rights.

In the United States, the freeze movement called for a drastic shift in the nuclear policies of the Reagan administration. However, the increasing criticism of nuclear weapons and of the US nuclear doctrine of mutual assured destruction (MAD), e.g. by the Conference of Catholic bishops, was later instrumentalized by President Reagan in his vision of a non-nuclear world after the deployment of a Strategic Defence Initiative.

During the missile controversy two major miscalculations occurred on the part of both NATO and Warsaw Pact leaderships.

The Soviet leadership erroneously assumed that both the independent peace movements in the United States and in Europe (the freeze movement and END) and the Soviet-inspired national peace councils or their associated organizations could become instrumental in the unilateral backtracking from the INF agreement (e.g. the Krefeld Appeal in West Germany). In 1979, the Soviet leadership lacked the political will to give up its SS-20 option unilaterally. When it finally adopted the idea of a conditional nuclear moratorium in 1980–1, its acceptance would have meant a major reassessment of the nuclear policies on the part of NATO governments. Due to the political miscalculation during the Brezhnev period, the new Soviet leadership under Mikhail Gorbachev had to pay a much higher political price for the removal of the Pershing 2s and GLCMs.

When President Reagan tabled the zero option proposal in November 1981, the hardliners in his administration believed that the Soviet Union would never accept a global zero option and that the Soviet rejection would be the best justification for going ahead with the implementation of the NATO decision. This tactic obviously no longer worked after General Secretary Gorbachev accepted the Western zero option at the Reykjavik summit.

Which factors contributed to the change: was it NATO's adherence to the INF decision, the efforts of the European and American peace movements, or was it the policies of the new Soviet leadership under Mikhail Gorbachev? What impact did these public movements have on the nuclear armament policies of the United States and the Soviet Union?

Neither the European and US peace movements nor the NATO adherence to the INF decision were decisive for the coming about of the INF Treaty.

However, the European and the American peace movements fundamentally changed their general attitude with respect to nuclear weapons by increasing the political price for the introduction of new nuclear systems. The critical transatlantic debate on the nature of deterrence (MAD doctrine) eased the way for non-nuclear conventional force structure alternatives.

Nevertheless, NATO's adherence to and the implementation of the INF decision of 1979 made Soviet C^3I systems and other time-urgent targets deployed in Eastern Europe and in the Western military districts of the Soviet Union vulnerable in the event of any nuclear confrontation in Europe. Due to the diplomatic and political inflexibility of Leonid Brezhnev and his advisers, the political price for the removal of NATO's Pershing 2 and GLCM systems also increased.

It was primarily the new Soviet leadership under Mikhail Gorbachev that was the driving force for the success of the INF agreement by taking Western tactical proposals seriously and by making significant compromises; by accepting President Reagan's proposal of a zero-option for INF and by suggesting a second zero option for systems with ranges of 500–1000 km; by giving up the call for an immediate inclusion of British and French systems; and by accepting global limits.

Nuclear weapons in Europe before and after the implementation of the INF Treaty

In the United States, support for the INF agreement and for a 50 per cent reduction in strategic nuclear systems in the context of a planned START agreement was often linked with the call for a modernization of the remaining short-range nuclear systems in Europe.

In early 1988, the Report of the Commission on Integrated Long-term Strategy for the United States (Iklé *et al.*, 1988, p. 30) stressed:

Even if NATO makes dramatic improvements in its conventional defenses, the Alliance will still want nuclear weapons (including weapons based in Europe) for at least two reasons. First, because nuclear weapons discourage the massing of forces in any attack. Second, because NATO's ability to respond with controlled and effective nuclear strikes would minimize the Soviet's temptations to use such weapons in discriminate attacks of their own on key elements of the Alliance's conventional capability.

However, the same report challenged several fundamental trans-atlantic strategic premises on the community of risk between the United States and its European NATO allies and on the avoidance of a regional nuclear war in Europe (Iklé *et al.*, 1988, p. 30):

However, there should be less ambiguity about the nature of the deterrent. The Alliance should threaten to use nuclear weapons *not as a link* to a wider and more devastating war—although the risk of further escalation would still be there—but mainly as an instrument for denying success to the invading Soviet forces. The *nuclear weapons would be used discriminately* in, for example, attacks on Soviet command centres or troop concentrations. The

Alliance's nuclear posture, like its posture for conventional war, will gain in deterrent power from new technologies emphasizing precision and control.

From a West German perspective, this report implies a shift of the role of nuclear weapons in alliance strategy from a purely political instrument of deterrence to weapons of military warfighting.

On 1 February 1988, US Secretary of Defense Frank C. Carlucci (1988, pp. 14–15) pointed to several consequences of the INF decision with respect to the modernization of the nuclear and conventional forces in Europe:

In making the Montebello Decision, NATO's defense ministers agreed that NATO must take steps to ensure the responsiveness, survivability, and effectiveness of the forces that would remain after NATO's unilateral reductions. The Supreme Allied Commander, Europe, was asked to develop recommendations on how best to structure these forces to maintain deterrence with a minimum number of nuclear weapons. His recommendations involved modernization of existing systems, improved development of nuclear forces within Europe, and enhanced survivability of these forces and their command, control, and communications.

Improvement measures which still require implementation include developing a follow-on to Lance, replacing a portion of our nuclear free-fall bombs with a tactical air-to-sea missile, and production of sufficient modern artillery rounds to allow retirement of older rounds. None of these programs are constrained by the INF treaty, because the agreement does not limit dual-capable aircraft or nuclear forces with ranges below 500 kilometers.

If NATO citizens resist vital defense modernization efforts for fear of upsetting Moscow, they invite eventual Soviet dominance.

These two US comments portray both the dilemmas of the debate on nuclear deterrence within NATO and the ongoing American-German dispute with respect to the current and future priorities: nuclear modernization versus further nuclear disarmament in Europe. Before turning to these two alternatives, we shall briefly analyse the Euro-nuclear balance prior to the INF agreement and after its implementation.

According to data published in *The Military Balance* (IISS, 1987, pp. 209–10; 1988, pp. 220–1) for July 1987, prior to the signing and ratification of the INF agreement with respect to the NATO guidelines area (MBFR talks) and for July 1988, after the signing, a clear Warsaw Pact superiority War existed with respect to nuclear systems with a range below 1000 km, while NATO was stronger in nuclear artillery. However, if the comparison is based on the whole of Europe (from the Atlantic to the Urals), the Soviet superiority also applies to nuclear artillery and nuclear-capable aircraft but not to maritime forces.

According to the provisions of the INF Treaty (*Strategic Survey 1987–1988*, p. 27) during the first 18 months (that is, by 30 November 1989) the following launchers have to be destroyed: 178 Pershing 1A launchers in the US and West German forces and 726 SS-12s and 200 SS-23s in the Soviet and other Warsaw Pact forces. By 31 May 1991, the United States will have to have destroyed an additional 689 Pershing 2s and GLCMs (or a total of 867 systems) and the Soviet Union an additional 910 SS-20, SS-4, SS-5 and SSC-X-4 systems (or a total of 1836 systems).

Which nuclear systems will still be available in Europe after the INF decision has been implemented, based on a static projection of the existing nuclear arsenals?

Independent of the INF Treaty the number of US nuclear warheads in Europe was unilaterally reduced by 1,000 warheads as part of the INF decision of December 1979 and by an additional 1,400 warheads after the Montebello decision of October 1983. By November 1991, the number of US nuclear warheads in Europe will be reduced from approximately 7,000 warheads in 1979 to 4,000 warheads. An additional 400–480 nuclear strategic warheads have been assigned to SACEUR since the late 1960s.

From a Soviet perspective a number of British and French nuclear systems have to be added that have continuously been modernized but that have been excluded from the INF Treaty. The following nuclear systems of the United States and the Soviet Union and of their allies will remain unconstrained by the INF treaty: the French IRBMs (18 SSBX-S3 launchers) and British and French SLBMs (more than 160 MIRVed launchers); the short-range ballistic missiles of the US and allied forces (93 Lance launchers) and of the Soviet Union and its allies (630 A/B launchers and 749 SS-21 launchers); the nuclear artillery (about 2,700 for NATO and 6,260 for Warsaw Pact forces); the air-based systems of the United States, Soviet Union, France and United Kingdom; the sea-based ballistic systems of France, the United States and Soviet Union that are not covered by the SALT/START process; the sea-based cruise missiles of both superpowers that are under debate within the START negotiations; and the anti-submarine warfare aircraft of the United States, its allies and of the Soviet Union.

Montebello and its consequences: compensatory nuclear rearmament?

In October 1983, at the 34th meeting of the NPG in Montebello, NATO's defence ministers agreed to maintain the survivability, retaliation capability and effectiveness of its remaining launchers and warheads. What factors contributed to this decision and which candidates for modernization have been considered in the United States and in NPG deliberations after the Montebello decision?

Both the US Army and US Air Force have been interested in replacements for their short-range ballistic systems deployed in Europe (follow-on imperative) in order to maintain existing missions. Strategic considerations have also been an important determinant, for example the adaptation of NATO's flexible response strategy to the changes that have occurred in the American nuclear employment doctrine since 1974 (Schlesinger doctrine and PD-59). Finally, tactical-operative concepts of the US armed forces (AirLand Battle and Counterair '90) and NATO's planning guidelines (e.g. FOFA) for conventional, chemical and nuclear strikes against follow-on forces have called for new dual-capable short-range missiles.

After signing of the INF agreement representatives of the US Army and US Air Force, supported by conservative politicians in the US Congress, called for compensatory armaments, especially for short-range nuclear systems in Europe, in order to enhance the credibility of the American nuclear guarantee for Europe (extended deterrence). According to US press reports and statements by Pentagon spokesmen, the following elements of a comprehensive compensatory armament programme for NATO Europe have been considered. In early 1988, Dan Quale, the then conservative Republican Senator, estimated that $75 billion would have to be spent in the next fifteen years on: the modernization of nuclear artillery; the introduction of a follow-on system to the Lance with a longer range; an enhanced survivability of the dual-capable conventional and nuclear aircraft with new air-to-ground missiles; strengthened conventional forces, e.g. by the deployment of an extended air defence; and the development of credible conventional options for a flexible response, including the integration of improved air-, sea- and land-based cruise missiles.

In early February 1988, the Supreme Allied Commander Europe, General Galvin, in a statement to the US Senate Armed Services Committee, called for: a nuclear air-surface missile for tactical fighter planes in order to supplement the penetration capability of FB-111 type bombers; an improved Lance missile with a range under 500 km; the procurement of the Army Tactical Missile (ATACM); the modernization of the nuclear artillery; and modernized conventional bombs and artillery shells (Meecham, 1988a; 1988b). Since the early 1980's, the ATACM has been discussed as a potential follow-on system to the Lance tactical missile. In 1987, the US armed forces had deployed 144 Lance launchers globally and 108 in Europe. An additional 55 launchers were available in the forces of its European allies. For these launchers about 700 Lance missiles were available in NATO Europe. The ATACM replacement was considered with ranges from 300 to less than 500 km both for nuclear and conventional warheads. Within NATO, the governments of the United States, the United Kingdom and France supported the modernization of NATO's short-range nuclear missiles while the government of West Germany and especially its Foreign Ministry opposed any isolated modernization decision. At the NATO summit in March 1988 the heads of government of the NATO countries called for equal ceilings for short-range nuclear forces in the context of a conventional balance and of a global removal of chemical weapons as part of a NATO *Gesamtkonzept* for arms control and disarmament. Since March 1988, within the CDU/CSU parliamentary group supporters of a replacement of the Lance SNF, such as its deputy chairman, Volker Rühe, linked this to the demand for a drastic reduction in the remaining nuclear artillery by about one-half. The Bush administration will be confronted with the task of obtaining the support of the West German government for a modernization decision linked to an arms control concept or a unilateral withdrawal option for nuclear artillery shells. If a modernization decision should be made the Soviet Union may either respond with a radical nuclear disarmament proposal for the remaining short-range ground-, sea- and air-based nuclear systems and artillery shells in Europe or opt for a military reaction in terms of new Soviet systems.

In the eighth edition of the Pentagon report *Soviet Military Power: An Assessment of the Threat* (US Department of Defense, 1988, p. 109), the following claims were made with regard to the balance of non-strategic nuclear forces (NSNF):

The vast majority of the NSNF missiles in Europe are deployed with Warsaw Pact forces. Compared to NATO's 88 operationally deployed LANCE missile launchers, the Warsaw Pack deploys about 1,400 FROG, SCUD, and SS-21 missile launchers west of the Urals. About 1,000 of these short-range launchers are assigned to Soviet units.

The fourth major change (since 1981) is the increased number of refire missiles deployed by the Soviets for their short-range (less than 500 kilometres) missile launchers in the forward areas. The refires for these launchers have been increased by between 50 and 100 per cent over the past several years. Consequently, the Pact has been able to plan on using these missiles, armed with non-nuclear warheads, to strike NATO air defenses, airfields, and command and control nodes without sacrificing their ability to plan on using the same missiles, if needed, in theater nuclear strikes. The fifth major change in the NSNF category has been the nuclear capability of the Soviet artillery. The overall trend in NSNF has been the increase in Warsaw

Pact theater nuclear capability to the point where today they have a substantially greater capability than the NATO Alliance in this category, notwithstanding the asymmetrical reductions that will result from the elimination of the INF category of weapons.

These claims are not only in conflict with the IISS data and analyses but they also contradict previous claims of the same source. Its major task may be to propagate the call for new US short-range nuclear systems.

From the perspective of West Germany, the worst case would be a drastic reduction of strategic nuclear forces, a modernization of tactical missiles in central Europe with ranges just below 500 km, and a shift towards considerations in the United States that call for a regionalization of the risk of a nuclear war as indicated in Iklé *et al.* (1988).

NATO's internal divisions with respect to the modernization of SNF systems are due to different political and strategic interests between those countries that own and control nuclear weapons and those crypto-nuclear states (Subrahmanyam, 1984) on whose territory nuclear weapons are deployed and may be used without a veto of the countries concerned.

Will the implementation of the Montebello decision of October 1983 contribute to a strategic and conventional stability in Europe and to confidence-building structures of defence?

Nuclear modernization: stabilizing distrust-creating military structures and doctrines

If the Soviet Union should respond to a NATO SNF modernization decision with continued modernization of its SNF systems and both a quantitative increase and qualitative improvements of its short-range nuclear-capable launchers, the call for an extended air defence for NATO Europe may re-emerge; and if the efforts for a second *détente* should fail, an offensive/defensive arms race for nuclear capable ballistic missiles and tactical BMD systems may follow (see Brauch, 1987; 1989a; 1989b).

The transatlantic strategic debate that has emerged since the Reykjavik summit in October 1986 has focused on the role of nuclear weapons as elements of deterrence and reassurance, on the configuration of the armed forces and on tactical-operative concepts in a future security regime in Europe. The public debate in the crypto-nuclear states in Europe, and particularly in West Germany and the Netherlands, has questioned the role of nuclear weapons as elements of a credible and publicly acceptable defence posture. A central element of

NATO's flexible response doctrine, its nuclear first-use option, is rejected by more than 70 per cent of the West German electorate, while membership of NATO enjoys somewhat broader support. The public debate that has been provoked by the INF dual-track decision had a major impact on public opinion in the prospective deployment countries for the modernized SNF in Europe, especially in West Germany (Vogt, 1989). The decreasing public support for defence issues in West Germany, the manpower shortage of the 1990s (Grass, 1989) and the many fiscal challenges (Bebermeyer, 1989) may contribute to a major crisis of legitimacy of the armed forces in the 1990s (Vogt, 1989). A new debate on the deployment of short-range nuclear missiles in West Germany at a time when a START agreement may be reached between the Soviet Union and United States, could hardly be justified to a sceptical electorate.

In addition, severe fiscal and public constraints both in the United States and especially in West Germany would have to be overcome in the implementation of such a development. However, even if these domestic constraints were overcome, a decrease in arms race stability and during a crisis an increase of crisis instability may be logical consequences. Such a development would not lead to confidence-building defence concepts but rather to distrust, creating structures that could prevent a second *détente* in Europe. This could result in a reduced political leverage of European countries, and the Europeans would once again become the objects of their own future rather than the subjects in a process of developing a structure of a just and permanent European system of peace and security.

Lessons from the INF case for a continuation of the nuclear disarmament process

What political lesson can be drawn from the experience of the arms control process since the SALT I Treaty was signed and ratified in 1972 and from the changes in the domestic, transatlantic, intra-European, and East–West environment of the security debate for a second era of *détente* in the 1990s? At least two lessons emerge from the arms control process.

The first is that the political price for the INF agreement in terms of new nuclear systems (compensatory armament) should not be allowed to undermine the process for a second *détente* in Europe.

The call for compensatory armaments by the US military and by conservative circles in the US Congress, and the insistence on a NATO *Gesamtkonzept* for nuclear arms control and disarmament by several

European governments—particularly West Germany—are due to differences in geography, political status, strategic interests and public opinion.

While from the point of view of the three Western nuclear powers a modernization of the SNF systems would enhance the credibility of the extended deterrence posture of the US nuclear forces and contribute to the realization of NATO's FOFA concept, from the West German point of view—especially of the liberals (FDP) in the Kohl government and even more so for the opposition parties, the SPD and the Greens—a deployment of these new nuclear systems in West Germany could exclusively threaten West Germany by adding to the risk and contributing in a crisis to efforts to contain a nuclear war to Europe, particularly to central Europe. These concerns and even West German suspicions concerning decoupling from the community of risk were strengthened in January 1988 in the Iklé report on *Discriminate Deterrence* (Iklé *et al.*, 1988). Influenced by the difference in perception, a majority of the West German electorate fears that the process of compensatory nuclear armament in central Europe would undermine the prospects for a second *détente* in Europe. Several conservative politicians would be prepared to accept only a partial replacement of the Lance nuclear missiles if the nuclear artillery shells were unilaterally reduced by about 50 per cent. At least in the Federal Republic there appears to be a preference for the second lesson to emerge from the arms control process.

This is that, in order to maintain the political momentum of the nuclear disarmament process, a combination of political vision and political leadership is needed, based on a political realism that tries to avoid the shortcomings of the first superpower *détente* of the 1970s.

While the Western nuclear powers appear to be reluctant to enter into any additional nuclear arms control agreements for Europe, many of the non-nuclear European NATO countries, especially the crypto-nuclear states, support the inclusion of the remaining nuclear systems in the arms control process of the 1990s. However, the political elites are split with respect to the functions that nuclear weapons should play in a future allied defence posture and with respect to the goals of additional nuclear arms control and disarmament agreements in Europe. While the Left, especially the Social Democrats, but not the French Parti Socialiste, would prefer a third zero option for SNF and nuclear artillery shells and the concept of limited nuclear weapon-free zones, the conservatives insist on a reduced, modernized and credible nuclear component that has to be forward-deployed in central Europe.

In the context of the proposed NATO *Gesamtkonzept* which will presumably be agreed upon by the summer of 1989, a new bargain will have to be struck between the Bush administration and its European allies that links European interests in nuclear disarmament and US, British and to some extent French interest in nuclear modernization and in a credible forward-deployed nuclear component.

The NATO *Gesamtkonzept* will most likely offer the political framework for future official Western initiatives for conventional, chemical and nuclear modernization, restructuring and disarmament. What alternative options for a gradual nuclear disarmament in Europe can be foreseen and should be pursued from an unofficial West German perspective?

Eleven proposals for the next steps towards nuclear disarmament in Europe

After the ratification of the INF Treaty those European states on whose territory nuclear weapons are deployed in peacetime and who have no right to veto their use should undertake political initiatives to contribute towards the realization of the political visions of both former President Reagan and President Gorbachev for a nuclear weapon-free world. In this respect both German states should consider initiatives to reduce the density of shorter range nuclear weapons from their territory.

Fifty years after the German aggression against Poland and the beginning of the Second World War, both German states should intensify, both at the official level between the heads of government, ministers of foreign affairs and defence and at the unofficial societal level, the dialogue on the mutual security concerns, on the structures of their armed forces in their respective military alliances and on the role of chemical and nuclear weapons in the military doctrines of both NATO and the Warsaw Pact. These informal consultations on arms control and security affairs should search for potential compromises between both military alliances. Within their respective military alliances both German governments should call for a gradualist arms control and disarmament strategy to facilitate and to stimulate the negotiations in the context of the talks on Conventional Forces in Europe (CFE) and on the Confidence and Security Building Measures (CSBMs) and disarmament in Europe (35 CSCE countries). Unilateral measures by either alliance, such as Gorbachev's announcement of unilateral reductions of 500,000 troops within two years, should be answered with unilateral signals of restraint by NATO with the goal of achieving binding arms control agreements.

The function of the remaining nuclear weapons in Europe should be limited to a pure political function of deterring an attack with nuclear weapons. For this minimal deterrence thousands of forward-deployed artillery shells and hundreds of short-range ballistic missiles are not needed.

With respect to a drastic reduction in nuclear artillery shells in Europe a compromise between politicians both in the United States and in Europe, especially in West Germany, could possibly emerge in the near future. The removal of the nuclear artillery shells would have to be linked with a reduction of the dual- or triple-capable launchers. Such a step would have direct implications for the structure of the forward-deployed allied forces. It would imply the removal of one component of a military posture that is often being perceived by the opponent as being offensive.

The credibility of deterrence does not require the presence of nuclear weapons but at least for a transition period the presence of the troops of several foreign countries on the territory of West Germany should be sufficient to deter any potential aggressor and to reassure the political elites.

The argument of some US experts that there should be 'no troops without nukes' implies that forward-deployed nuclear weapons are an indispensable element of the credibility of the extended deterrence posture of NATO. However, even after a zero option on SRBM from the Atlantic to the Urals—the West would have to dismantle 93 Lance and 32 Pluton launchers while the Soviet Union and its allies would have to destroy 630 A/B launchers and 749 SS-21 launchers—and after a total withdrawal of all artillery shells—2,700 by NATO and about 6,260 by the Warsaw Pact—Europe would still not be denuclearized. Several categories of nuclear weapons would remain: nuclear bombs delivered by land-based aircraft, those delivered by carrier-based strike aircraft, land-based naval bombers, ASW aircraft, the SLCMs and SLBMs of France, the United Kingdom, and the SACEUR-assigned US warheads as well as the Soviet SLBMs that could be targeted against NATO-Europe. According to my own count (see Table 9.1.), in these five categories NATO (the United States, France and the United Kingdom) has approximately 2,375 nuclear systems left and the Soviet Union about 2,978. More than 5,000 nuclear warheads would remain in the arsenals of both alliances.

Table 9.1. Substrategic nuclear weapons in Europe after the implementation of the INF agreement in June 1991 based on a modernisation freeze

Category	Deployment countries	MBFR area				From the Atlantic to the Urals			
		NATO		Warsaw Pact		NATO		Warsaw Pact	
		1987	(1988)	1987	(1988)	1987	(1988)	1987	(1988)
Land-based systems									
IRBM									
SSBS-S3	France					18	(18)		
GLCM									
SS-C-1b Sepal								100	(40)
SRBM									
Pluton	France					32	(32)		
Lance	USA	36	(36)			36	(65)		
Lance	Allies	51	(53)			57	(59)		
Scud B	USSR			76	(150)			475	(506)
Scud A/B	Allies			83	(83)			155	(158)
Frog/SS-21	USSR			104	(104)			531	(534)
Frog/SS-21	Allies			124	(140)			218	(234)
Artillery									
	USA	512	(644)			512	(644)		
	Allies	1445	(1546)			2188	(2378)		
	USSR			1068	(1840)			5850	(5100)
Land-based air	Allies			200	(288)			410	(498)
	USA	168	(156)			380	(368)		
	Allies	498	(668)			1163	(1014)		
	USSR			315	(225)			2125	(2004)
	Allies			178	(300)			223	(385)

Sea-launched maritime		European/Atlantic waters			
		NATO		Warsaw Pact	
		1987	(1988)	1987	(1988)
SLBM	France	[160]	(96)		
	UK	[160]	(64)		
	USSR			18	(18)
SLCM	USA	152	(41)		
	USSR			182	(58)
Carrier-based strike aircraft					
	USA	272	(352)		
	France	38	(64)		
	UK		(42)		
Land-based naval bombers					
	USSR			280	(286)
ASW aircraft					
	USA	80	(95)		
	Allies	140	—		
	USSR			150	(66)

Source: Calculated from the IISS data of 1987 (1988).

However, with the removal of the nuclear artillery shells and the SRBM missiles and warheads from the Atlantic to the Urals, an additional category of time-urgent primary targets would also be removed from the nuclear strike plans of both major nuclear powers and of both alliances.

The process of nuclear disarmament in Europe may not be limited to American and Soviet systems; at a later stage both British and French nuclear weapons should gradually be included.

While both France and the United Kingdom have been opposed to any extension of the nuclear disarmament process in Europe, they have indicated a readiness to reduce their nuclear forces after drastic reductions in the nuclear arsenals of both superpowers have taken place. After a START agreement, the British and French nuclear systems may have to be considered in the context of any future nuclear disarmament process in Europe. However, progress in further nuclear disarmament initiatives should not become hostage to the approval of these two nuclear states.

In the process of the negotiations on dual-capable nuclear systems not only all four nuclear powers in Europe but also those countries should be included on whose territory nuclear weapons are presently deployed.

Future negotiations on nuclear arms control and disarmament in Europe may therefore involve not only the nuclear powers: USA, USSR, UK and France, but also the following crypto-nuclear states: FRG, Italy, Belgium, the Netherlands, Greece and Turkey on behalf of NATO and the GDR, Czechoslovakia, Hungary, Poland and Bulgaria. Instead of among these 16 countries, the negotiations could also take place in the framework of the negotiations on conventional disarmament in Europe among the 23 countries.

At least three approaches of future nuclear arms control and disarmament efforts will have to be distinguished: national and alliance measures of self-restraint and unilateral restructuring of the forces; a strategy of mutual self-restraint, or gradualism (Osgood, 1962); and legally binding arms control and disarmament treaties.

National initiatives and gradualist steps can create positive preconditions for arms control and disarmament agreements but they cannot substitute for them. In the pursuit of arms control and disarmament agreement, three dangers should be avoided (Rathjens *et al.*,

1974): the introduction of new weapons systems as trump cards or bargaining chips (these often develop a life of their own once a specific alliance has been formed in their support); the tendency to level up or to agree to relatively high ceilings; and the danger of compensatory armaments.

After the INF agreement and after the approval of the final document of the third CSCE follow-up conference in Vienna the political efforts at deterrence, arms control and disarmament will concentrate on the following topics: the continuation of the START negotiations; the search for a global chemical weapons agreement; the continuation of the Stockholm process (CSBMs); and the initiation of talks on conventional disarmament in Europe.

Problems of substrategic nuclear arms in Europe have been raised by NATO in 1975 in the MBFR context (option 3) and they have been introduced by the Soviet Union and Warsaw Pact states since 1984 in the CSBM talks in Stockholm. During 1988, NATO countries could not reach agreement on whether the remaining nuclear weapons in Europe should become a topic for future East–West talks and, if so, where they should be dealt with.

At least three steps in a gradualist approach to nuclear disarmament in Europe are conceivable: a moratorium on both sides on the modernization of existing nuclear systems as a first step towards the goal of achieving a third zero option for short-range nuclear missiles and for nuclear artillery; the inclusion of the dual- and triple-capable launchers (artillery and aircraft) in the context of the talks on Conventional Forces in Europe (CFE); and talks among the five nuclear states after the conclusion of a START agreement.

Which unilateral steps may be undertaken by both the Soviet Union and the United States to reduce their respective superiority in specific segments of the substrategic nuclear balance (see Table 9.1) possibly in the context of a gradualist disarmament strategy?

As the next step towards the realization of a nuclear weapon-free world the Soviet Union should initiate a positive political signal by withdrawing from East Germany, Czechoslovakia, Poland and Hungary its short-range nuclear weapons down to the level of comparable US and French systems (Lance and Pluton) (levelling down).

NATO should respond to this unilateral step with a decision not to modernize its SNF, e.g. not to replace the Lance with ATACM. After this demonstration of mutual restraint both the United States and the

Soviet Union should enter into bilateral negotiations with the goal of a third zero option.

In the 1950s, both politicians and scientists (for example Rapacki, Gomułka, Kennan and Kissinger) tabled proposals for a nuclear disengagement in Europe (Hinterhoff, 1959), and for a nuclear weapon-free corridor from the Baltic, across central Europe to the Balkans. In the Palme Report (Independent Commission, 1982), several proposals for nuclear weapon-free zones in Europe and for a nuclear weapon-free corridor are incorporated. What role could such steps play in the context of a European disarmament strategy?

The establishment of nuclear weapon-free zones in Europe (in Scandinavia, the Balkans and central Europe) could be a necessary but not sufficient condition for a process of reducing nuclear capabilities in Europe.

A nuclear weapon-free corridor in central Europe could make a modest contribution towards crisis avoidance and stability. However, such a first step would be even more credible if the forward-deployed systems were not just rebased but dismantled. The dismantling of dual-capable forward-deployed systems would also contribute towards a change in existing force structures towards a less provocative posture.

A third zero option on ballistic missiles with a range below 500 km in Europe would require the destruction of many launchers that are dual- or triple-capable (nuclear, chemical and conventional).

Such a step would remove time-critical targets from the territory of third countries in Europe. With the dismantling of a whole category of multiple-capable launchers an important step would be initiated with the goal of a restructuring of the armed forces in central Europe. A third zero option would contribute both to crisis and arms race stability.

Therefore, as a first credible step towards a nuclear weapon-free corridor in central Europe all launchers for nuclear battlefield systems (e.g. artillery) should be removed and dismantled and all warheads deactivated.

This proposal would also initiate major changes in the force structures and in the tactical operative concepts. However, these two steps would not lead to a complete denuclearization of Europe. As we have seen above, even then about 5,000 air- and sea-based nuclear launchers would remain in the arsenals of both military alliances in Europe.

In the context of the talks on Conventional Forces in Europe (CFE) among the 23 countries belonging to both military alliances a third step might be considered: a reduction of the dual-capable aircraft or the gradual removal of all land-based nuclear forces.

This third step would lead to a denuclearization of those crypto-nuclear countries on whose territory nuclear weapons are presently deployed (see Bahr's minority report in the Palme Report (Independent Commission on Disarmament and Security Issues, 1982)).

The neutral and non-aligned states in Europe could play a major role in the verification of these three additional steps towards nuclear disarmament in Europe in the context of a European Verification Force modelled on the peace-keeping forces of the United Nations.

As a consequence of the Stockholm Agreement of September 1986 and of the INF Treaty of December 1987, a system of multilateral and bilateral verification measures has been adopted that include on-site inspections with a few hours' notice. The existing verification requirements could be further enhanced by a special European verification force that should also involve the European neutral and non-aligned states who are a part of the IAEA inspection regime. Independent data could be collected by a special European verification satellite that could be developed by the European Space Agency (ESA) in close co-operation with the Inter-Cosmos Council.

Concluding remarks

Nuclear disarmament in Europe is an indispensable element of a political structure of confidence and stability in Europe. Therefore, these proposals are put forward to initiate a process leading to a gradual reduction of existing nuclear potentials in Europe and to constraints on or the prevention of any future nuclear modernization.

These steps would also have positive repercussions for the multi-capable launchers and they would therefore directly affect the structure of the armed forces and the tactical-operative concepts of both military alliances with the goal of less offensive and provocative forces towards a confidence-building military posture.

Since the ratification of the INF agreement there are real political prospects for further nuclear disarmament measures in Europe. With the improvement of the East–West climate, the increasing sensitivity of European public opinion towards nuclear weapons, and the fiscal constraints confronting both military alliances, many factors supporting arms control solutions have recently emerged. Nevertheless, as long as the modernization issues have not been solved it is still uncertain whether the political leadership in East and West will learn and implement the lessons of the first *détente* period in the 1970s.

Bibliography

Bebermeyer, Hartmut, 1989. 'German Armed Forces—Resource Planning in Crisis' in Hans Günter Brauch and Robert Kennedy (eds), *Alternative Conventional Defense Postures for the European Theater. Vol. 1: The Military Balance and Domestic Constraints*. New York: Taylor & Francis.

Brauch, Hans Günter, 1981. 'Plädoyer für eine Modernisierung des NATO-Doppelbeschlusses—Zehn Handlungsoptionen für die deutsche Sicherheitspolitik', *Vorgänge*, vol. 20, no. 52.

Brauch, Hans Günter, 1983. *Die Raketen kommen! Vom NATO-Doppelbeschluss bis zur Stationierung*. Cologne: Bund.

Brauch, Hans Günter, 1984. 'Bemühungen um eine nukleare Rüstungskontrolle—Ein einführender Überblick (1945–1982) in Hans Günter Brauch (ed.), *Kernwaffen und Rüstungskontrolle. Ein interdisziplinäres Studienbuch*. Opdalen: Westdeutscher Verlag.

Brauch, Hans Günter, 1986. *30 Thesen und 10 Bewertungen zur Strategischen Verteidigungsinitiative (SDI) und zur Europäischen Verteidigungsinitiative (EVI)*, AFES-PRESS Report no 2. Starnberg: AFES-PRESS.

Brauch, Hans Günter, 1987. 'From SDI to EDI—Elements of a European Defense Architecture' in Hans Günter Brauch (ed.), *Star Wars and European Defence—Implications for Europe: Perceptions and Assessments*. London: Macmillan; and New York: St Martin's Press, pp. 436–99.

Brauch, Hans Günter, 1989a. 'Europäische Raketenabwehr—eine trügerische Alternative' in Studiengruppe Alternative Sicherheitspolitik (ed.), *Vertrauensbildende Verteidigung—Reform deutscher Sicherheitspolitik*. Gerlingen: Bleicher-Verlag.

Brauch, Hans Günter, 1989b. *Evaluation of Antitactical Ballistic Missile Defense Technologies and Concepts for NATO Europe in Terms of Strategic Stability*, AFES-PRESS Report no. 27. Mosbach: AFES-PRESS.

Brzezinski, Zbigniew, 1983. *Power and Principle, Memoirs of the National Security Adviser 1977–1981*. New York: Farrar-Straus-Giroux.

Buteux, Paul, 1983. *The Politics of Nuclear Consultation in NATO, 1965–1980*. Cambridge: Cambridge University Press.

Carlucci, Frank C,, 1988. 'INF Treaty will Relieve Nuclear Command Pressure' in *US Policy Information and Texts*, no. 21 (2 February 1988), pp. 11–16.

Carter, Jimmy, 1982. *Keeping Faith*. Toronto: Bantam.

Grass, Bernd, 1989. 'The Personnel Shortage of the Bundeswehr till the Year 2000' in Hans Günter Brauch and Robert Kennedy (eds), *Alternative Conventional Defense Postures for the European Theater. Vol. 1: The Military Balance and Domestic Constraints*. New York: Taylor & Francis.

Hinterhoff, Eugene, 1959. *Disengagement*. London: Stevens & Sons.

Hoffman, Hubertus, 1986. *Die Atompartner. Washington-Bonn und die Modernisierung der taktischen Kernwaffen*. Koblenz: Bernard & Graefe.

Holm, Hans Henrik and Petersen, Nikolaj (eds), 1983. *The European Missiles Crisis—Nuclear Weapons and Security Policy*. New York: St Martin's Press.

Holst, Johan Jörgen, 1983. 'The double-track decision revisited', in Hans Henrik Holm and Nikolaj Petersen (eds), *The European Missiles Crisis*. New York: St Martin's Press.

Iklé, Fred C. *et al.*, 1988. *Discriminate Deterrence—A Report of the Commission on Integrated Long-Term Strategy*. Washington: US Government Printing Office.

Independent Commission on Disarmament and Security Issues, 1982. *Common Security*, London: Pan (Palme Report).

International Institute for Strategic Studies, 1987. *The Military Balance 1987–1988*. London: IISS.

International Institute for Strategic Studies, 1988a. *The Military Balance 1988–1989*. London: IISS.

International Institute for Strategic Studies, 1988b. *Strategic Survey 1987–1988*. London: IISS.

Joxe, Alain, Metge, Pierre and Santos, Alberto, 1987. 'Eurostrategies Americaines', *Cahiers d'Etudes Stratégiques*, no. 12.

Matthée, Volker, 1985. *Die Neutronenwaffe zwischen Bündnis-und Innenpolitik*. Herford: Mittler & Sohn.

Meecham, Michael, 1988a. 'Treaty Hearings Focus on NATO Force Structure', *Aviation Week & Space Technology*, vol. 128, no 7.

Meecham, Michael, 1988b. 'U.S. Outlines Modernization Plans: Allies Told Nothing is 'Concrete', *Aviation Week & Space Technology*, vol. 128, no. 11.

Newhouse, John, 1973. *Cold Dawn—The Story of SALT*. New York: Holt, Rinehart and Winston.

Osgood, Charles, 1962. *An Alternative to War and Surrender*. Urbana, University of Illinois Press.

Payne, Samuel B, Jr, 1980. *The Soviet Union and SALT*. Cambridge, Ma: MIT Press.

Rathjens, George, Chayes, Abram and Ruina, Jack, 1974. *Nuclear Arms Control Negotiations*. Washington DC: Carnegie Endowment on International Peace.

Risse-Kappen, Thomas, 1988a. *Null-Lösung. Entscheidungsprozesse zu den Mittelstreckenwaffen 1970–1987*. Frankfurt/New York: Campus.

Risse-Kappen, Thomas, 1988b. *Die Krise der Sicherheitspolitik. Neuorientierungen und Entscheidungsprozesse im politischen System der Bundes-*

178 *Hans Günter Brauch*

Ruehl, Lothar, 1980. 'Der Beschluss der NATO zur Einführung nuklearer Mittelstreckenwaffen', *Europa-Archiv*, vol. 35, no. 4.

Ruehl, Lothar, 1987. *Mittelstreckenwaffen in Europa*. Baden-Baden: Nomos.

Scheer, Hermann, 1981. 'NATO-Doppelbeschluss: Landestützte Raketen gehören nach Alaska. Ein Plädoyer für die Stationierung der Systeme auf See', *Die Zeit*, 29 May.

Schmidt, Helmut, 1987. *Menschen und Mächte*. Berlin: Siedler.

Schwartz, David N., 1983. *NATO's Nuclear Dilemmas*. Washington, DC: The Brookings Institution.

Smith, Gerard, 1980. *Doubletalk. The Story of SALT I*, Garden City, NY: Doubleday.

Subrahmanyam, K., 1984. 'Eine Bestandsaufnahme der Politik der Nichtweitergabe von Atomwaffen—eine indische Perspektive' in Hans Günter Brauch (ed.), *Kernwaffen und Rüstungskontrolle. Ein interdisziplinäres Studienbuch*. Opsdalen: Westdeutscher Verlag.

Talbot, Strobe, 1984. *Deadly Gambits. The Reagan Administration and the Stalemate in Nuclear Arms Control*. New York: Alfred A. Knopf.

US Department of Defense, 1988. *Soviet Military Power—An Assessment of the Threat 1988*. Washington, DC: US Government Printing Office.

Vogt, Wolfgang R., 1989. 'Peace and Security in a Process of Change? Hypotheses and Data on the Legitimacy of Security policy in the FRG' in Hans Günter Brauch and Robert Kennedy (eds), *Alternative Conventional Defense Postures for the European Theater. Vol. 1: The Military Balance and Domestic Constraints*. New York: Taylor & Francis.

Wasserman, Sherri L., 1983. *The Neutron Bomb Controversy*. New York: Praeger.

Weizsäcker, Carl Friedrich von, L. 'Zum NATO-Doppelbeschluss: Die neuen Raketen gehören auf See. Gefahren der Rüstung in den achtziger Jahren', *Die Zeit*, 22 May.

Wolfe, Thomas W., 1979. *The SALT Experience*. Cambridge, MA: Ballinger.

Index